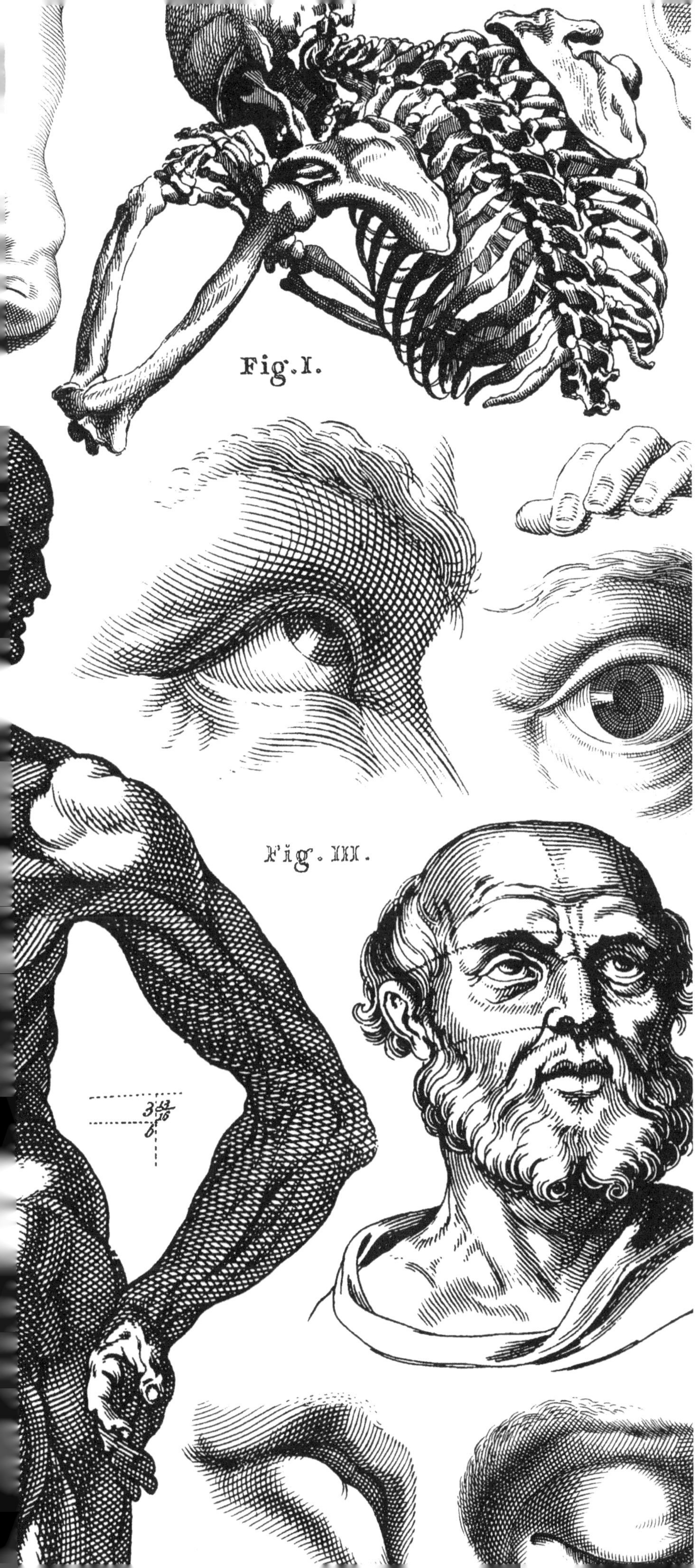

VOLUME NUMBER ONE

AF230747

DRAWING THE HUMAN FIGURE

AN IMAGE ARCHIVE FOR ARTISTS *And* DESIGNERS

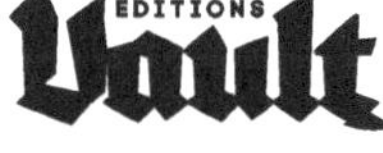

INTRODUCTION

Drawing the human figure has provided artists
throughout history with invaluable insight into
our physical form and the ability to capture subtle
nuances of emotion that words cannot express.
Mastery of this skill allows artists to capture
movement, gesture and changes in facial features
in great detail, helping them create powerful works
of art that are more accurate and expressive.
Understanding human anatomy and body language
enables artists to portray characters with greater
realism, making their artwork more life-like. It helps
them accurately convey emotion in a work of art
through perspective, proportion, light and shadow
and colour theory.

Drawn figures have captivated audiences since
prehistory. This timeless subject matter has seen
different variations in style and method throughout
the ages, from realistic portraiture to abstract
figures. Each new interpretation illuminates our
shared humanity while documenting and reflecting
on our changing times and ultimately bringing us
closer together through art.

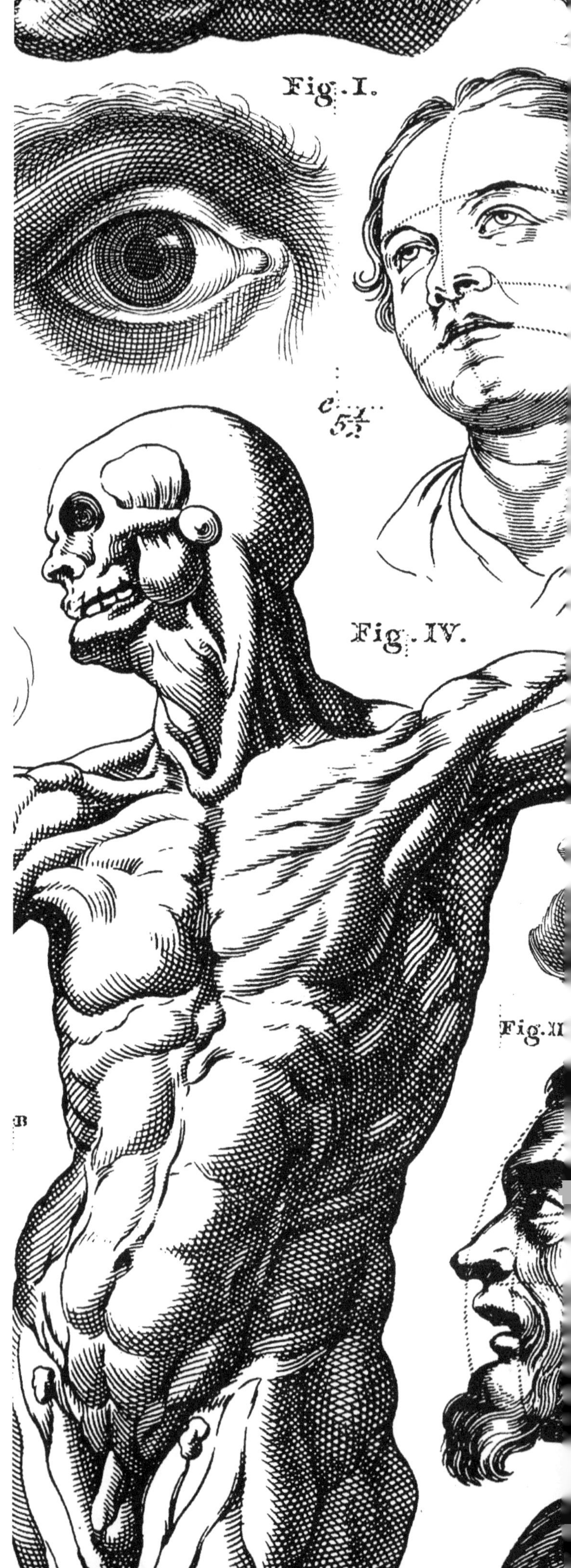

TABLE OF CONTENTS

Studies of the human figure	01-30
Studies of the human face	31-62
Studies of the eye and its expressions	63-68
Studies of the nose and mouth	69-74
Studies of the ear	75-78
Studies of the arm, hand and extremities	79-90
Studies of the leg, feet and extremities	91-102

DOWNLOAD YOUR FILES

Downloading your files is simple. To access your digital files, please go to the last page of this book and follow the instructions.

For technical assistance, please email:
info@vaulteditions.com

Copyright

Bibliographical Note

This book is a new work created by Vault Editions Ltd.

ISBN: 978-1-922966-09-4

DRAWING THE HUMAN FIGURE

VAULT EDITIONS

DRAWING THE HUMAN FIGURE

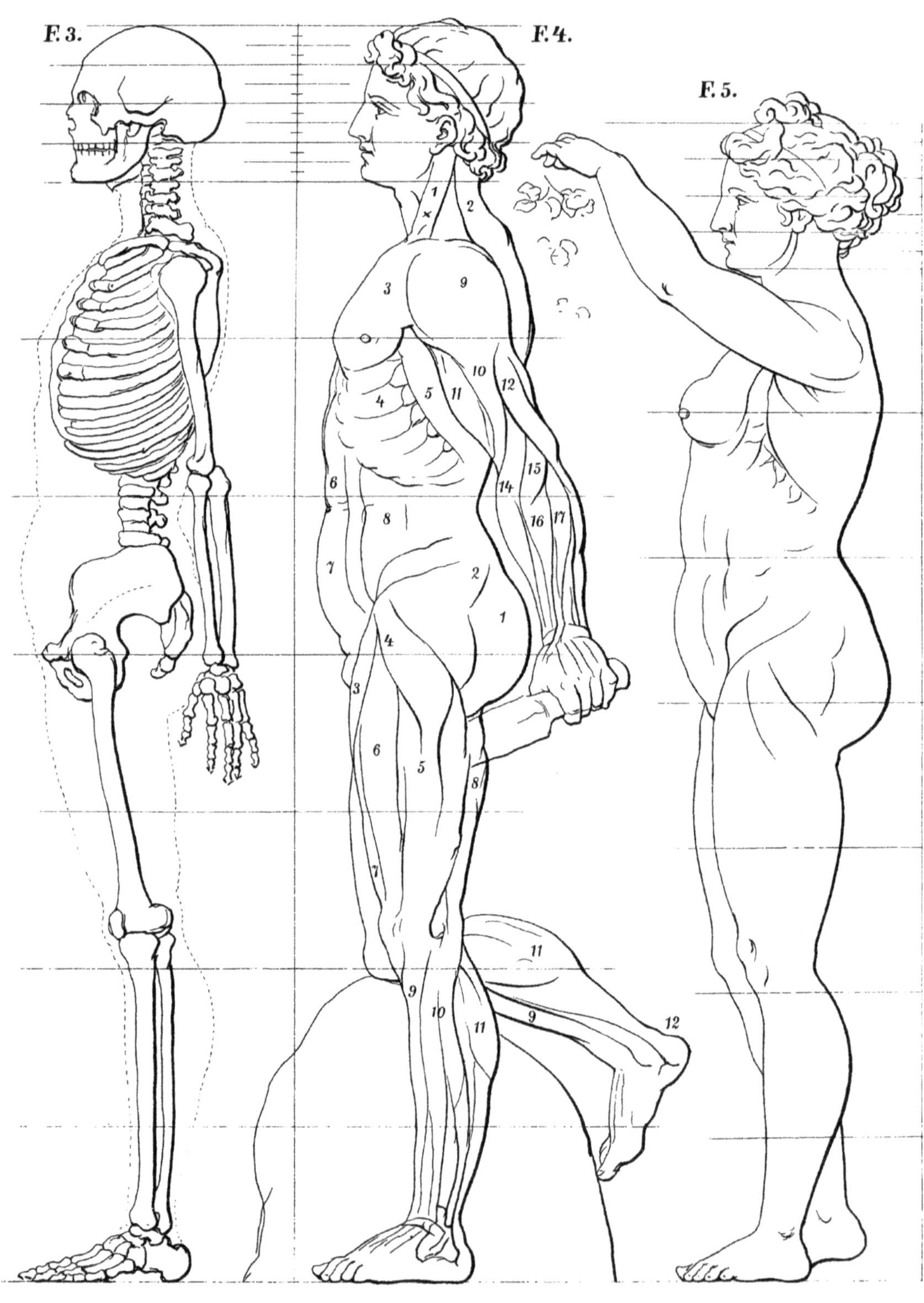
F. 3.
F. 4.
F. 5.

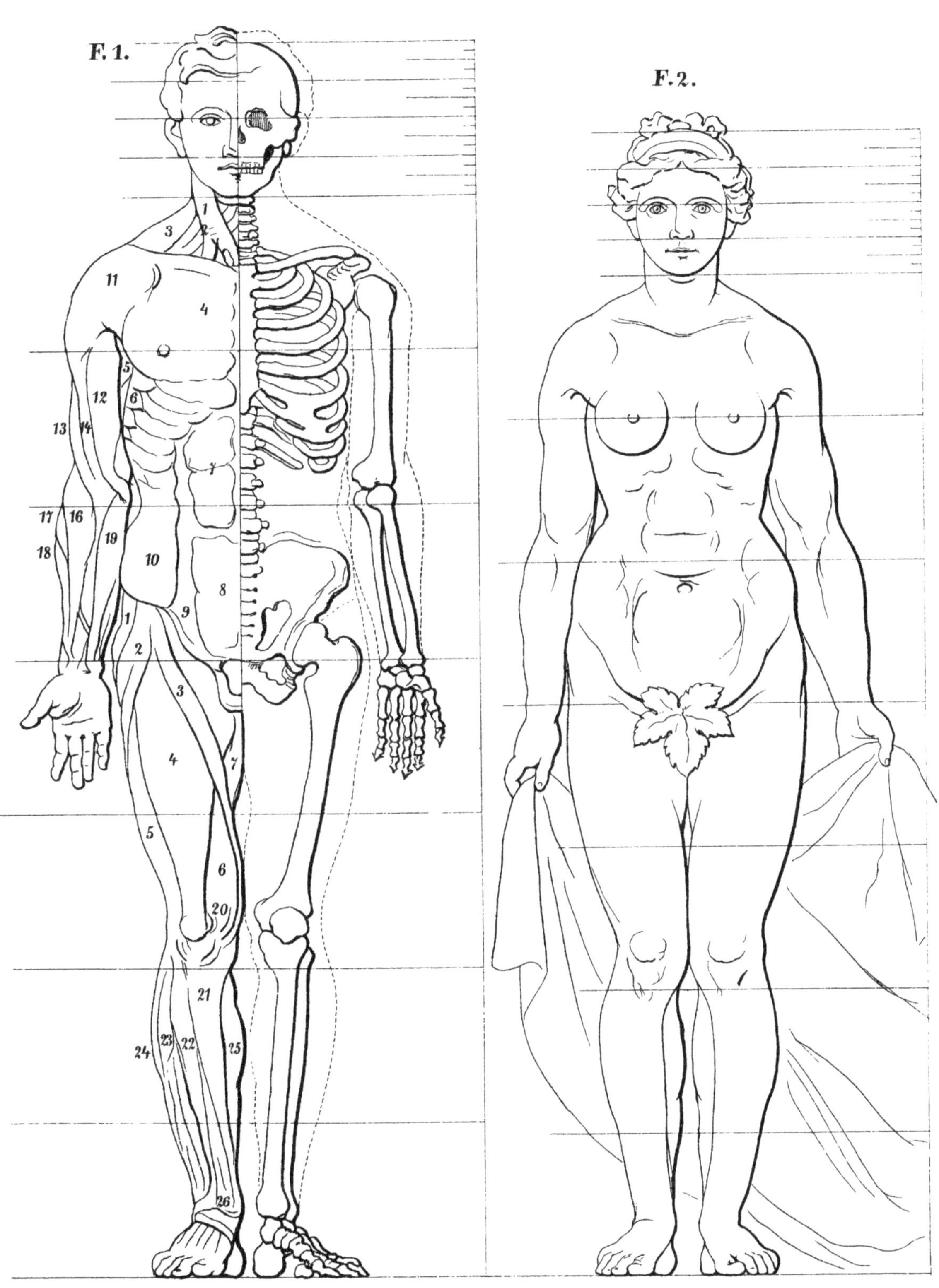
F. 1.
F. 2.

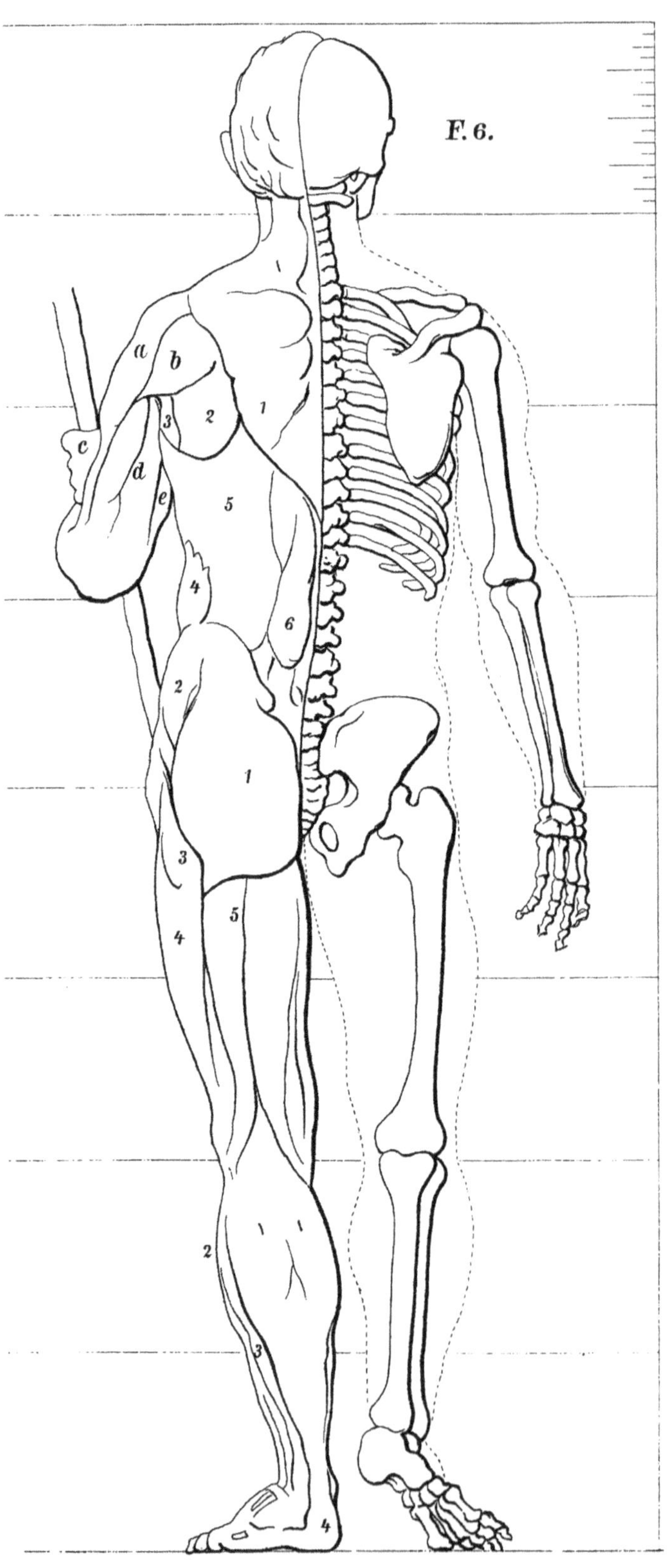
F. 6.

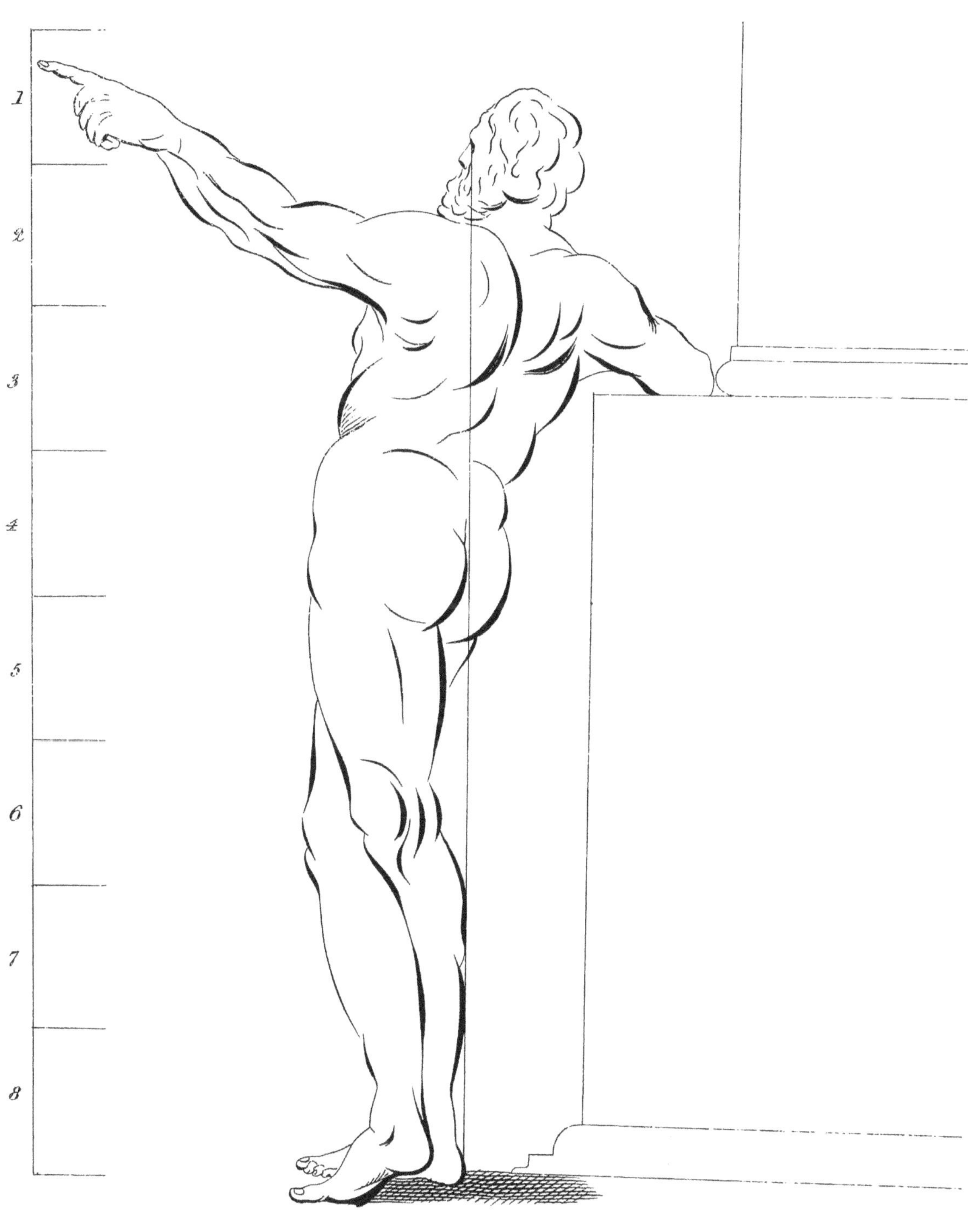
1
2
3
4
5
6
7
8

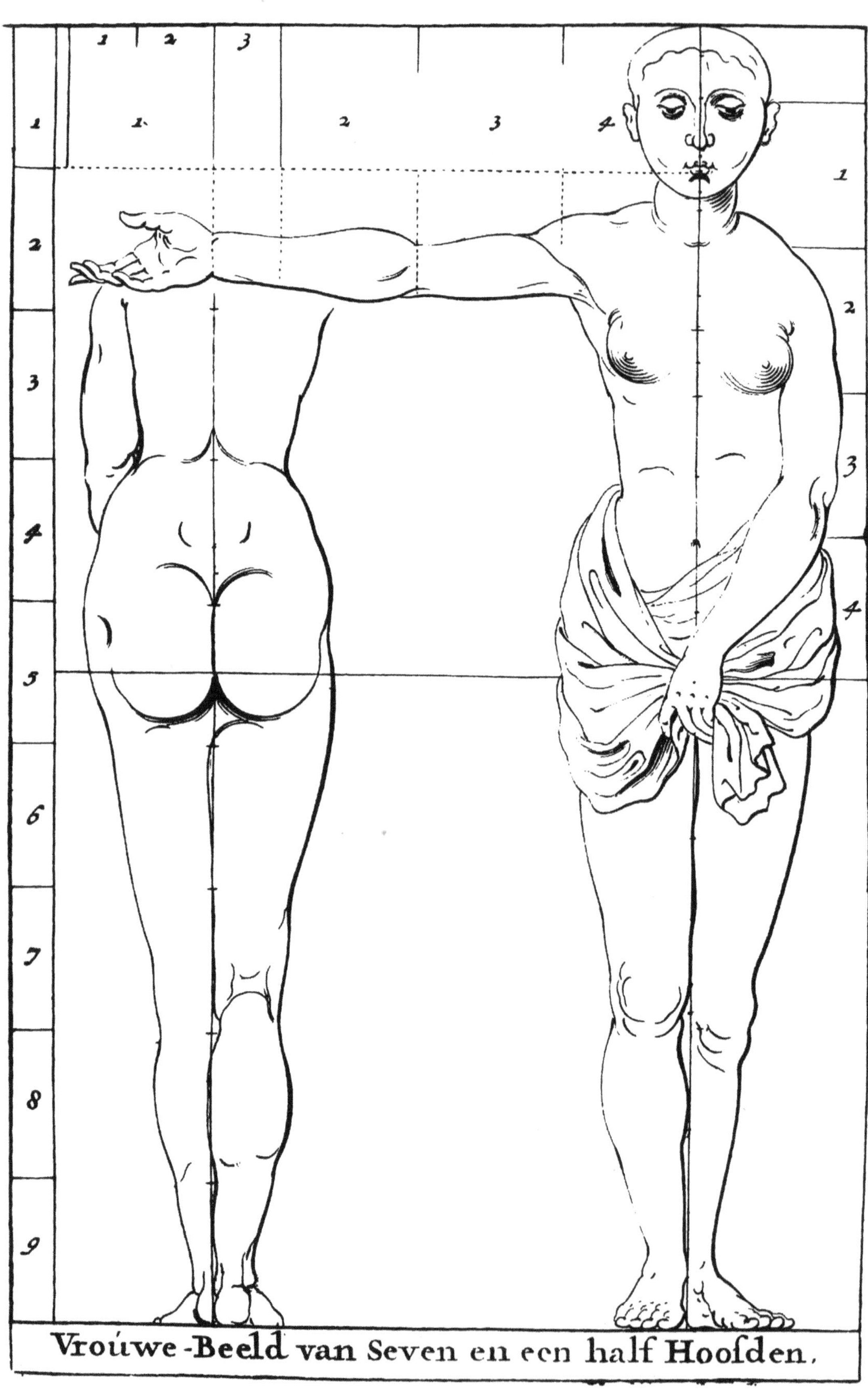
Vrouwe-Beeld van Seven en een half Hoofden.

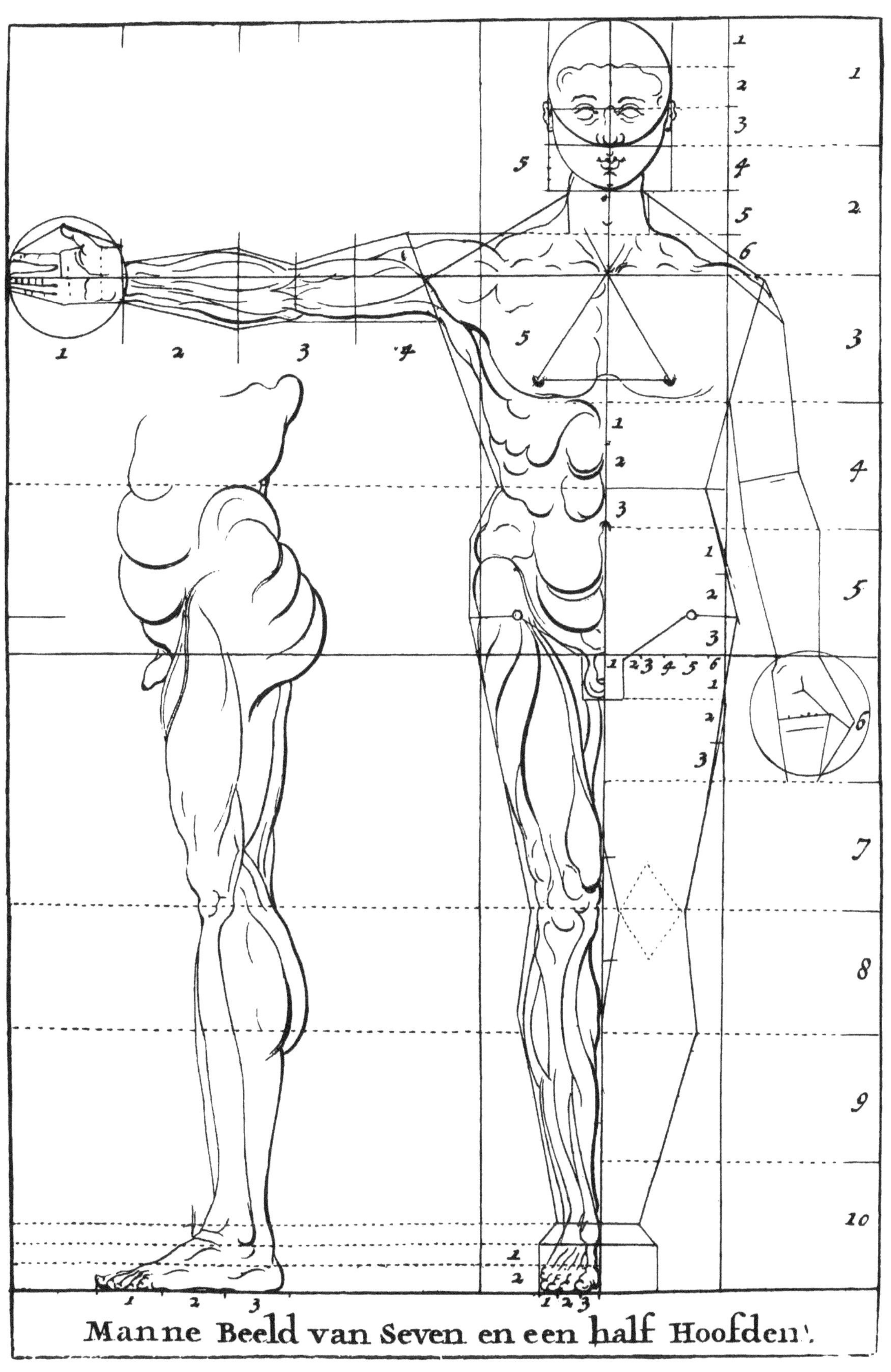
Manne Beeld van Seven en een half Hoofden.

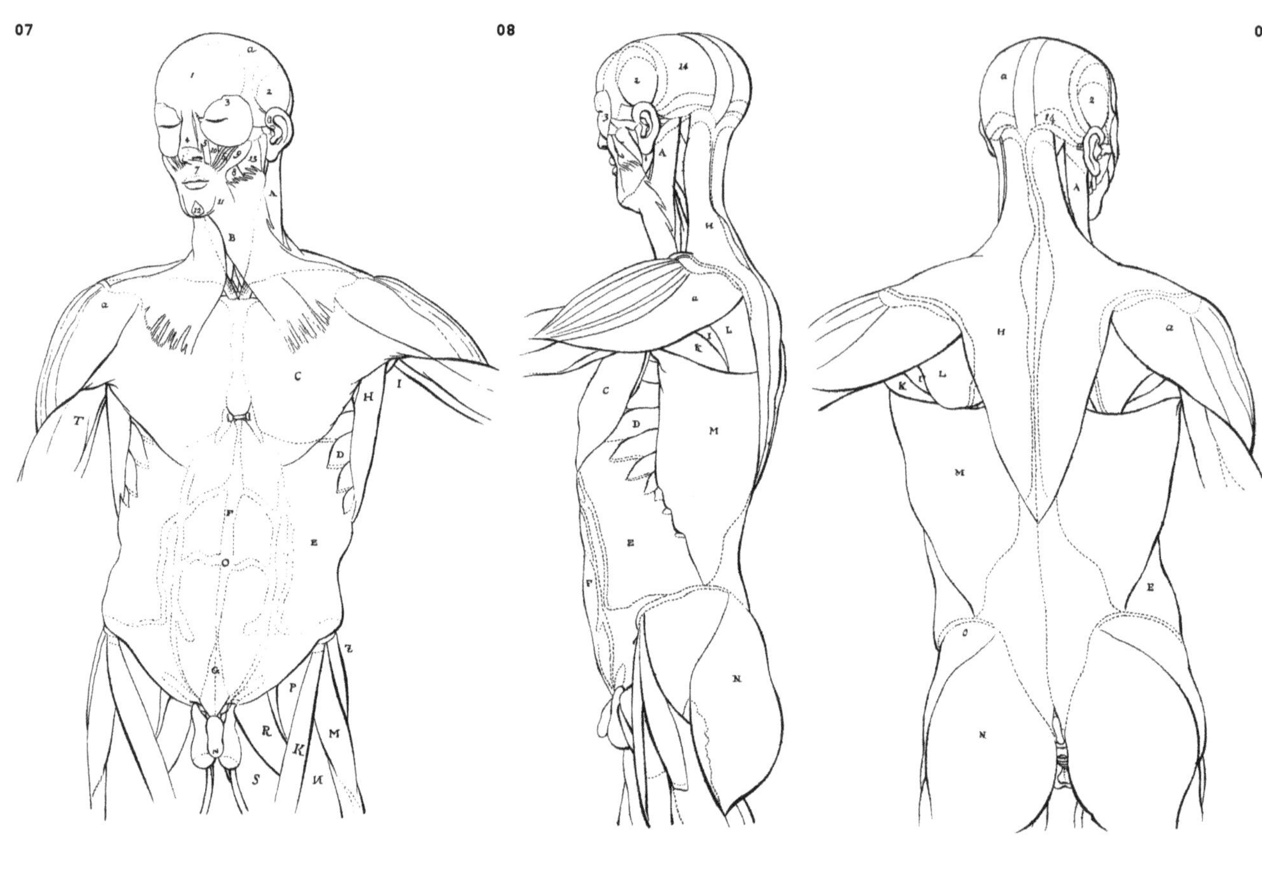

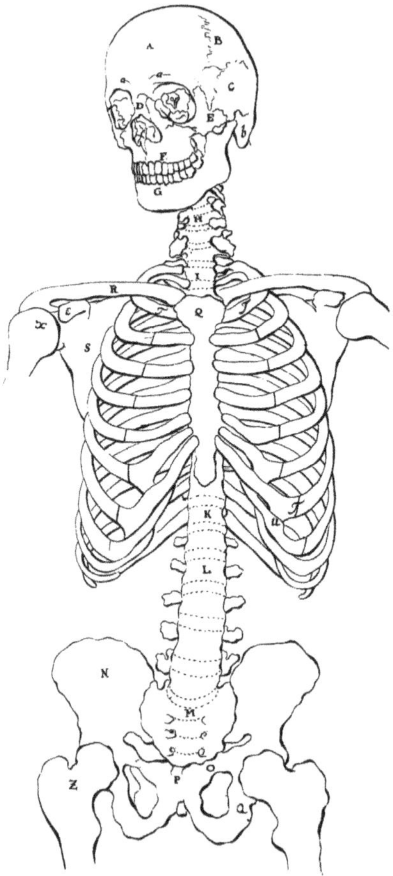

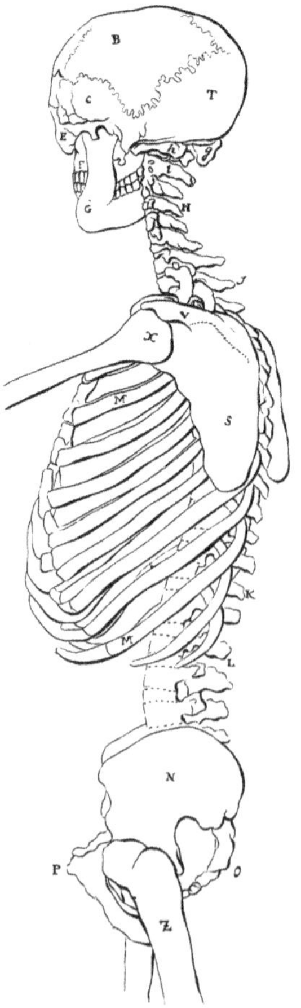

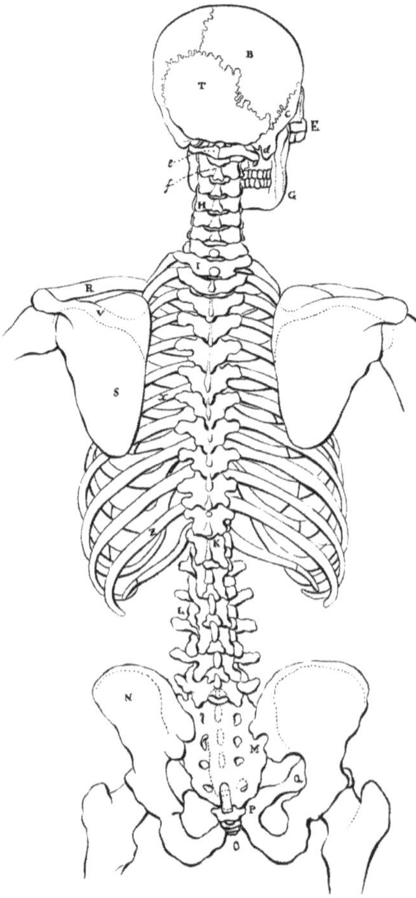

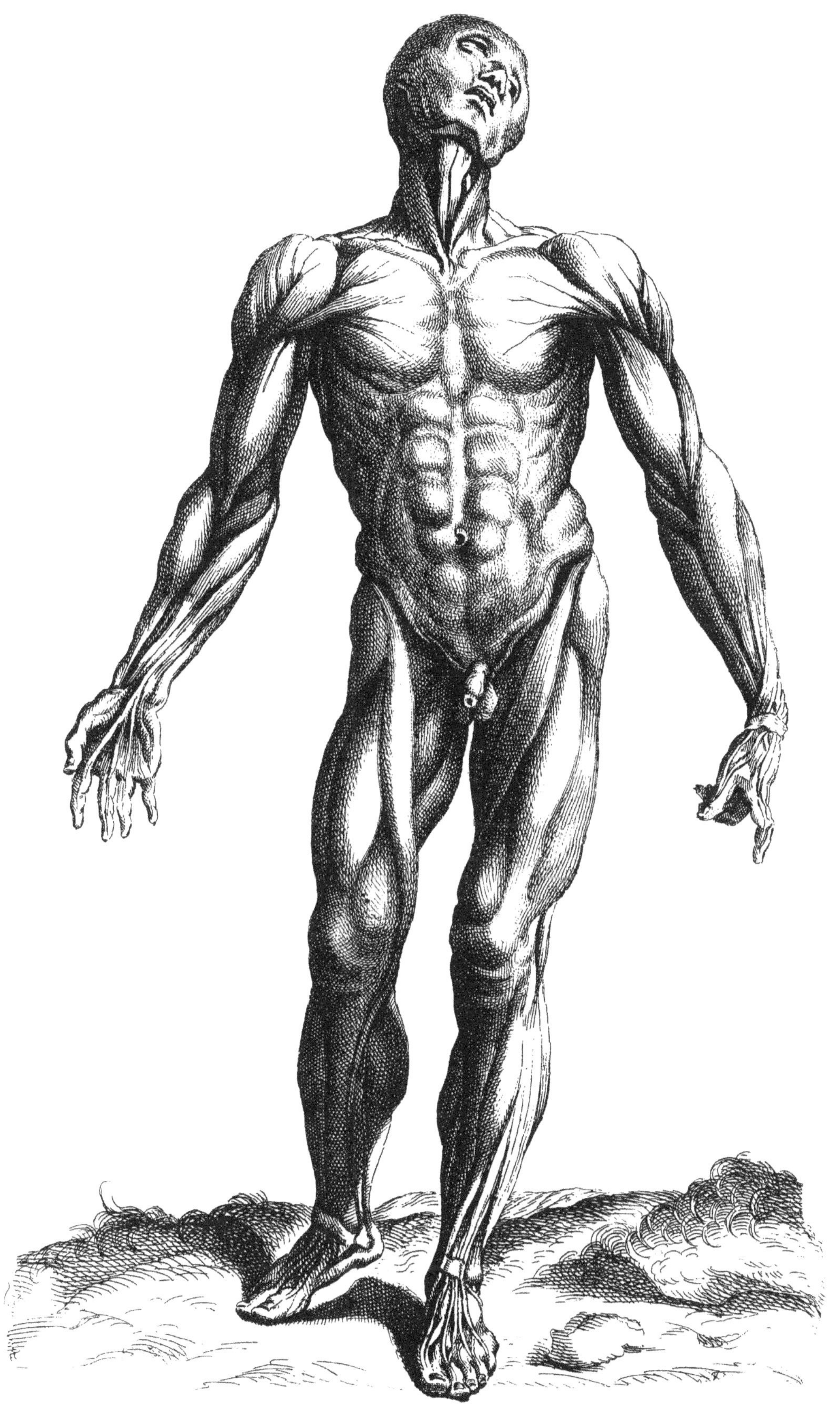

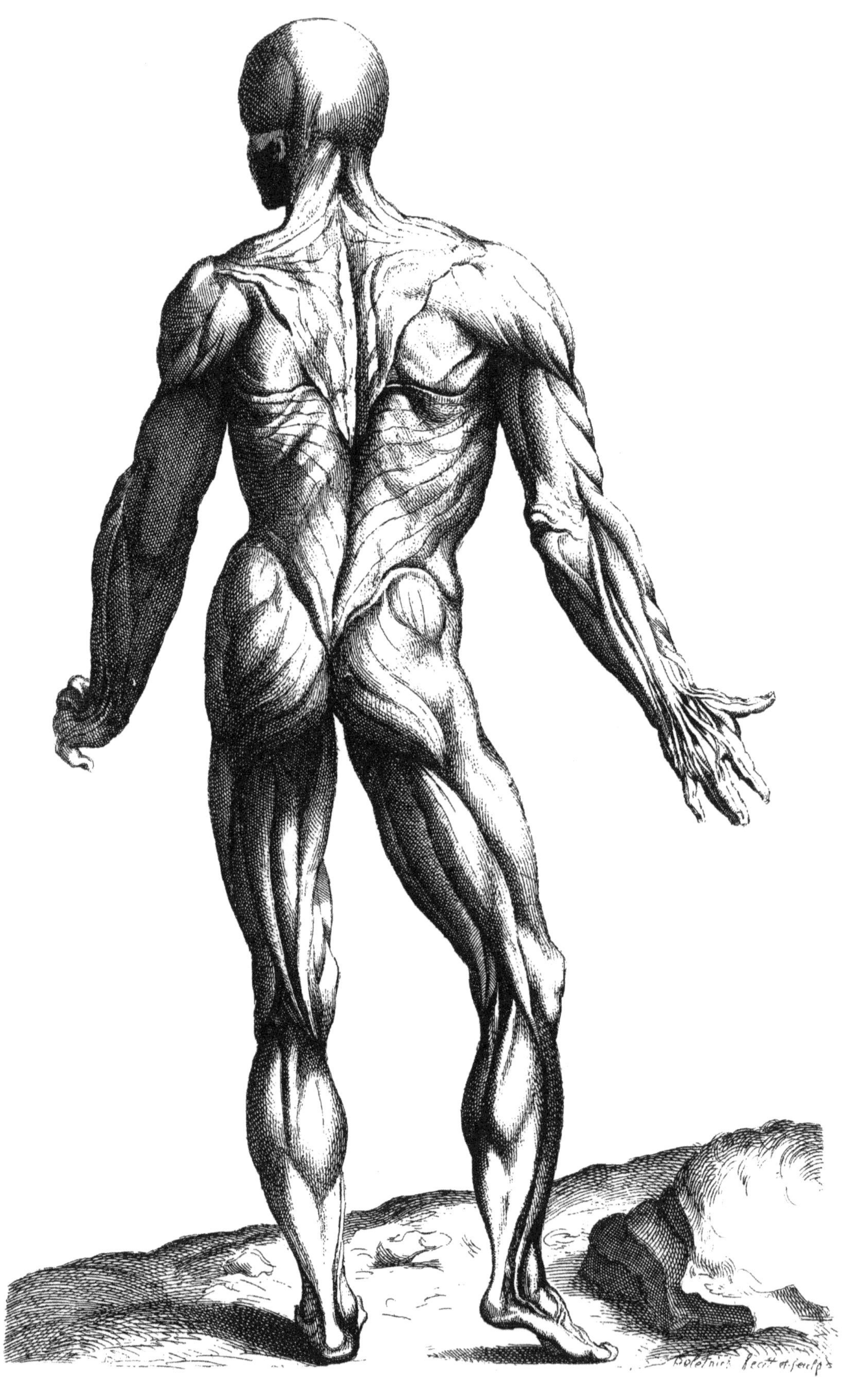

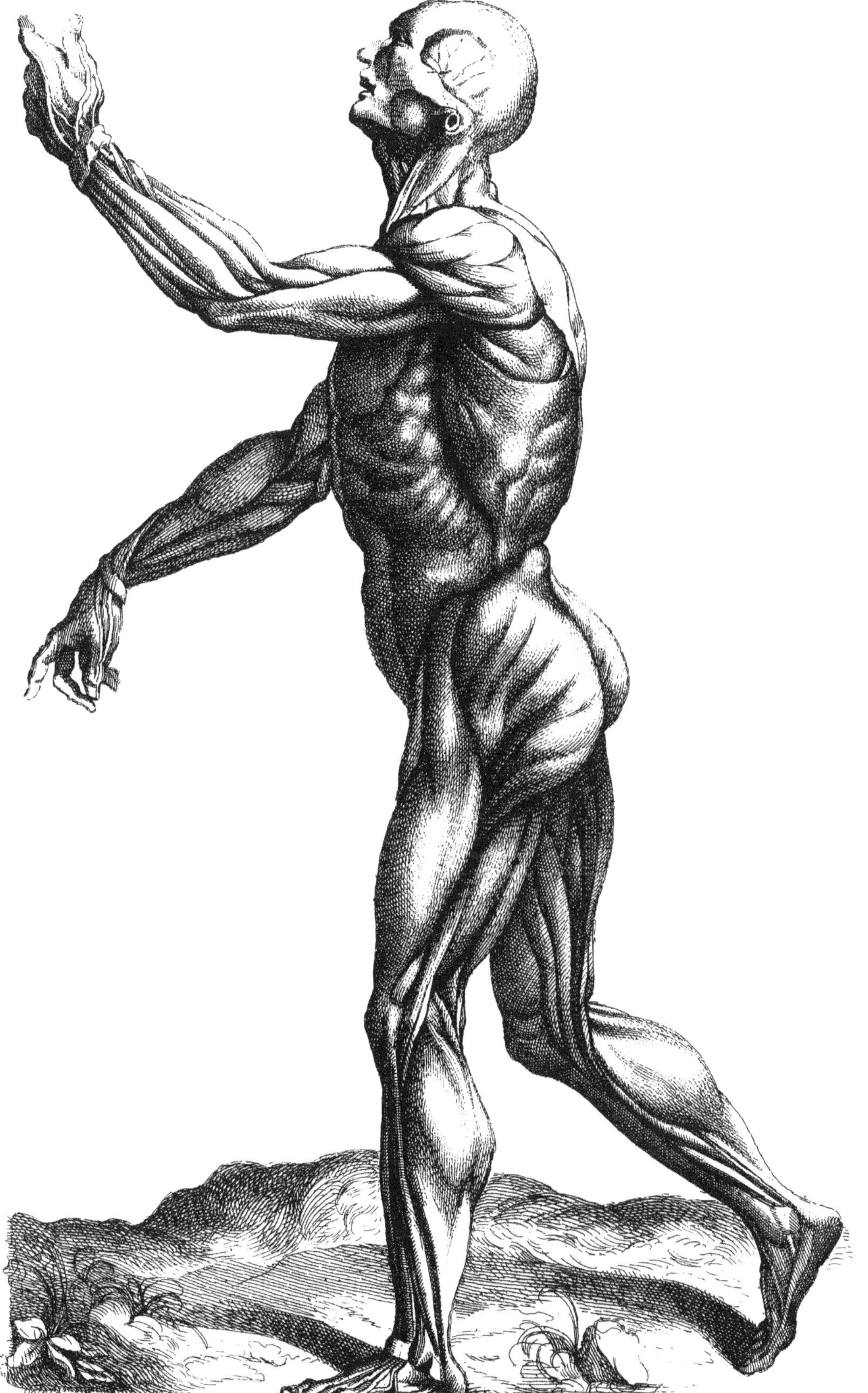

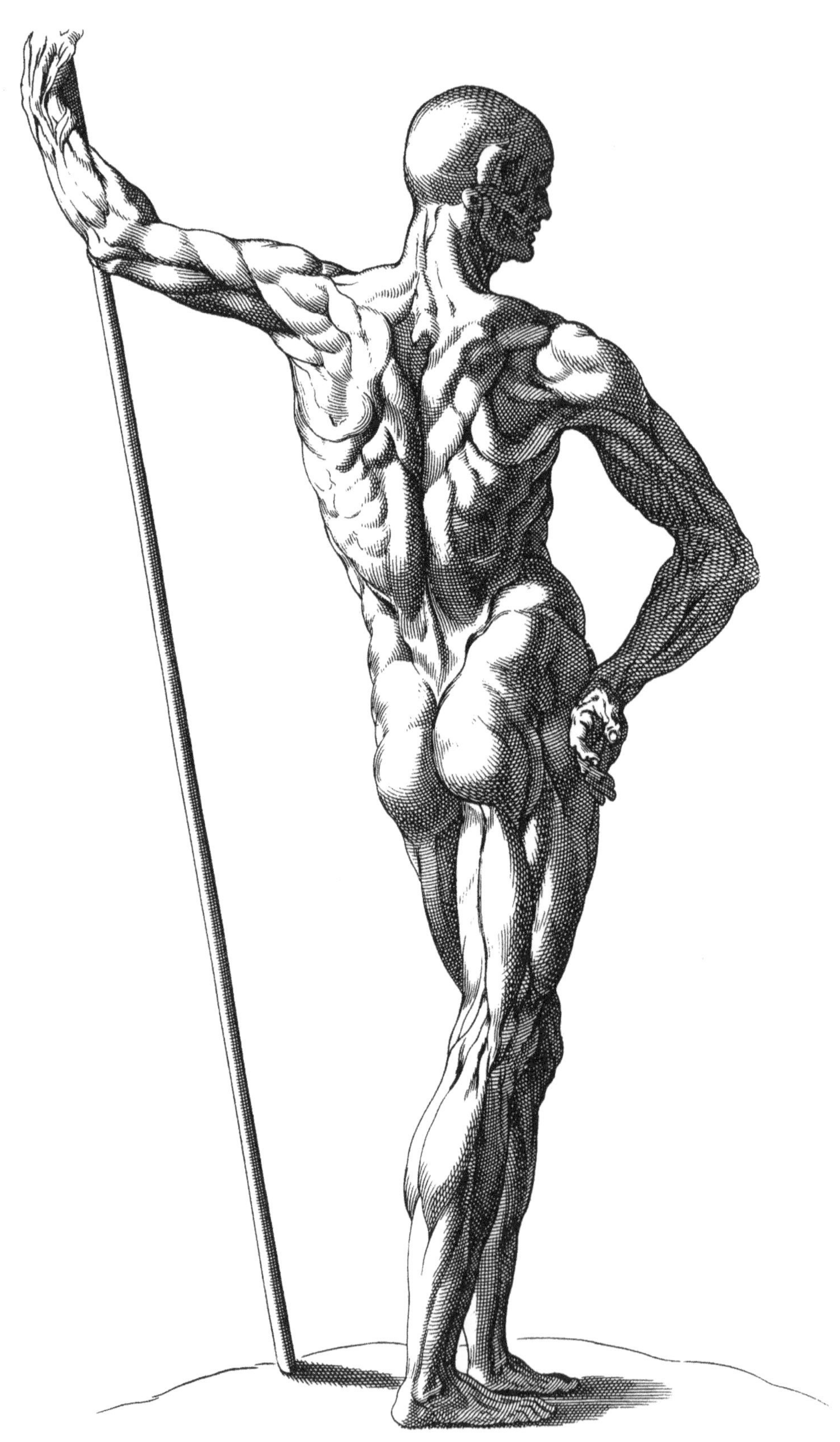

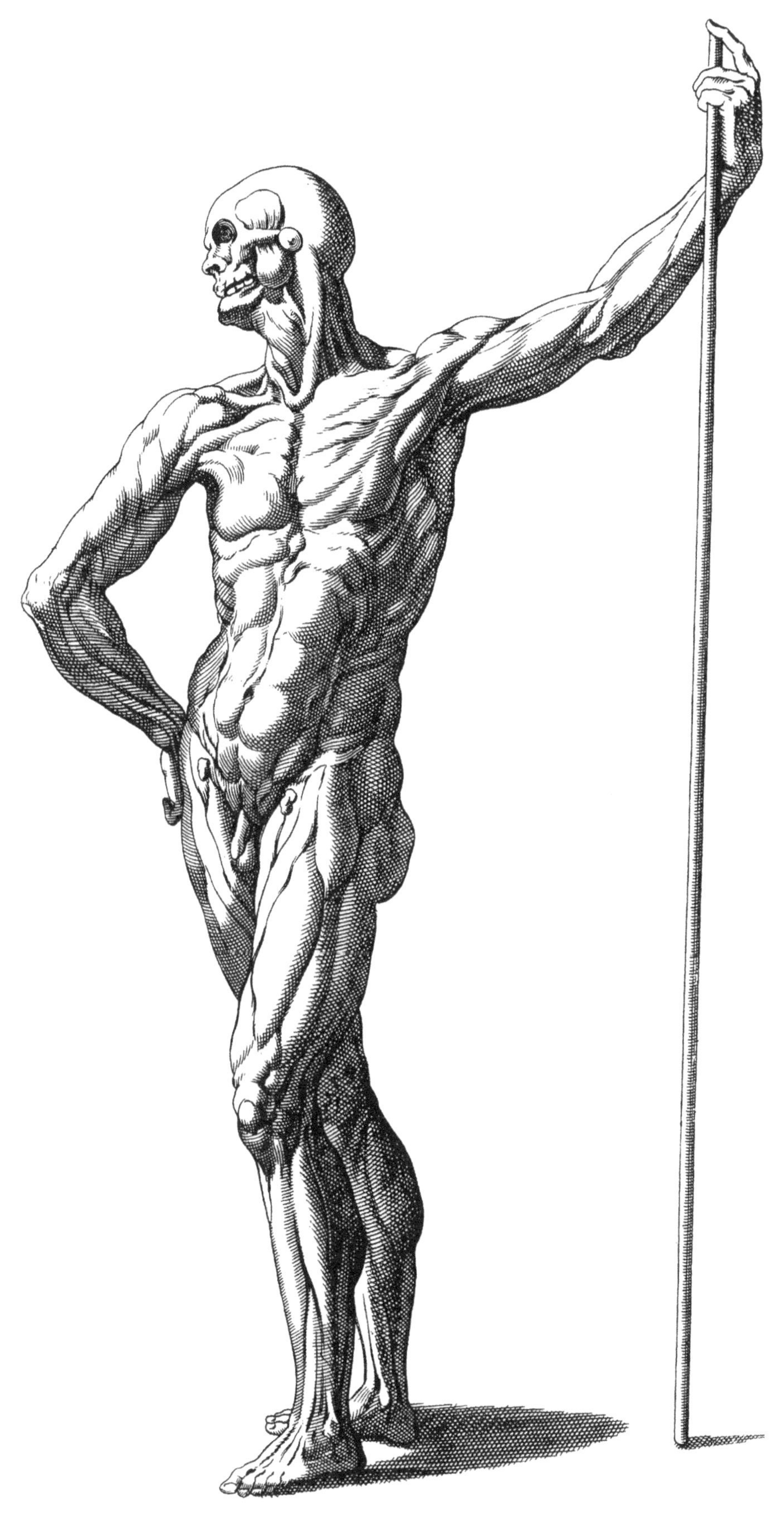

18

0
17
Head
Inch 1
16
1
12
13
1 Head
11
11
2
1
9
9
1
2
2
3
2
5
15
14
3
10
5
3
10
6
3
7
8
4
18
26
18
20
26
20
23
19
19
24
23
24
22
21
27
25
27
25
5
28
29
29
28
6
7
G.JEWITT. delt sc
7
0   1   2   3   8
4

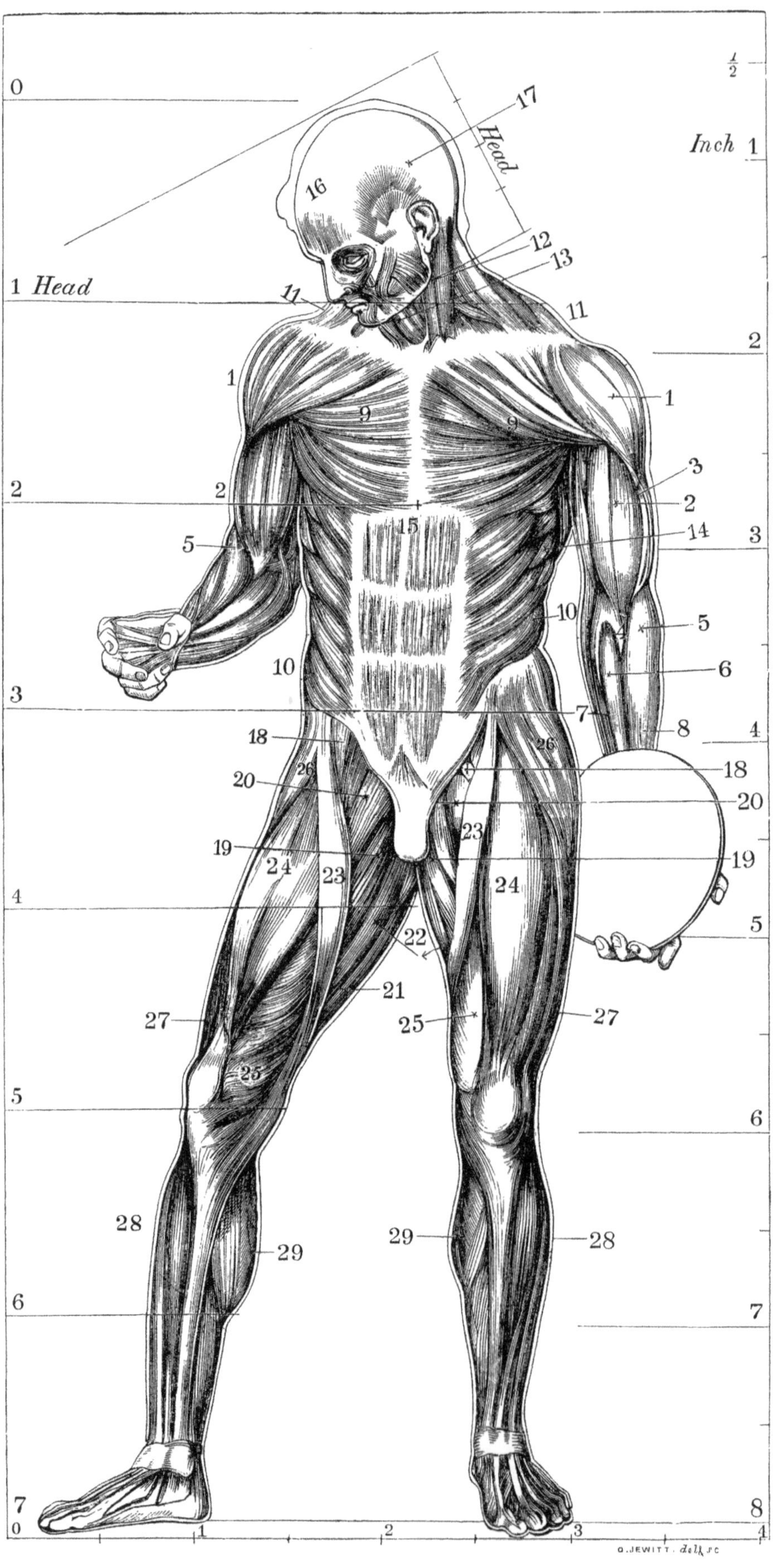

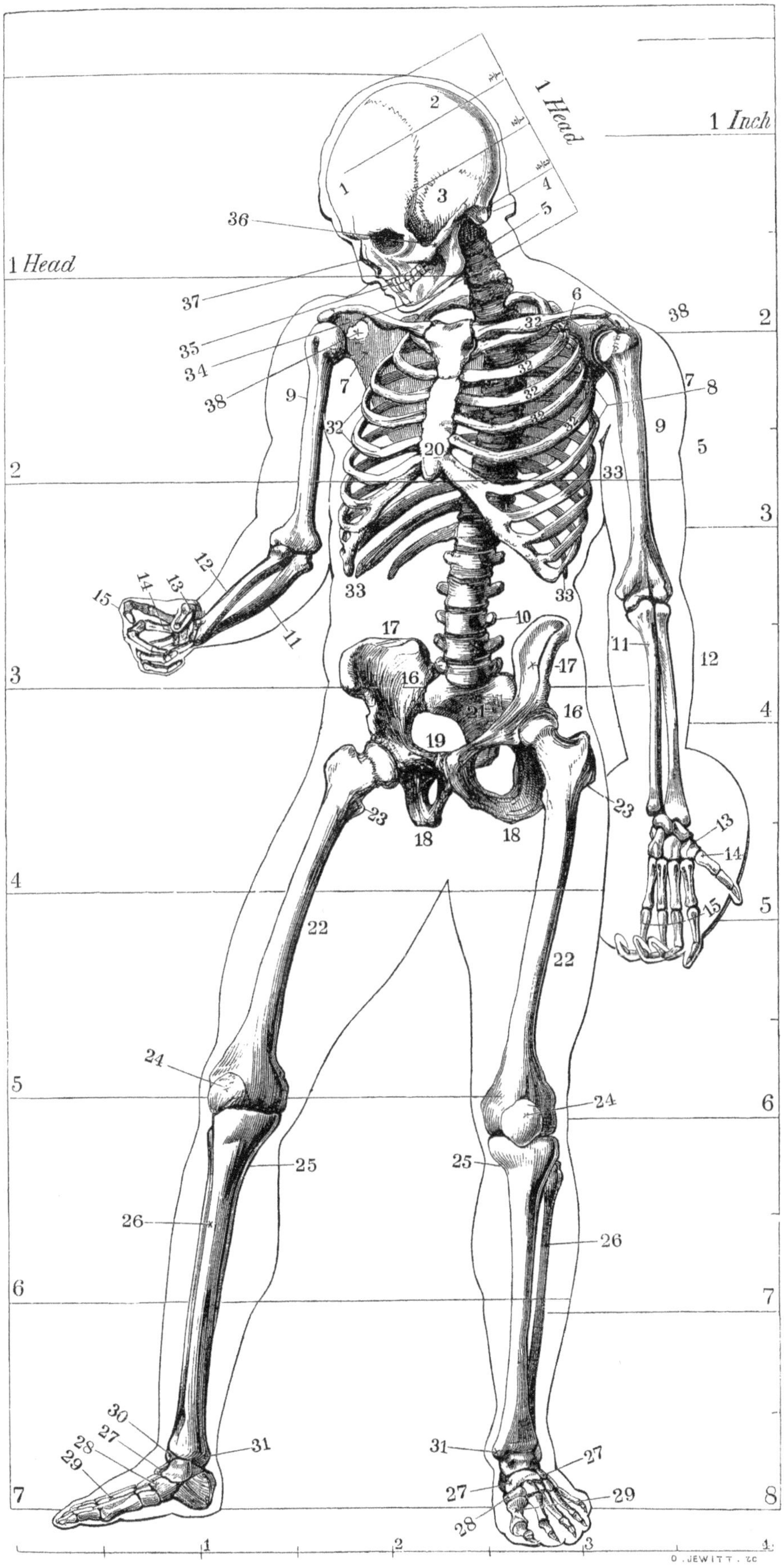

1 Head

1 Inch

1 Head

O. JEWITT. SC

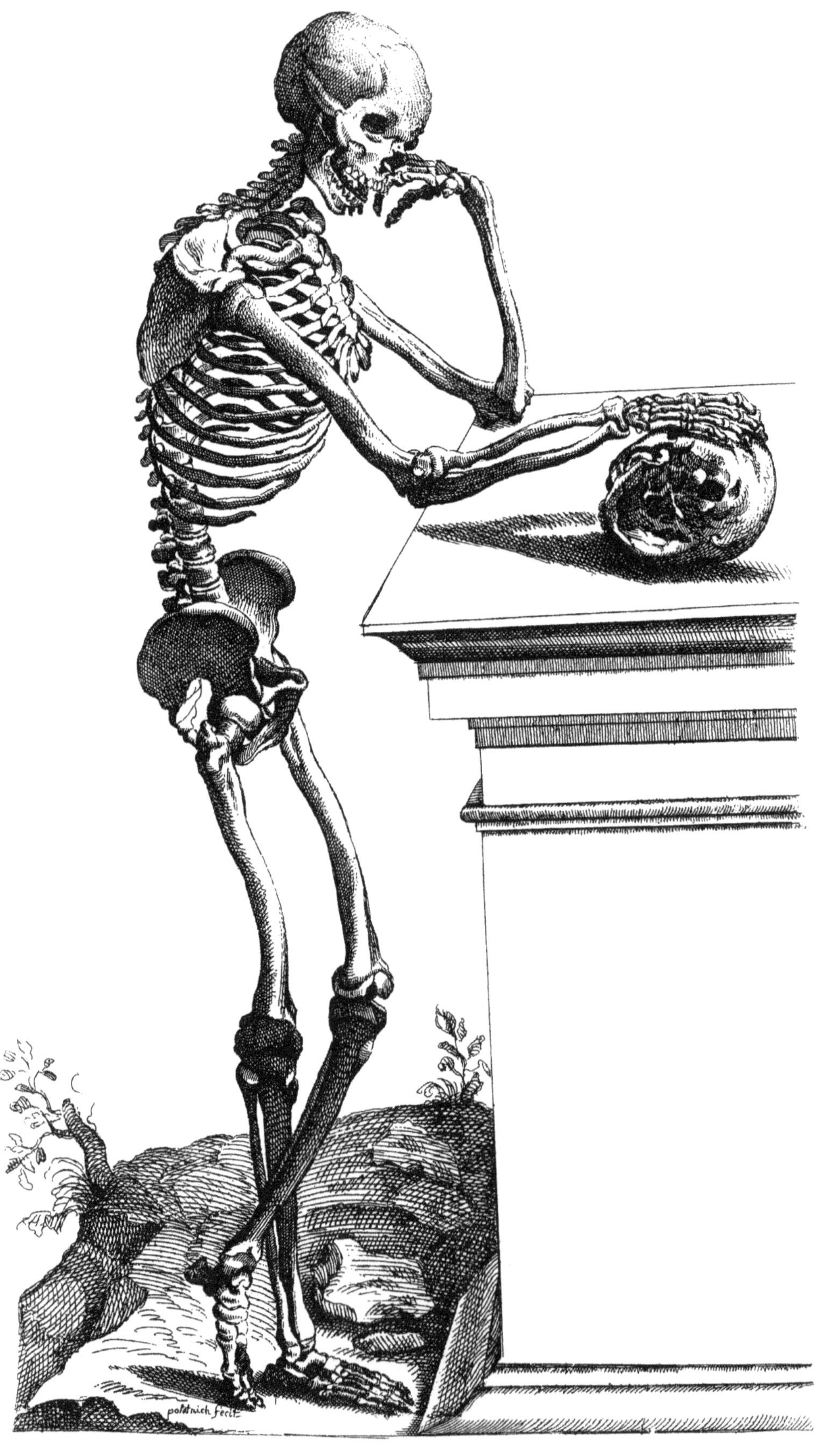

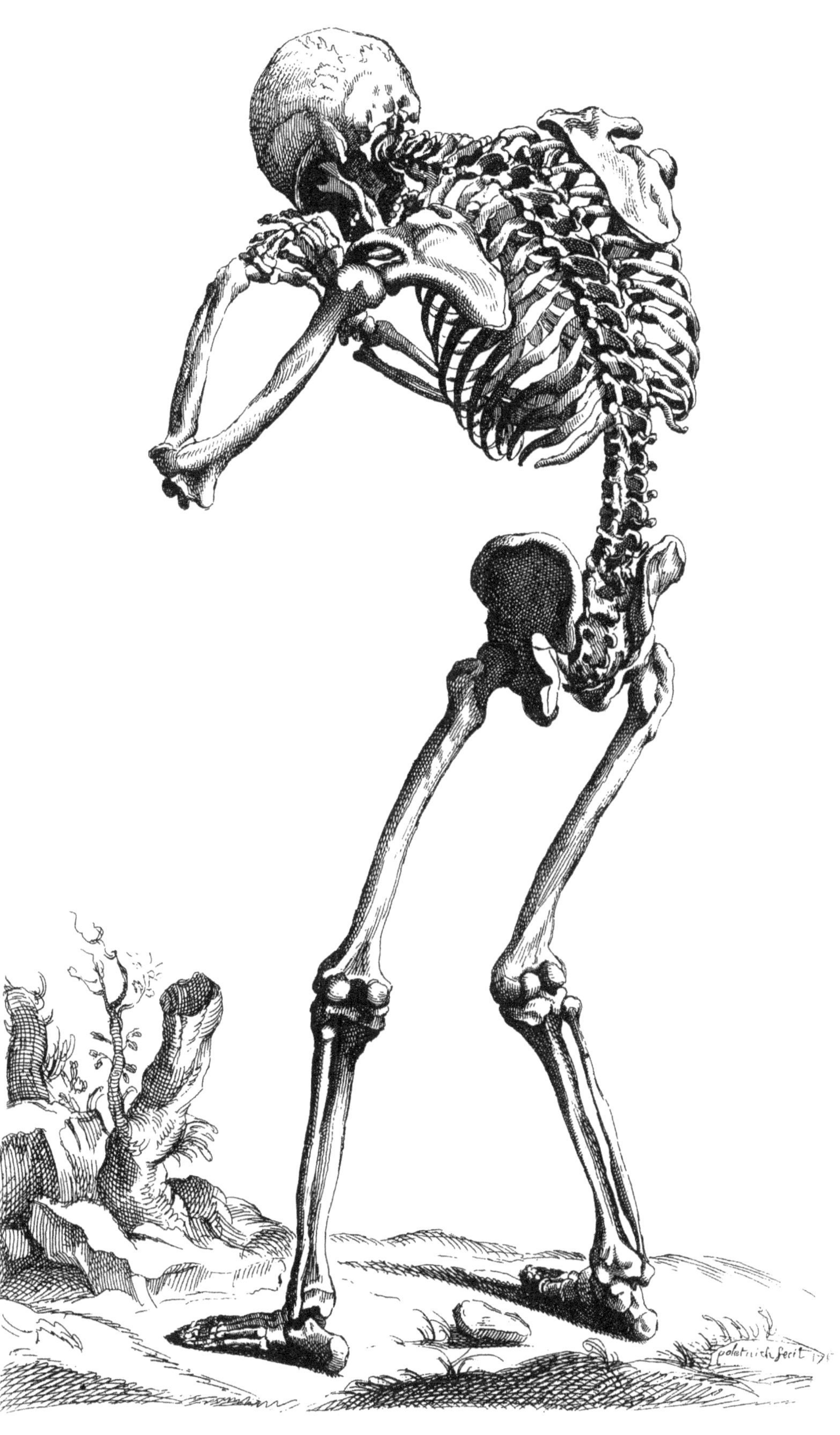

22

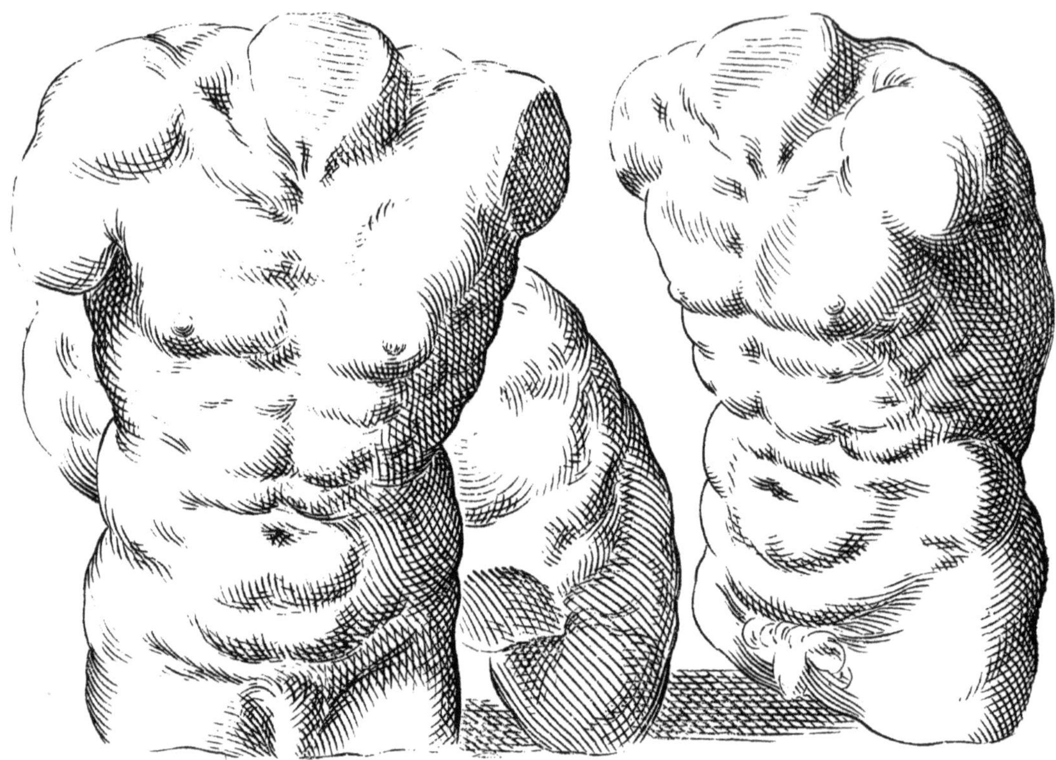

23

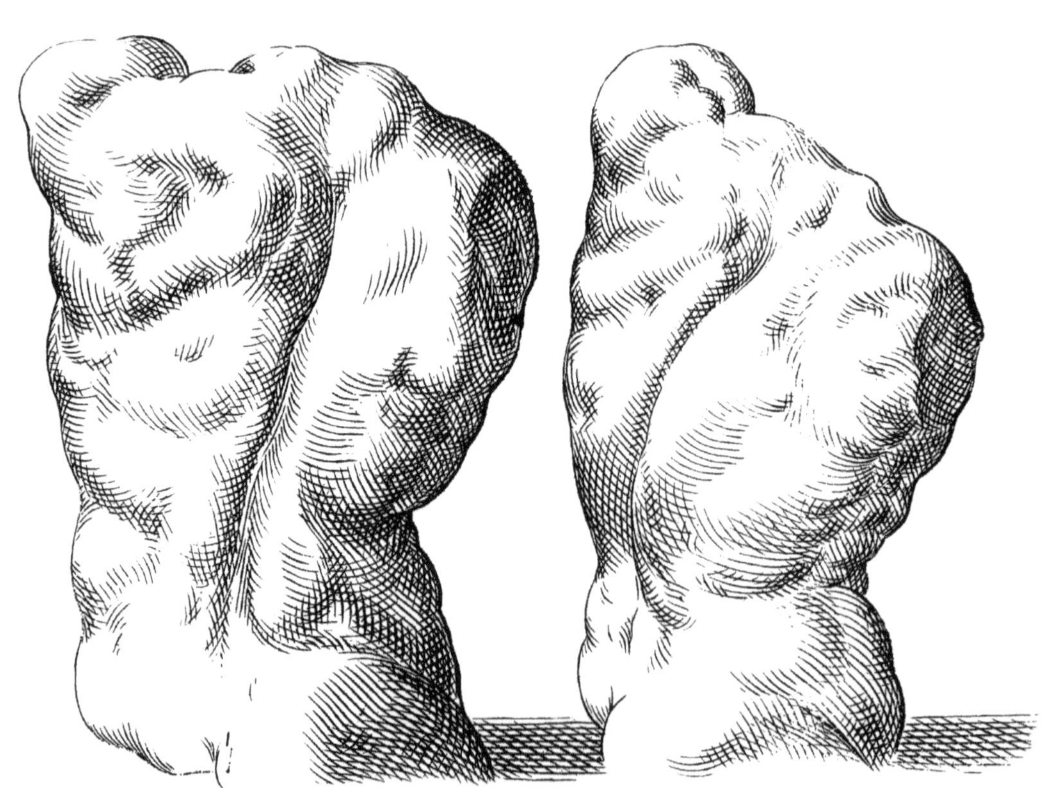

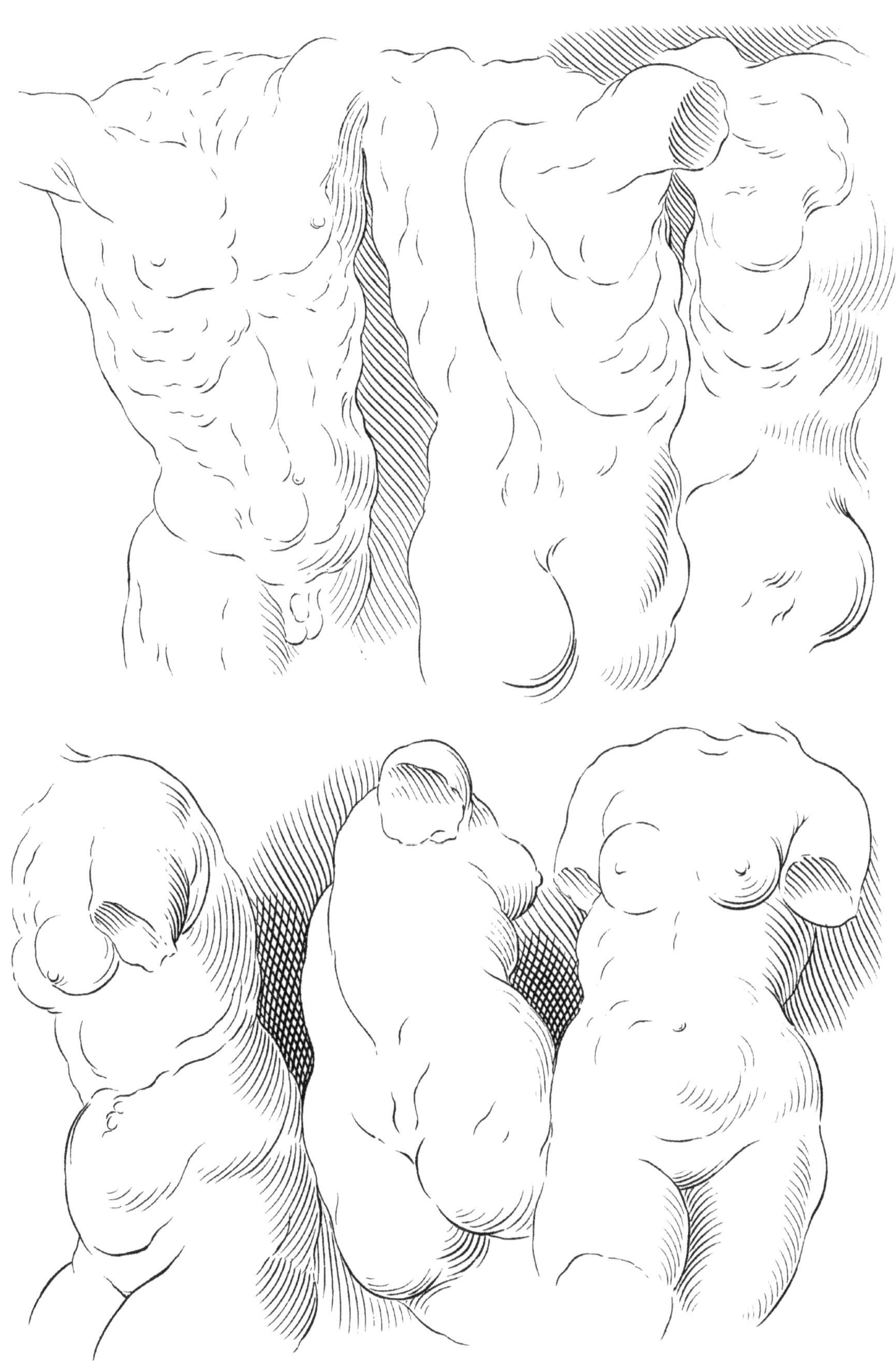

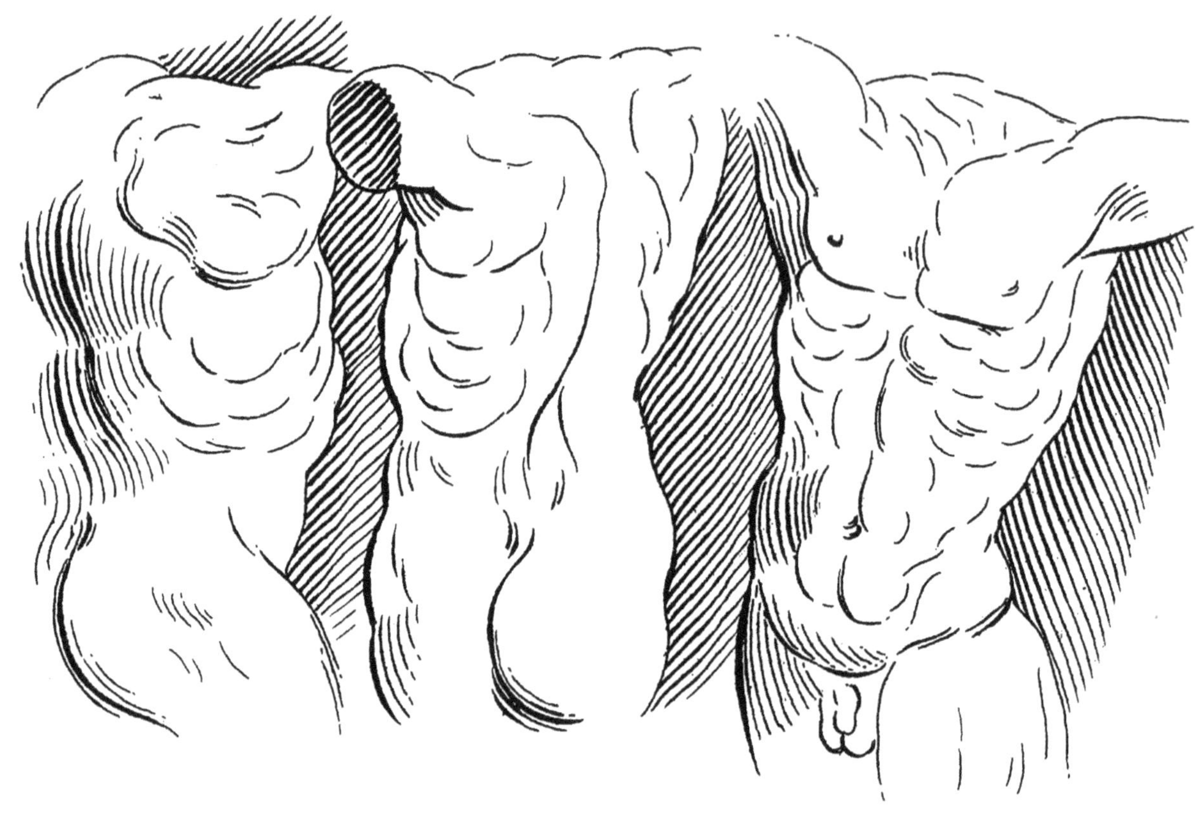

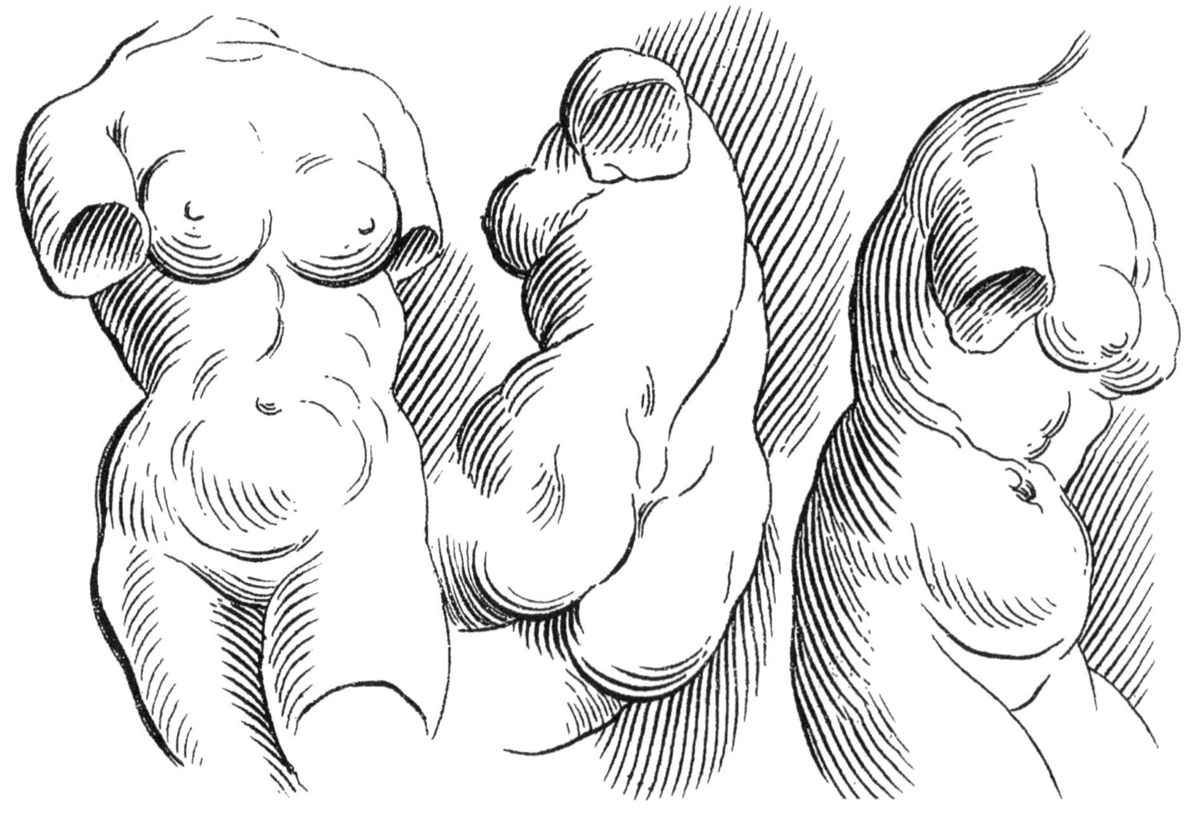

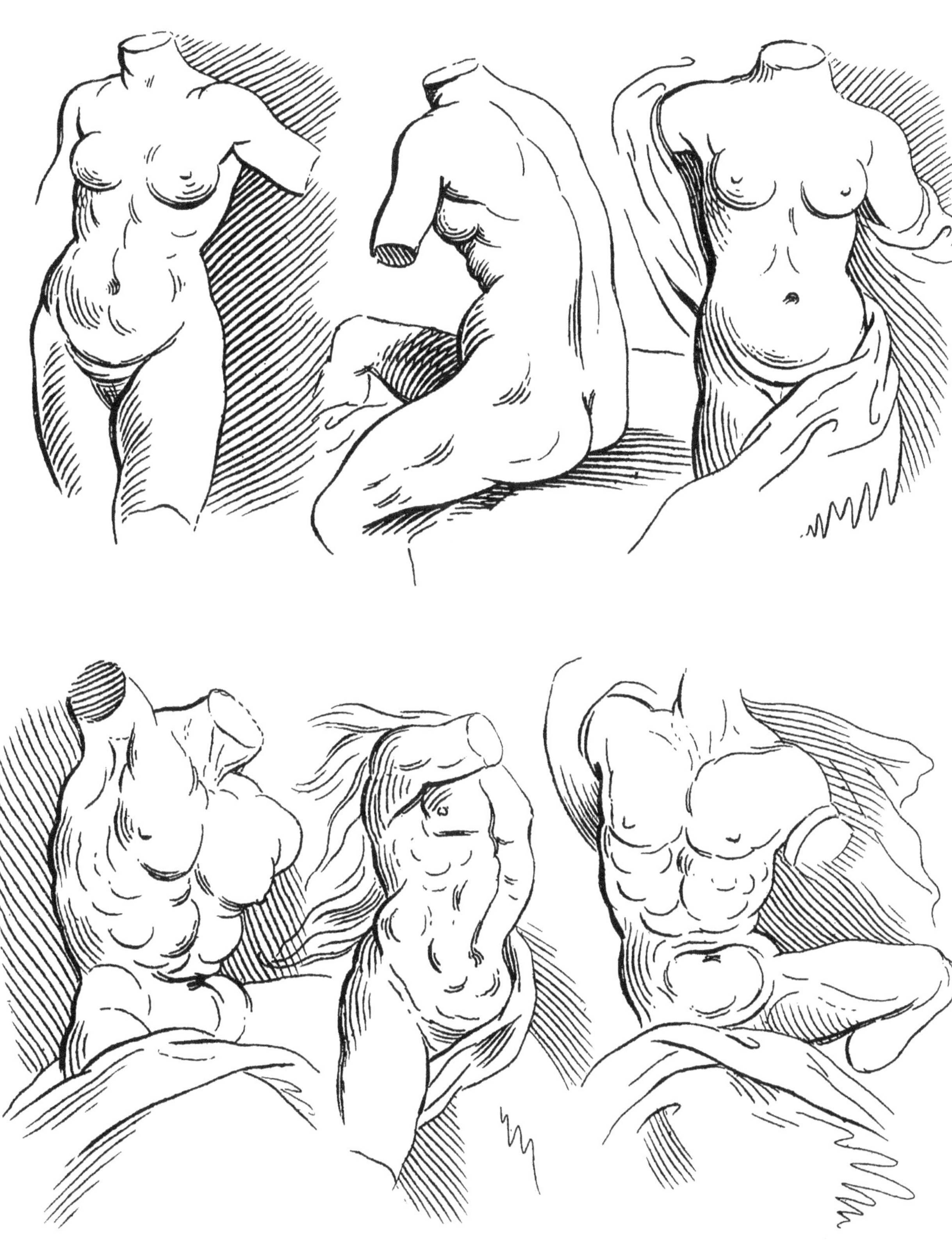

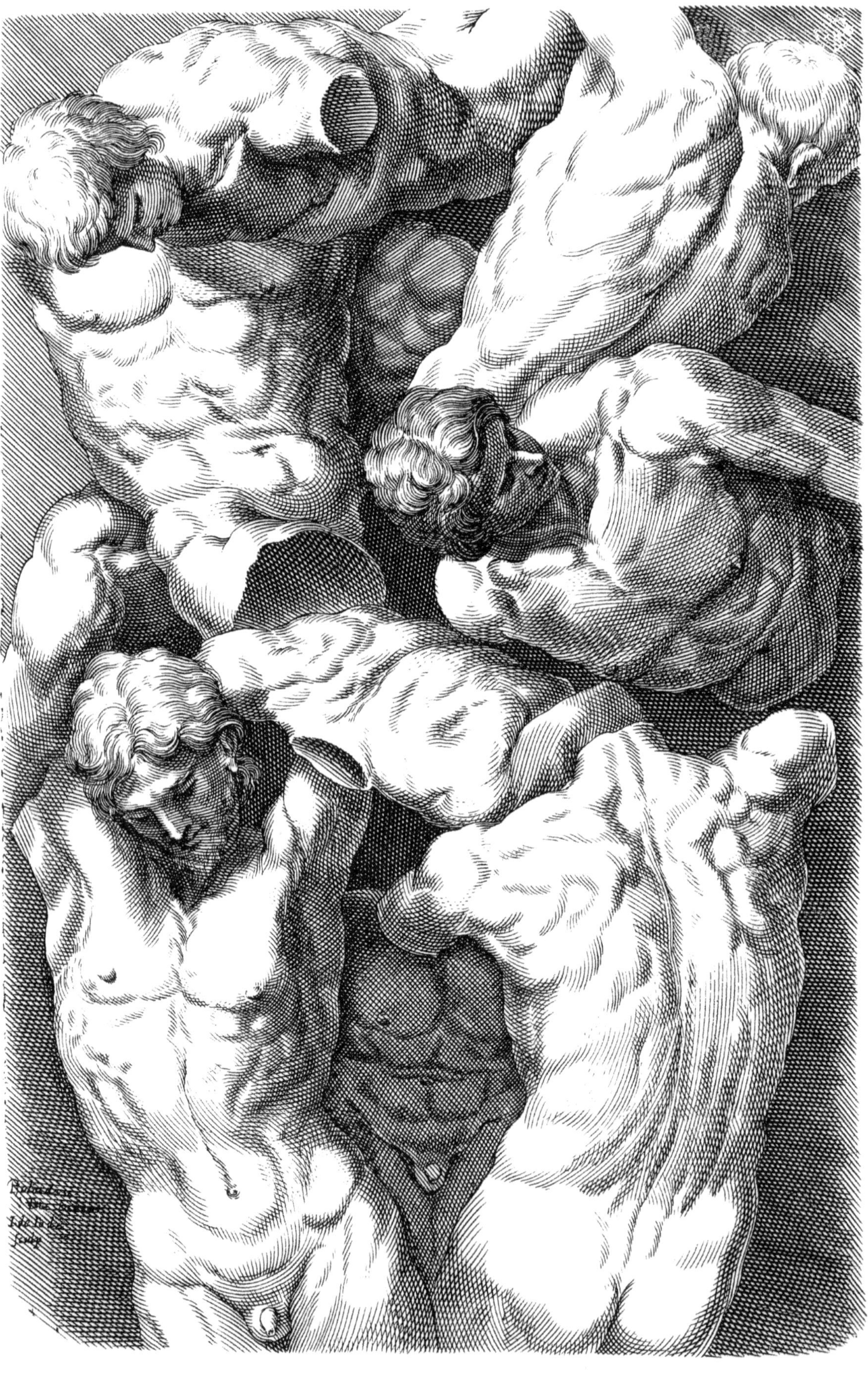

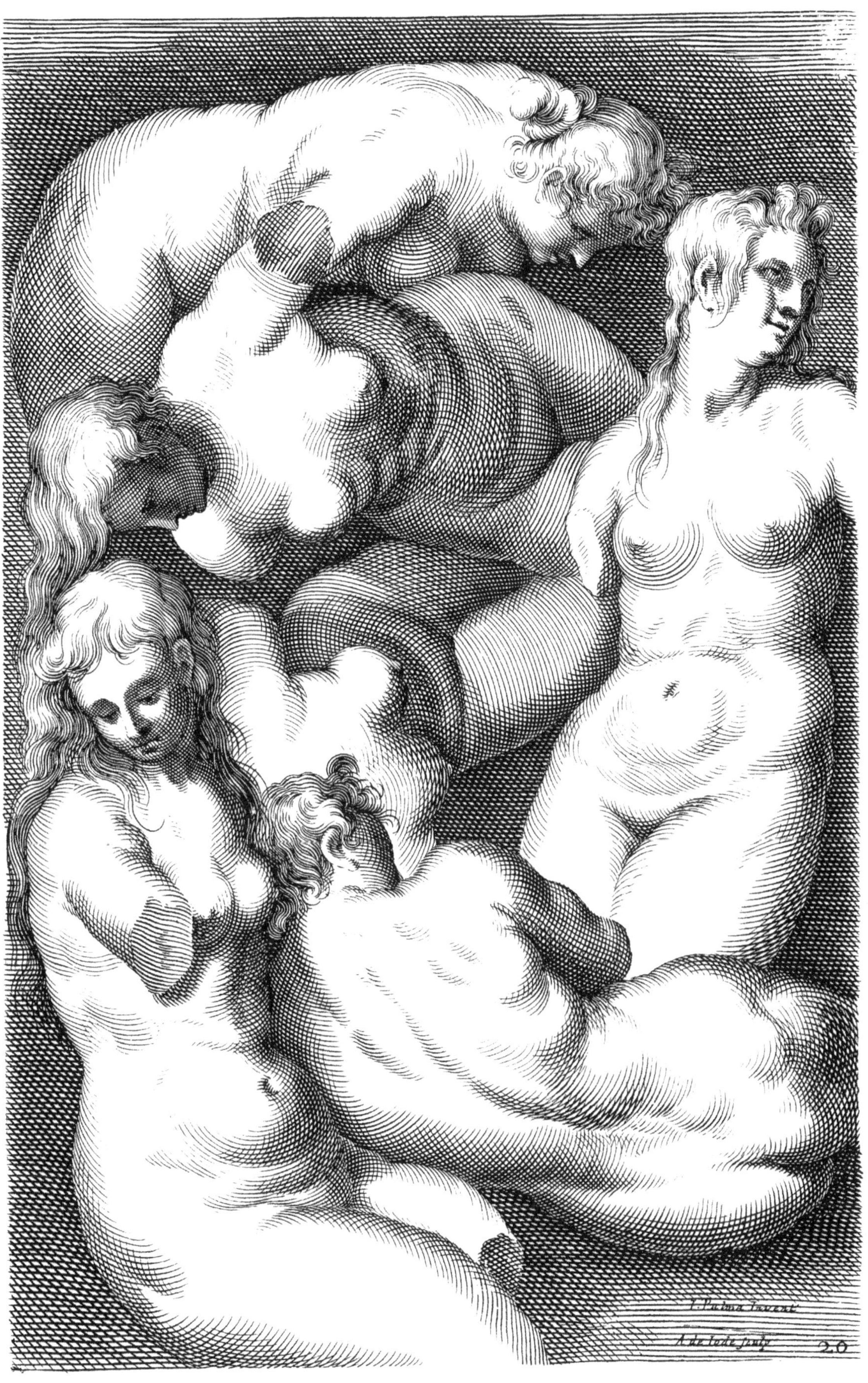

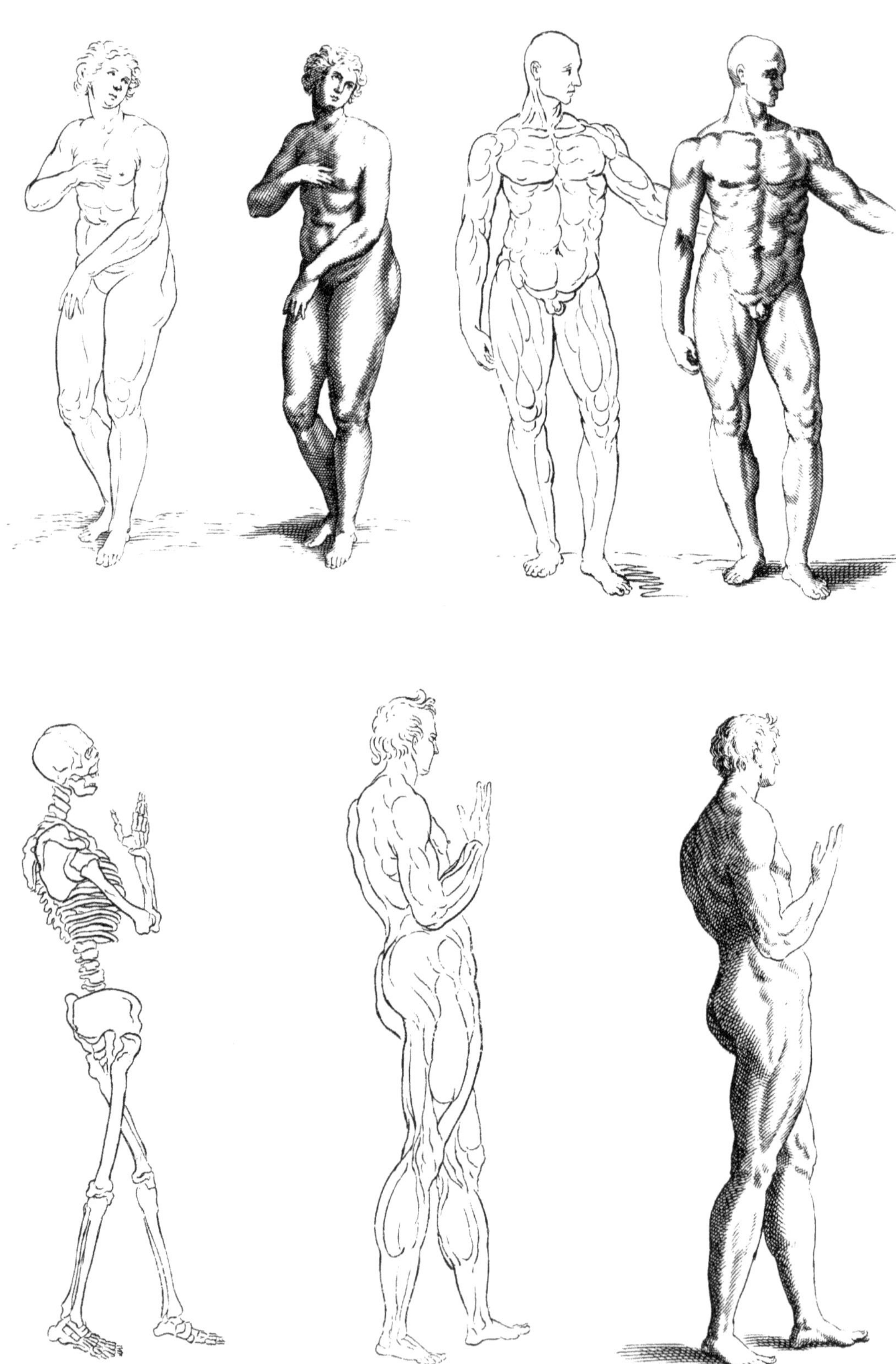

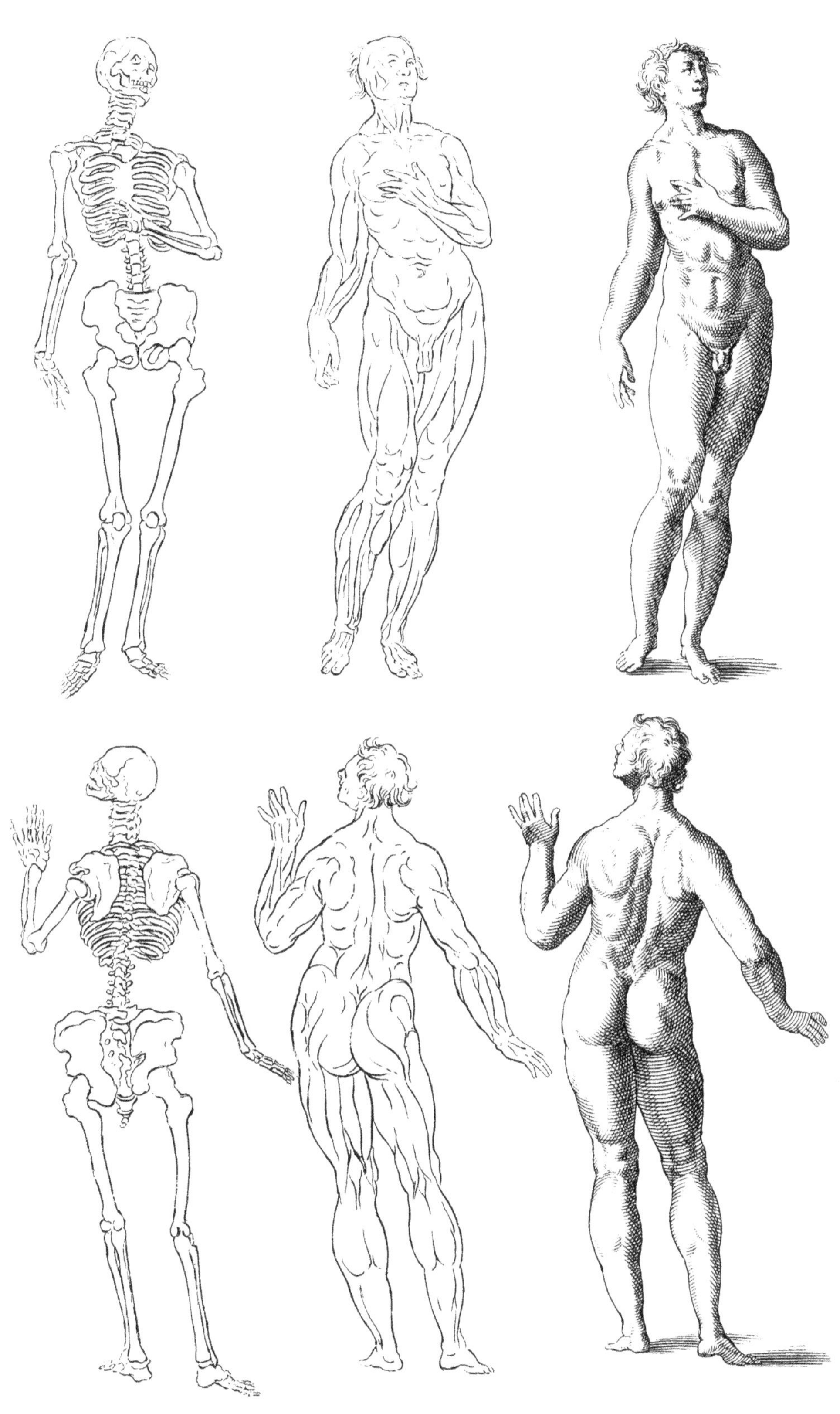

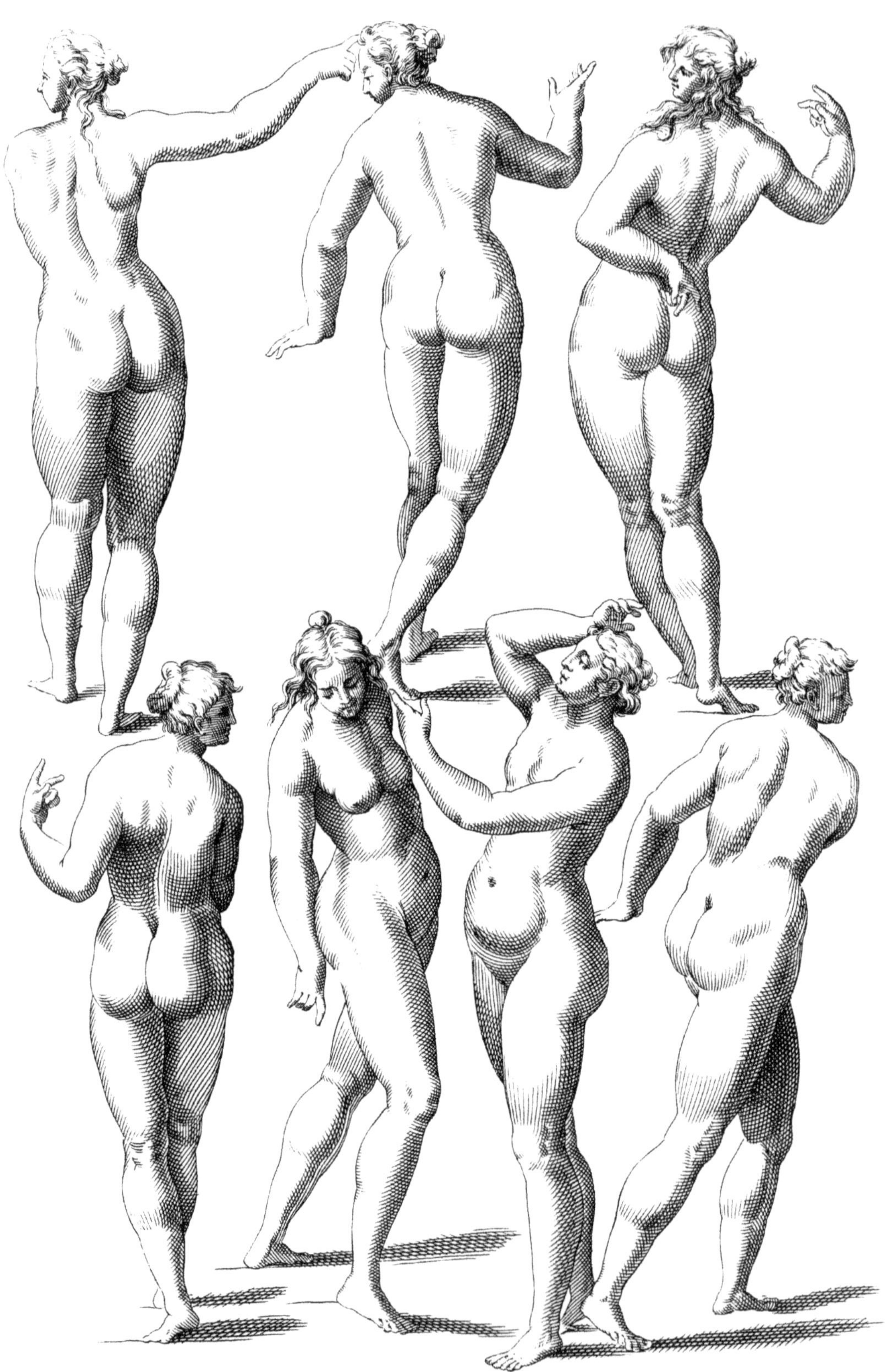

32

33

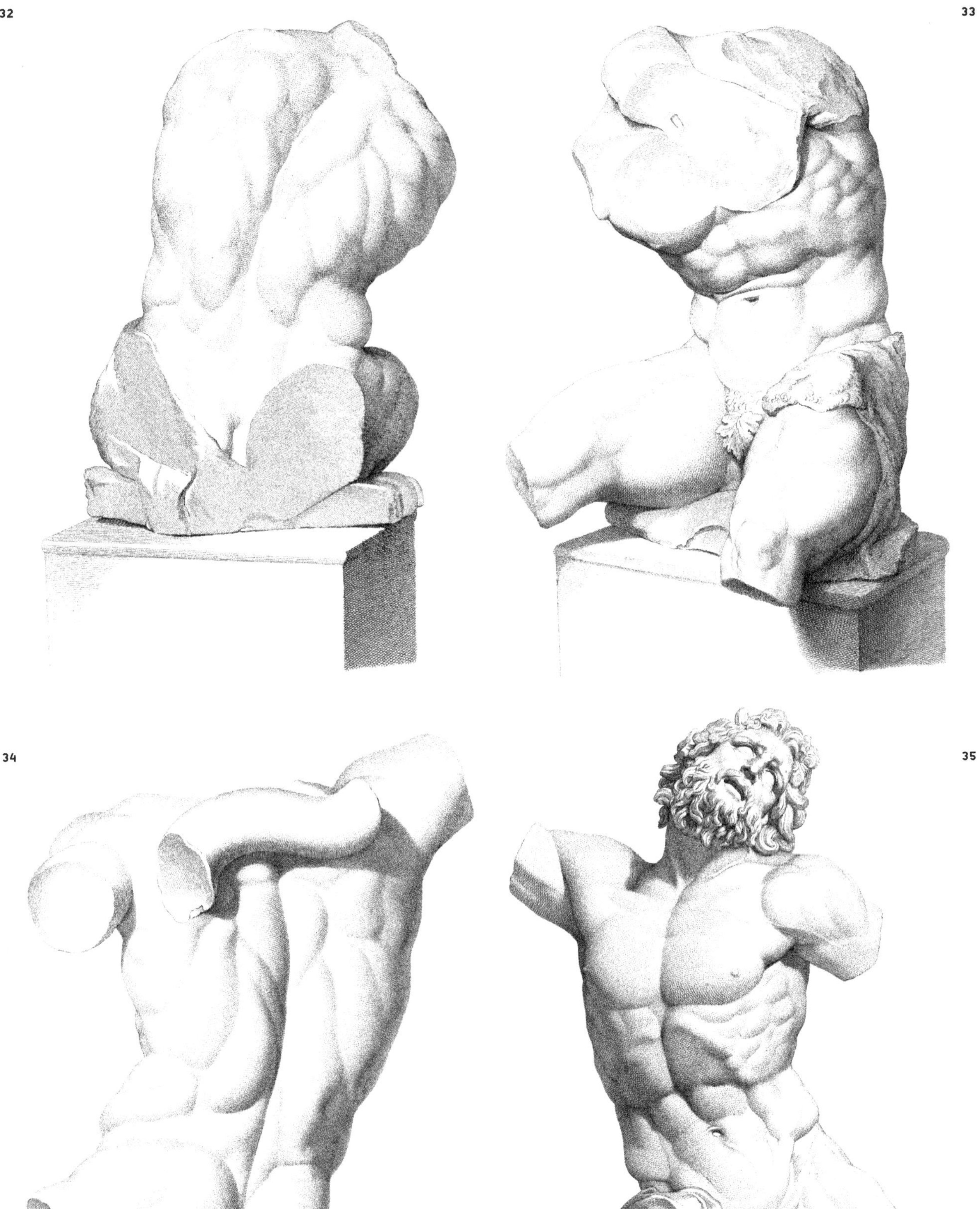

34

35

DRAWING THE HUMAN FIGURE

36

37

38

39

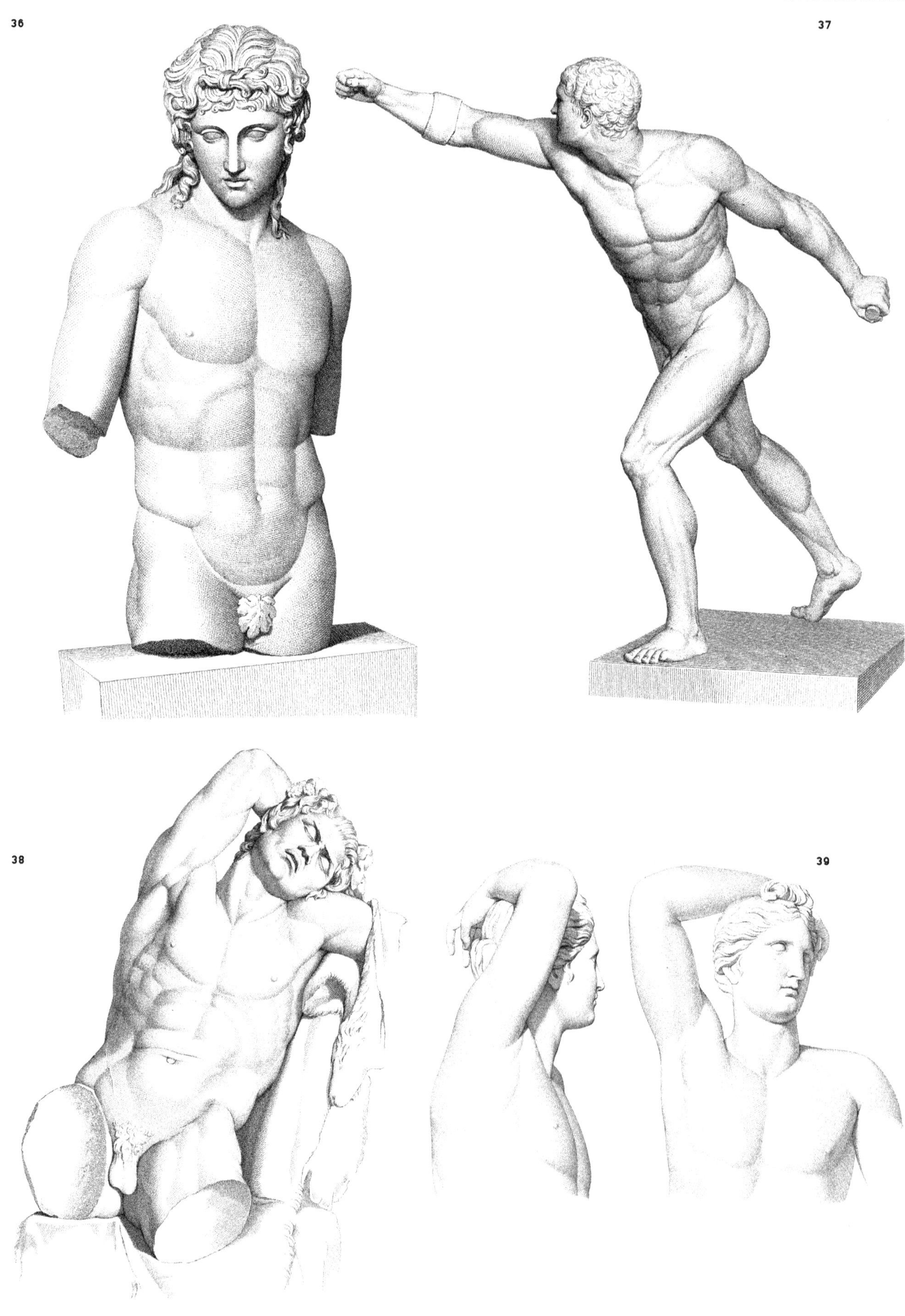

40

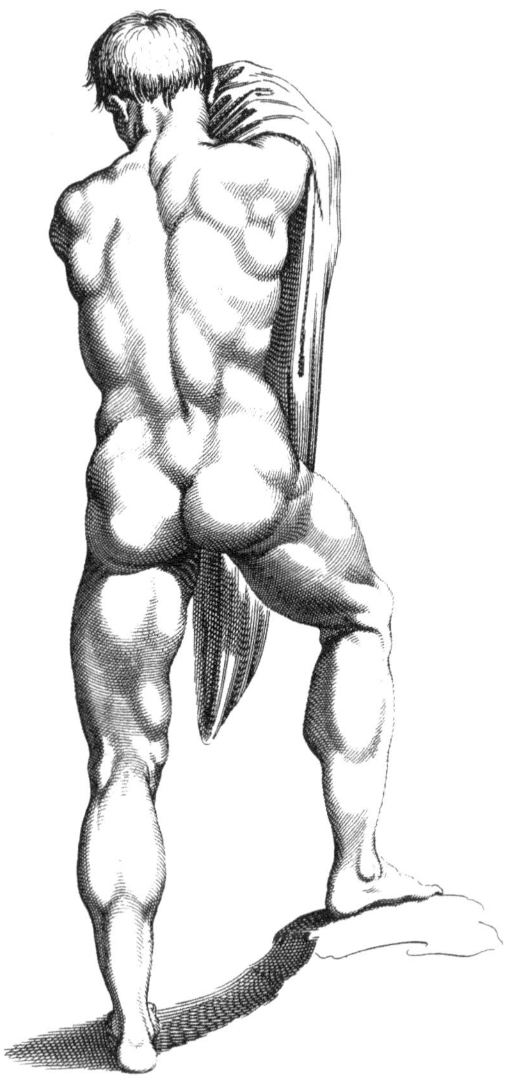

41

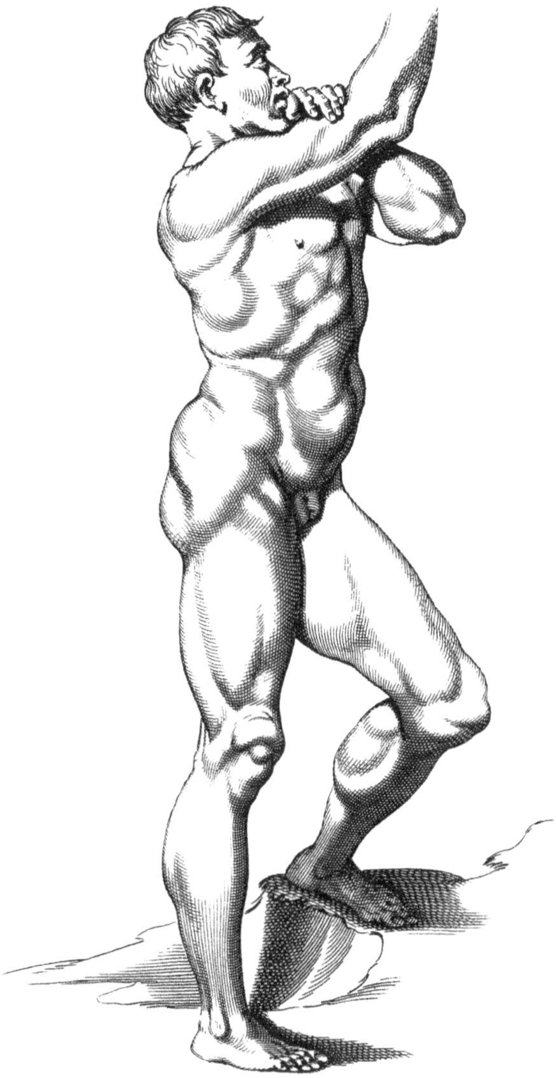

42

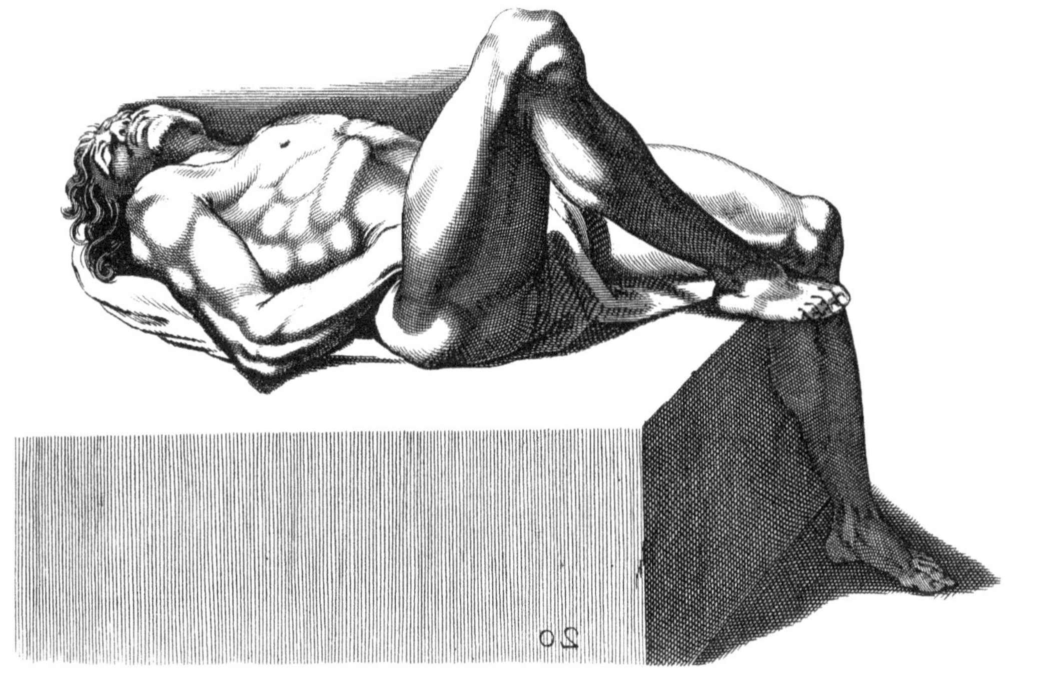

43

44

46

45

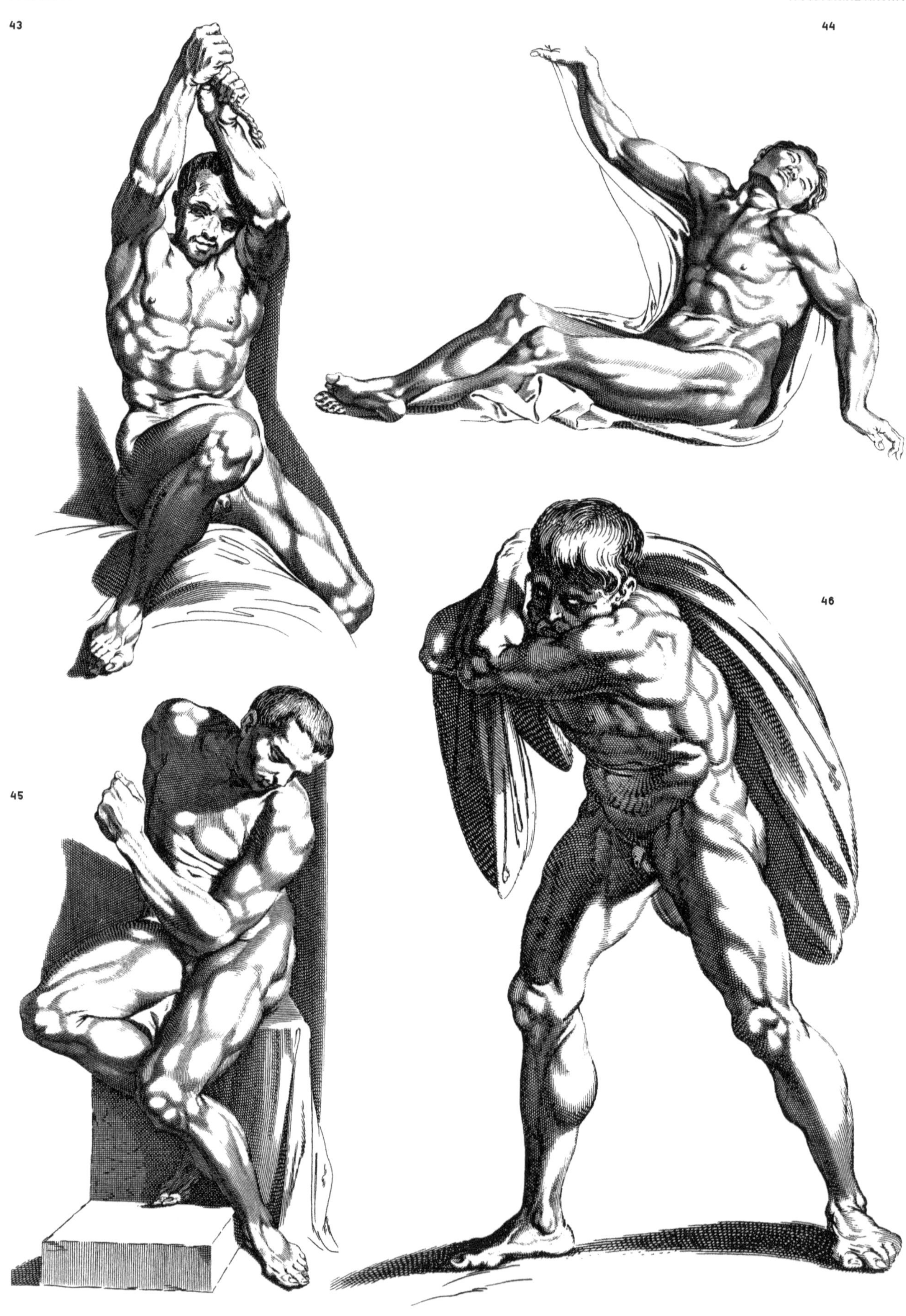

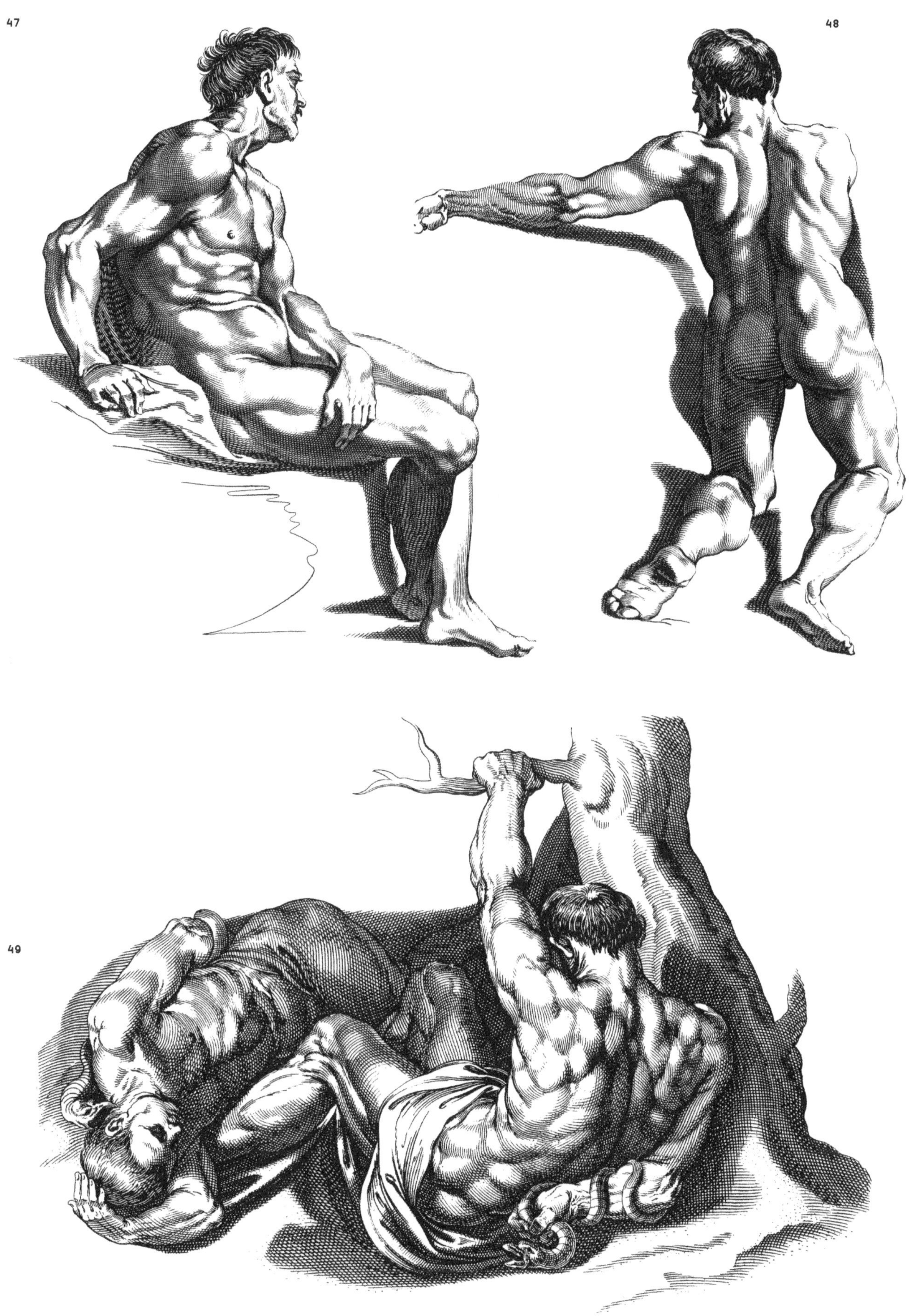

50

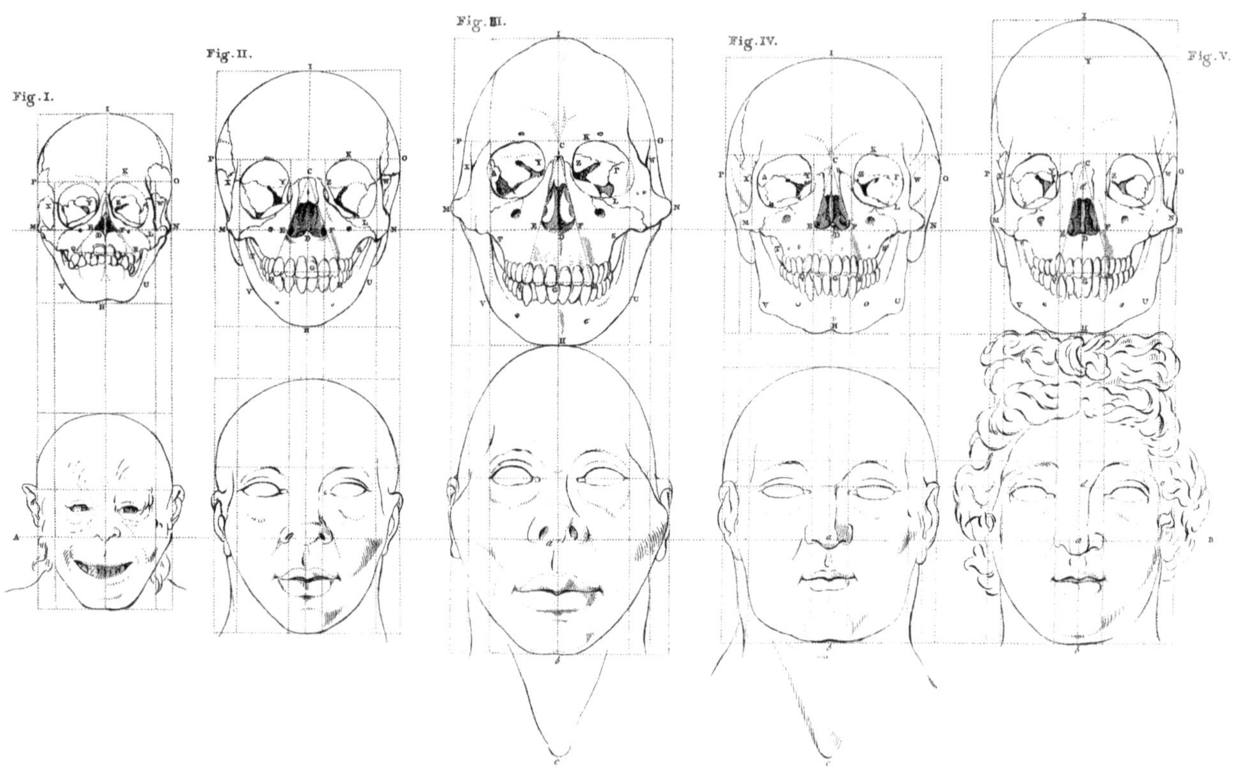

51

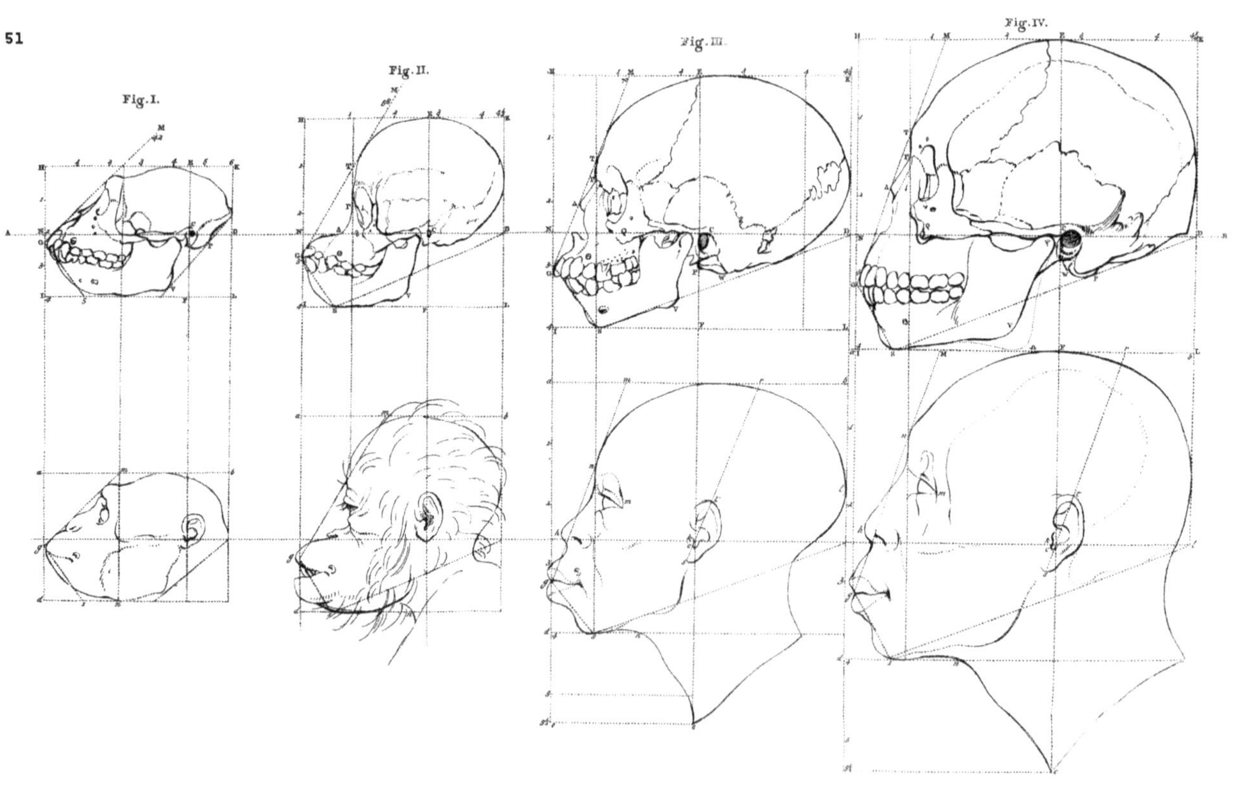

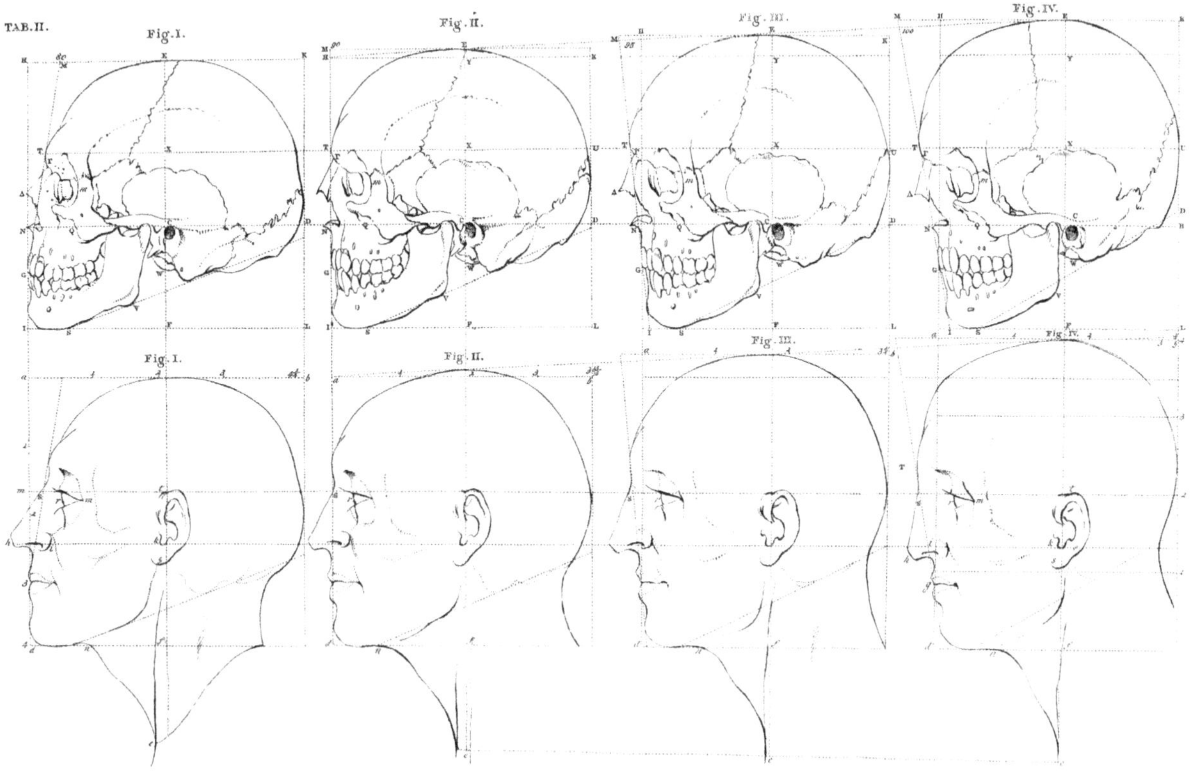

TAB.II.   Fig.I.   Fig.II.   Fig.III.   Fig.IV.
Fig.I.   Fig.II.   Fig.III.   Fig.IV.

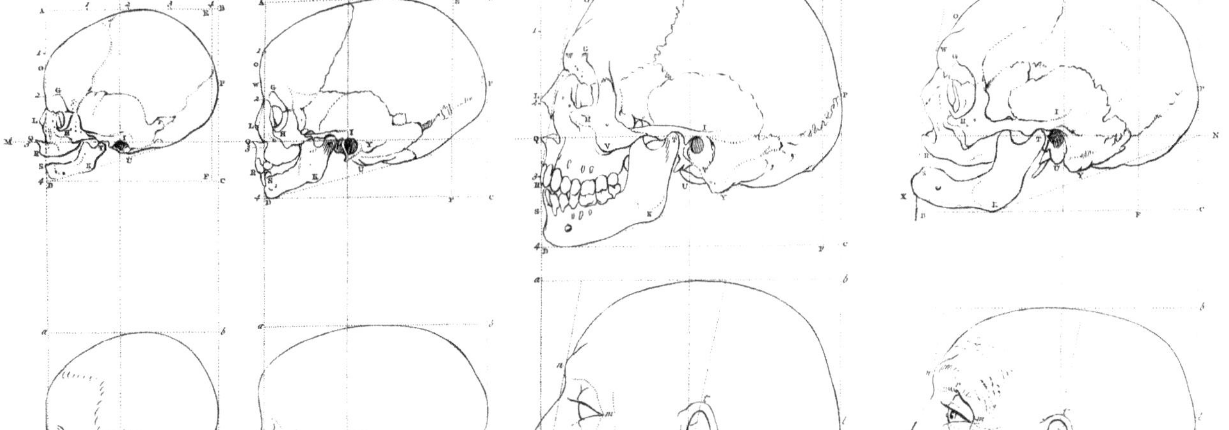

Fig.I.   Fig.II.   Fig.III.   Fig.IV.

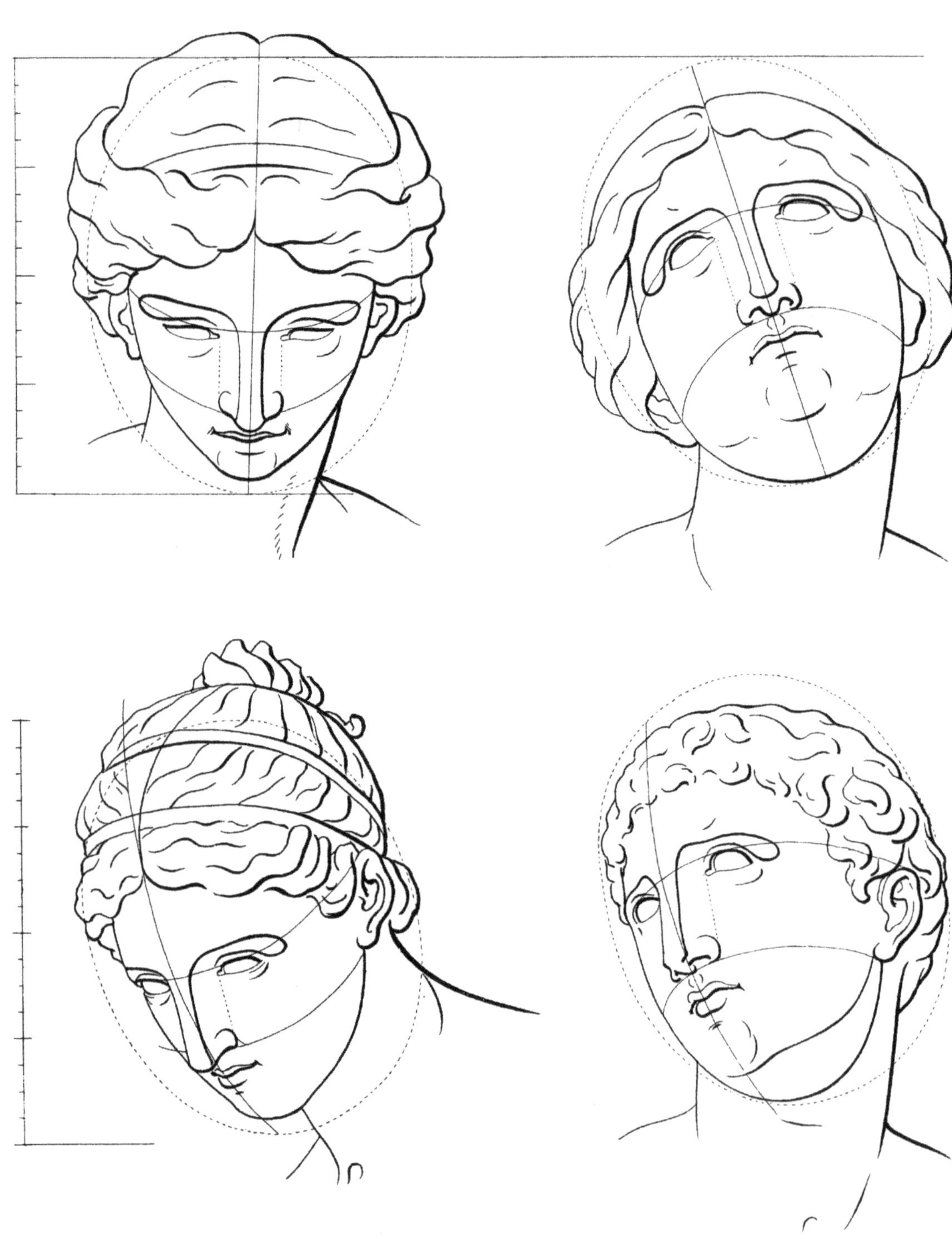

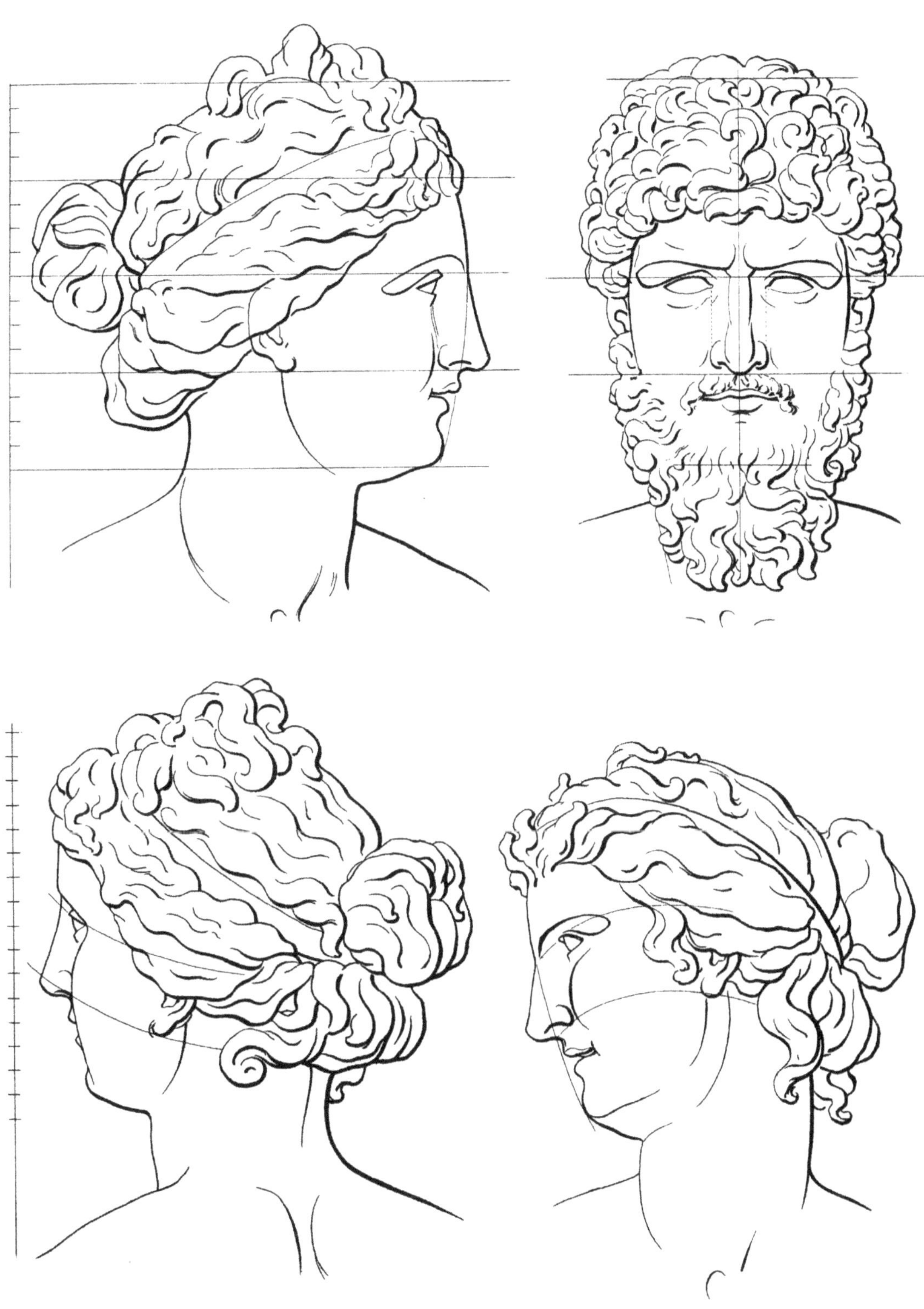

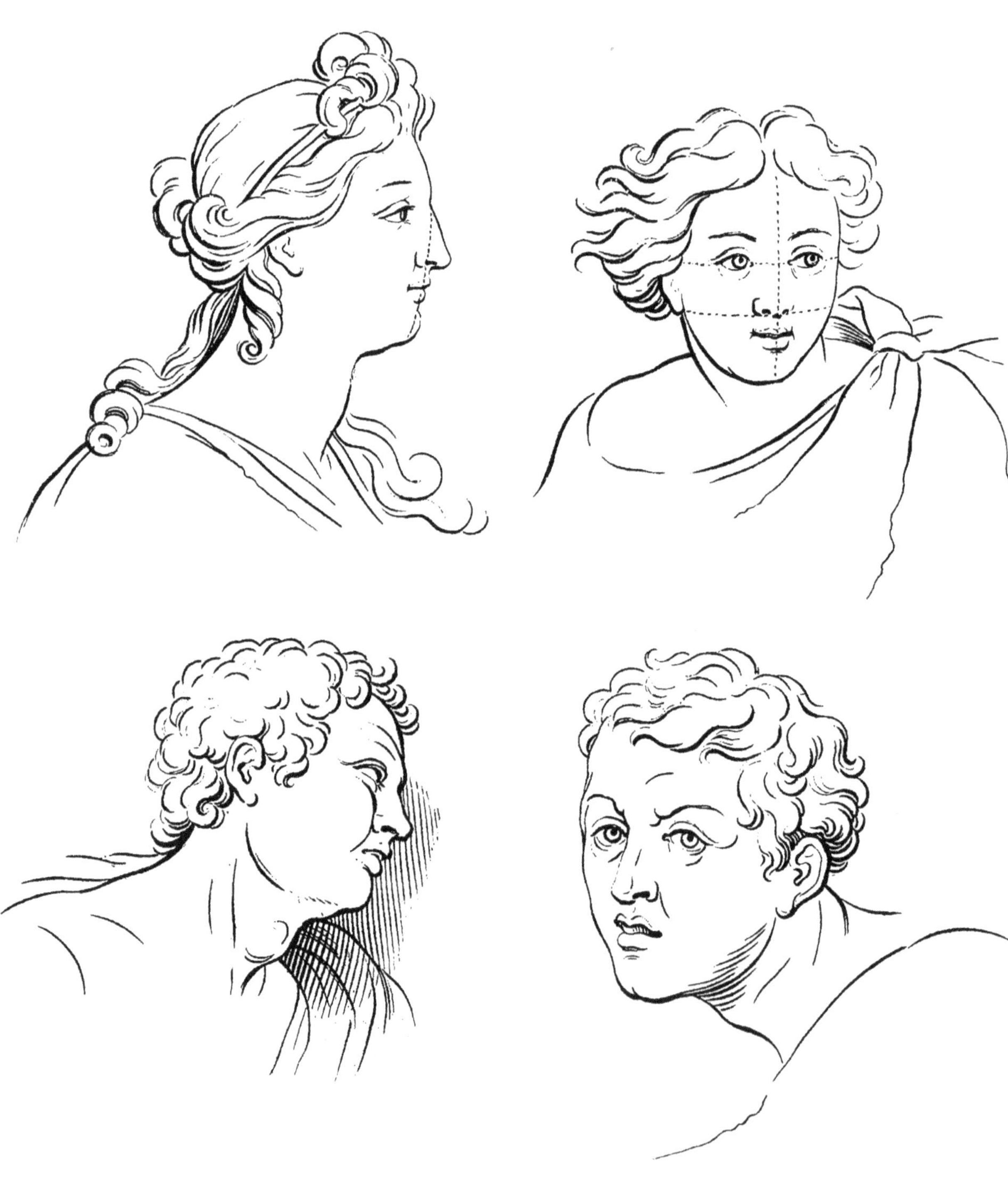

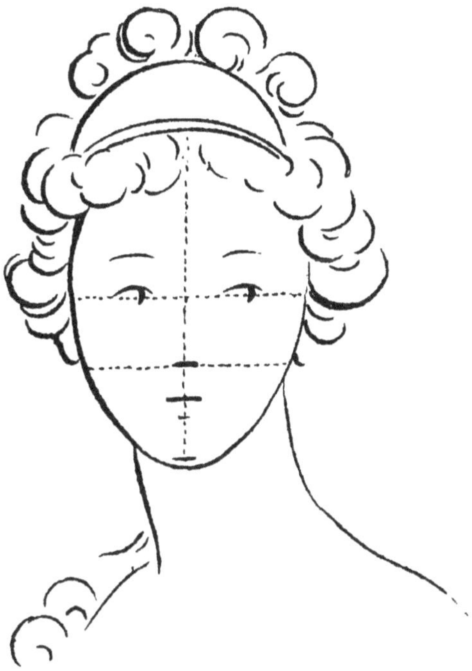

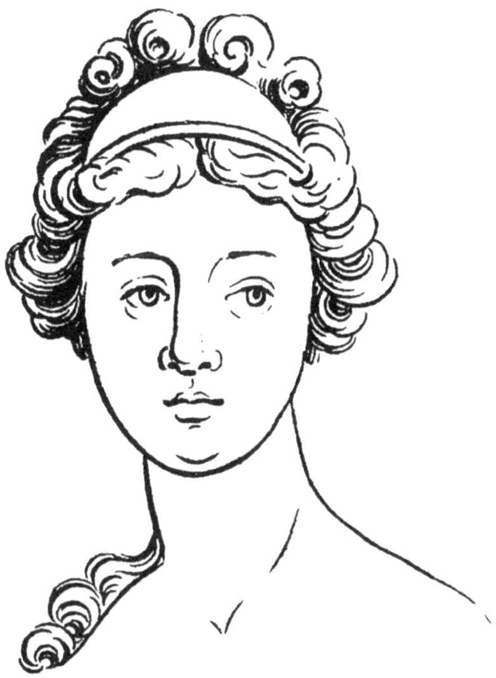

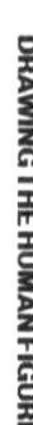
DRAWING THE HUMAN FIGURE

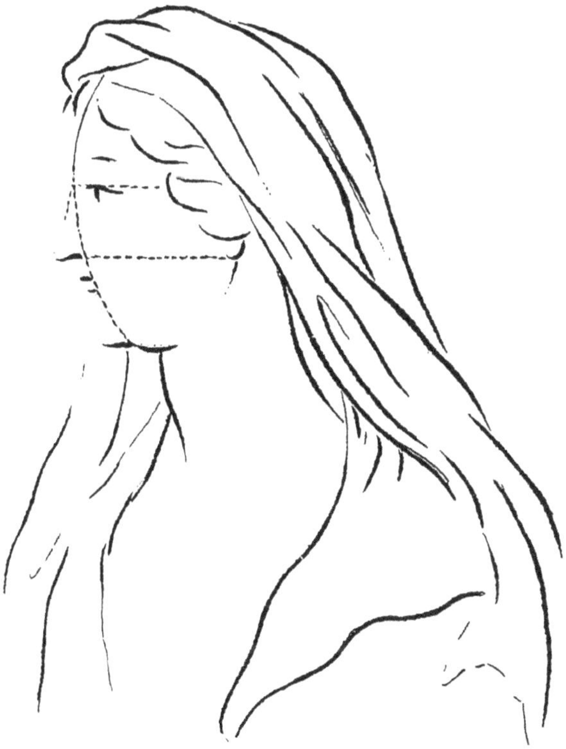

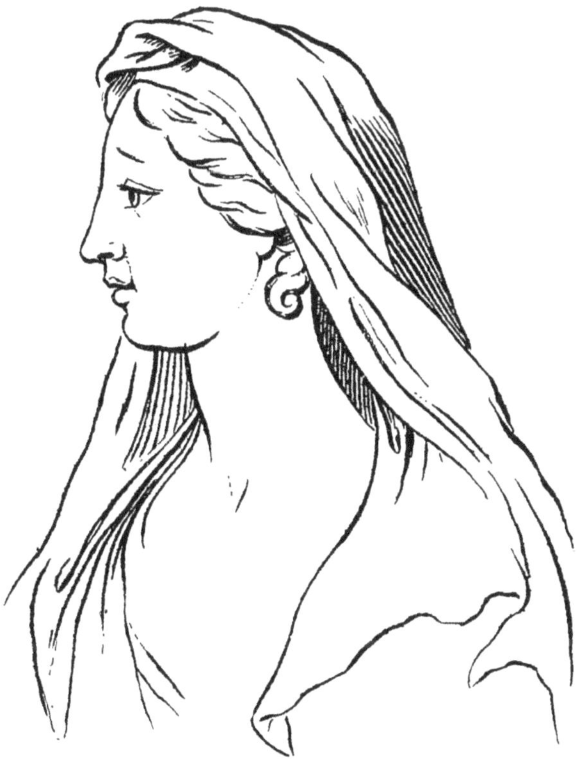

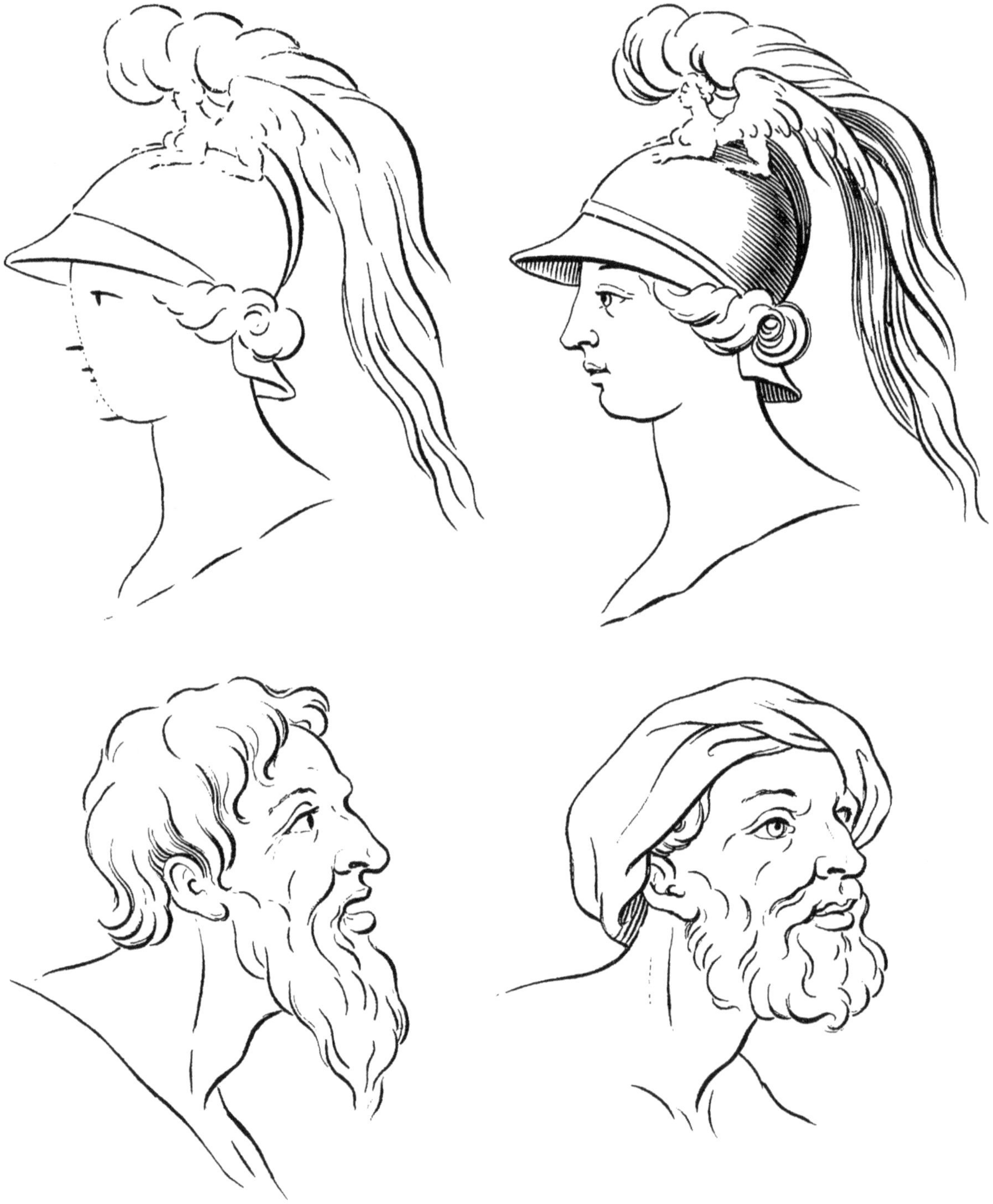

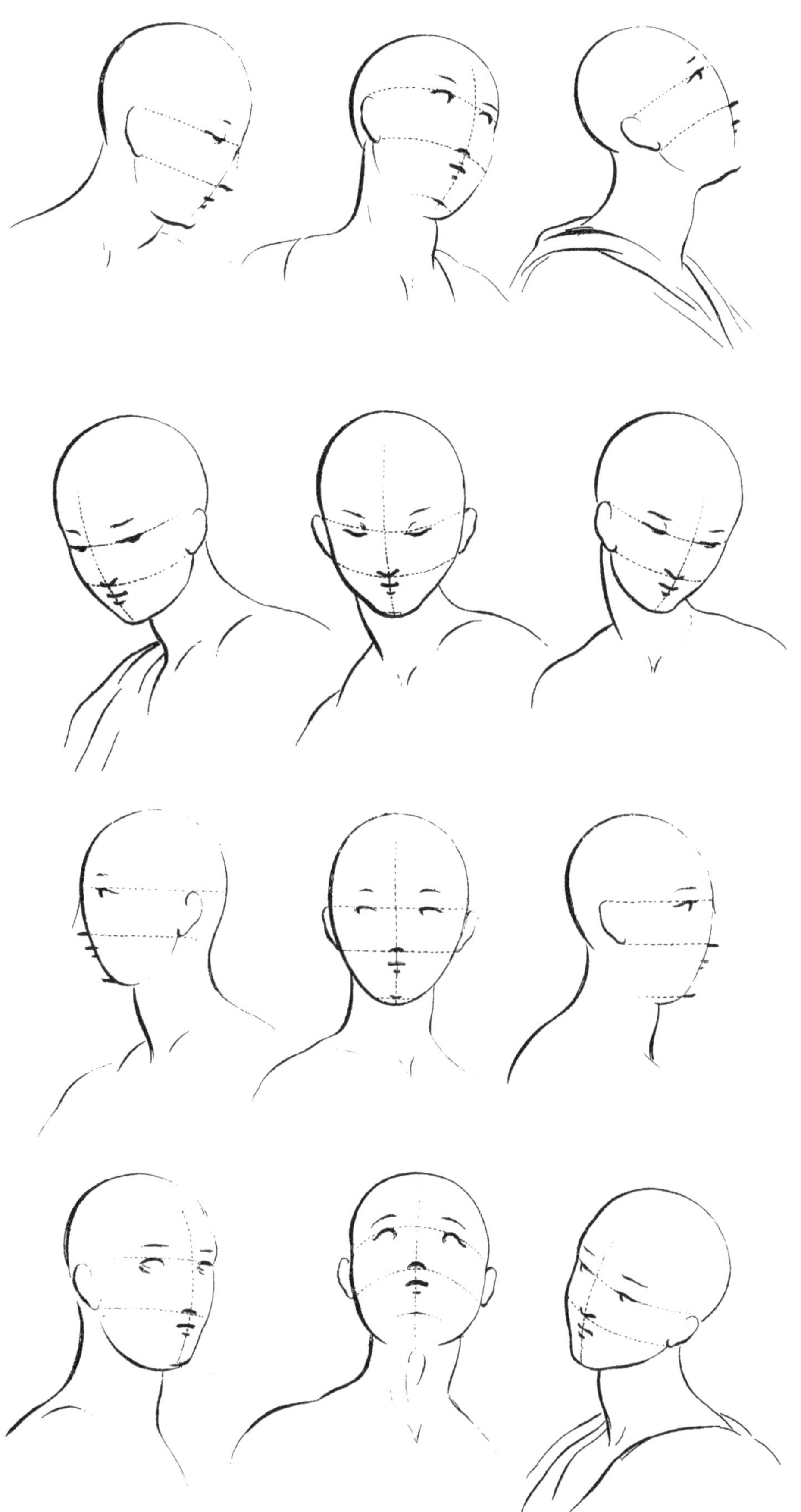

DRAWING THE HUMAN FIGURE

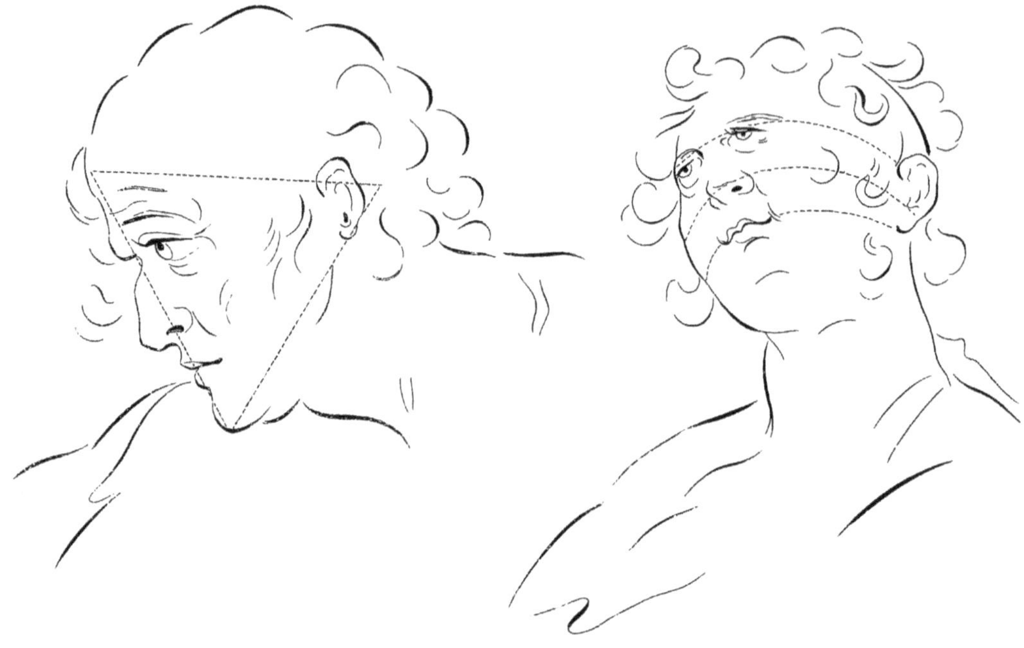

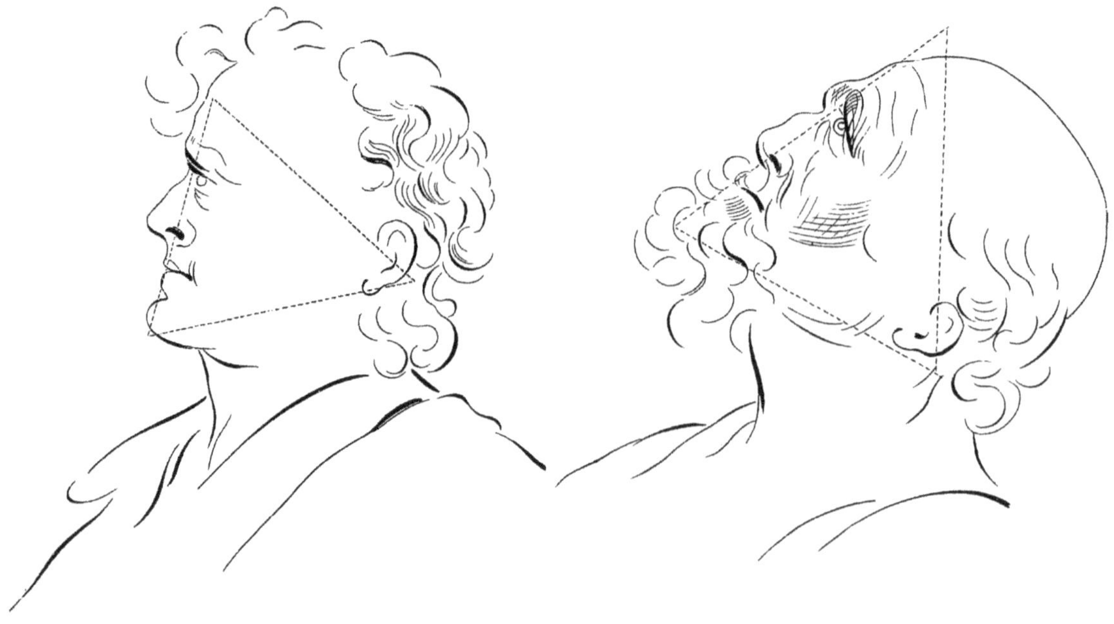

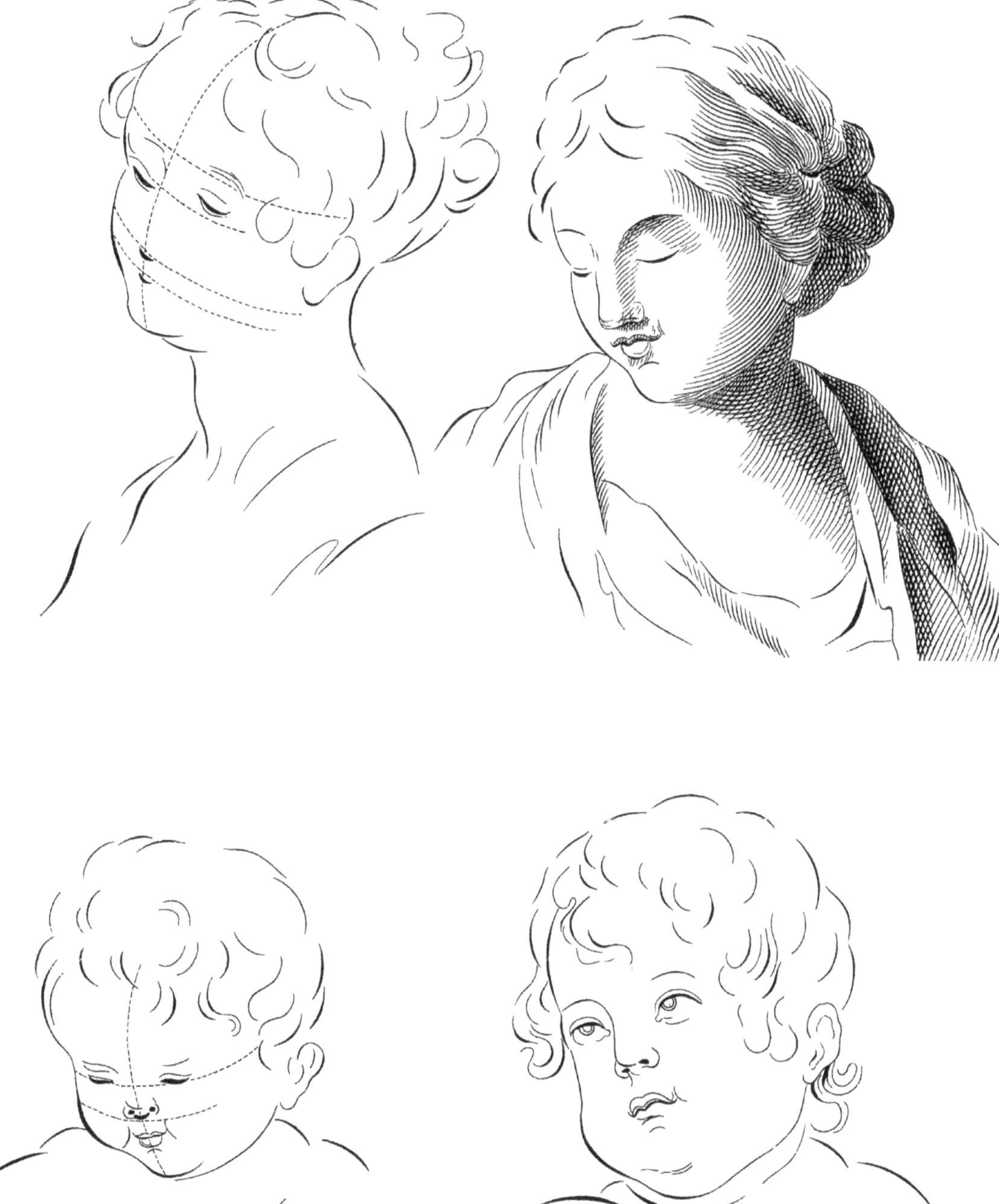

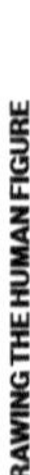
DRAWING THE HUMAN FIGURE

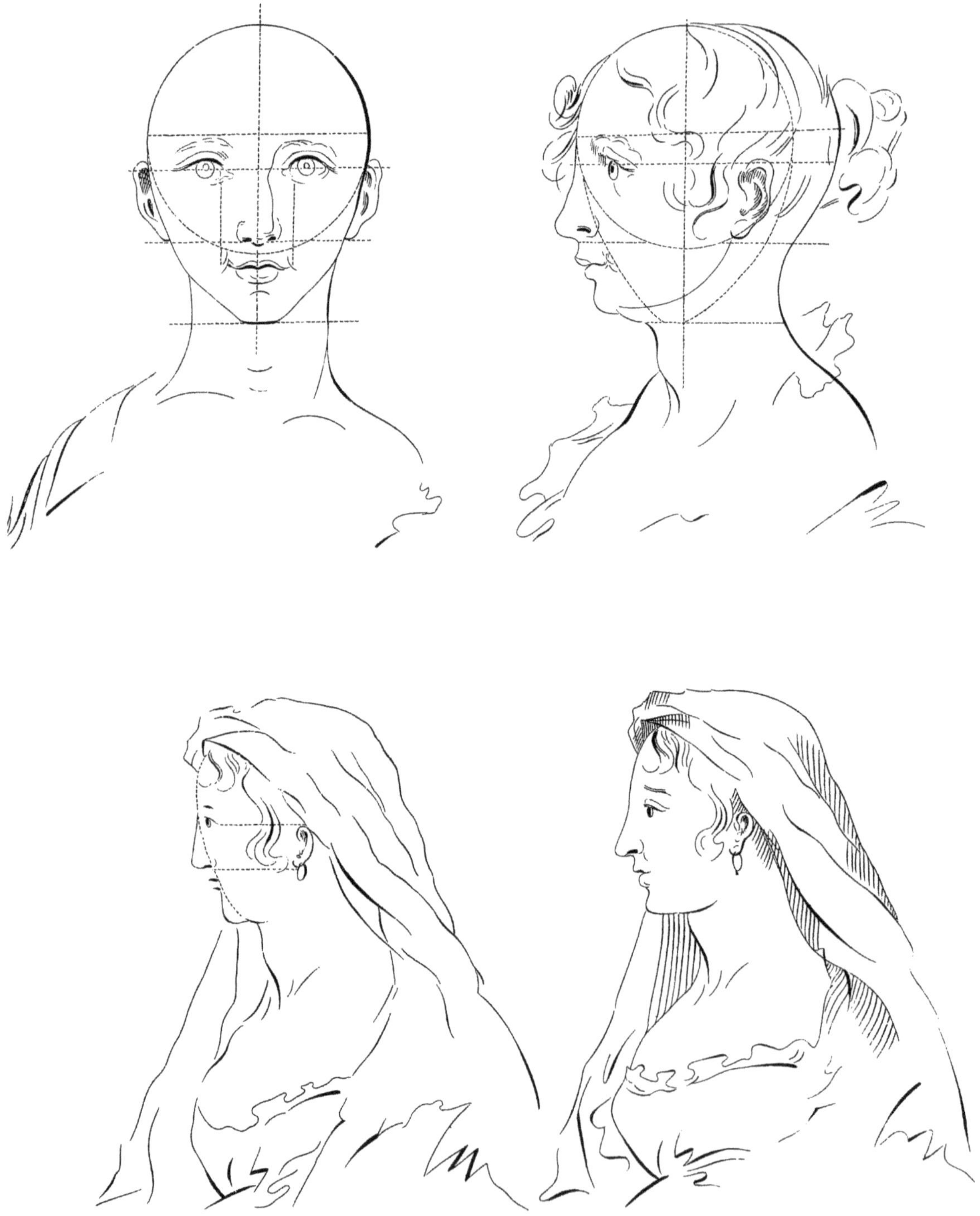

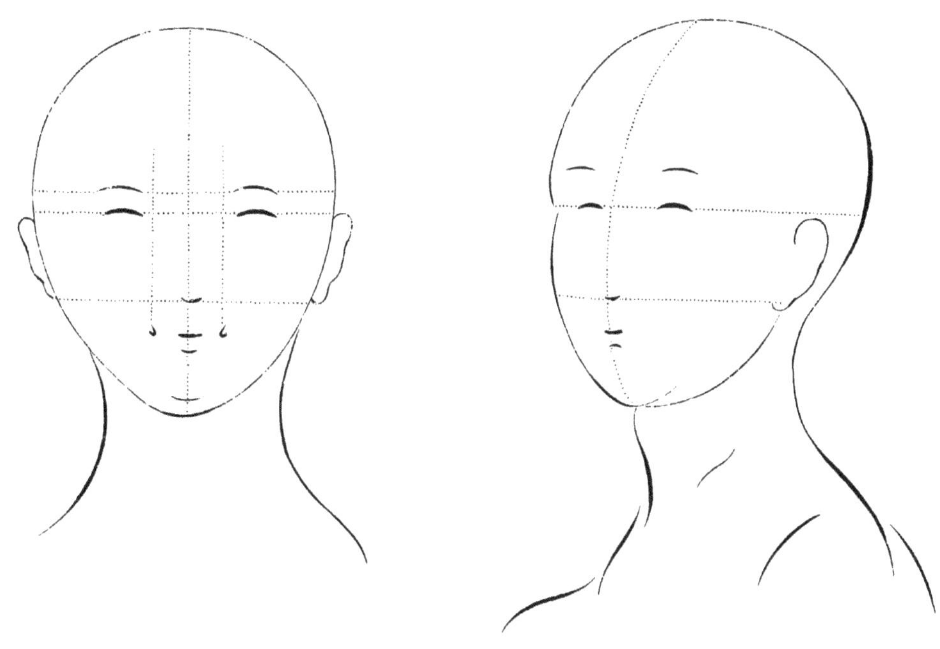

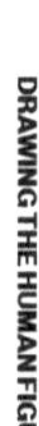

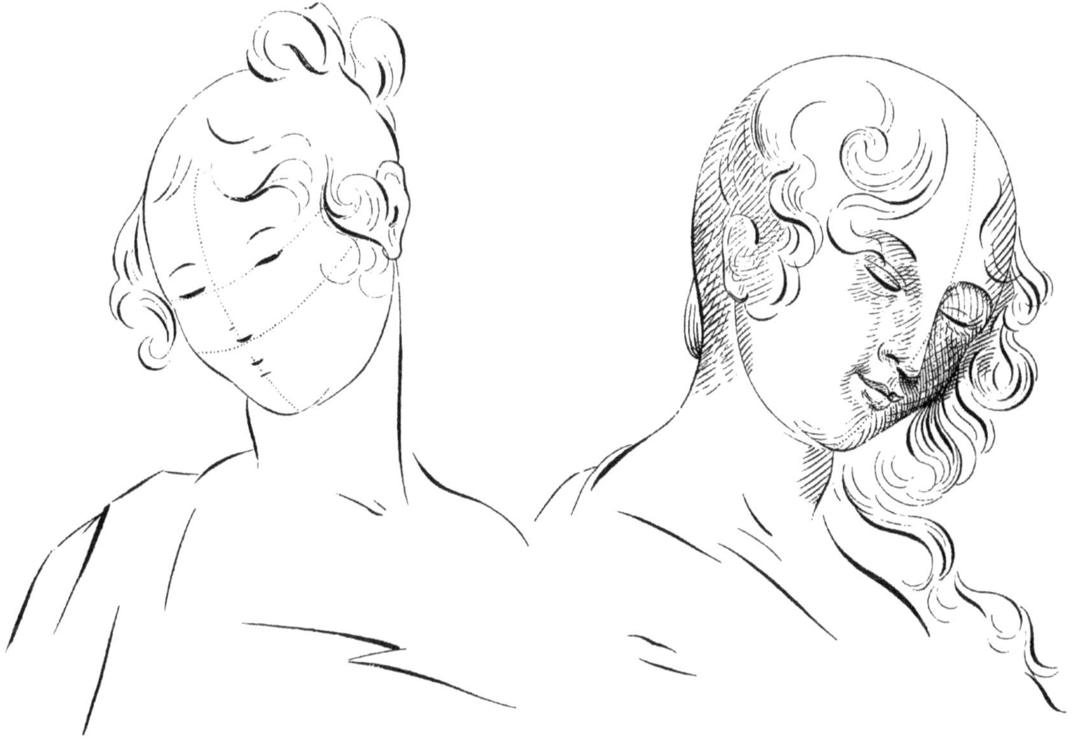

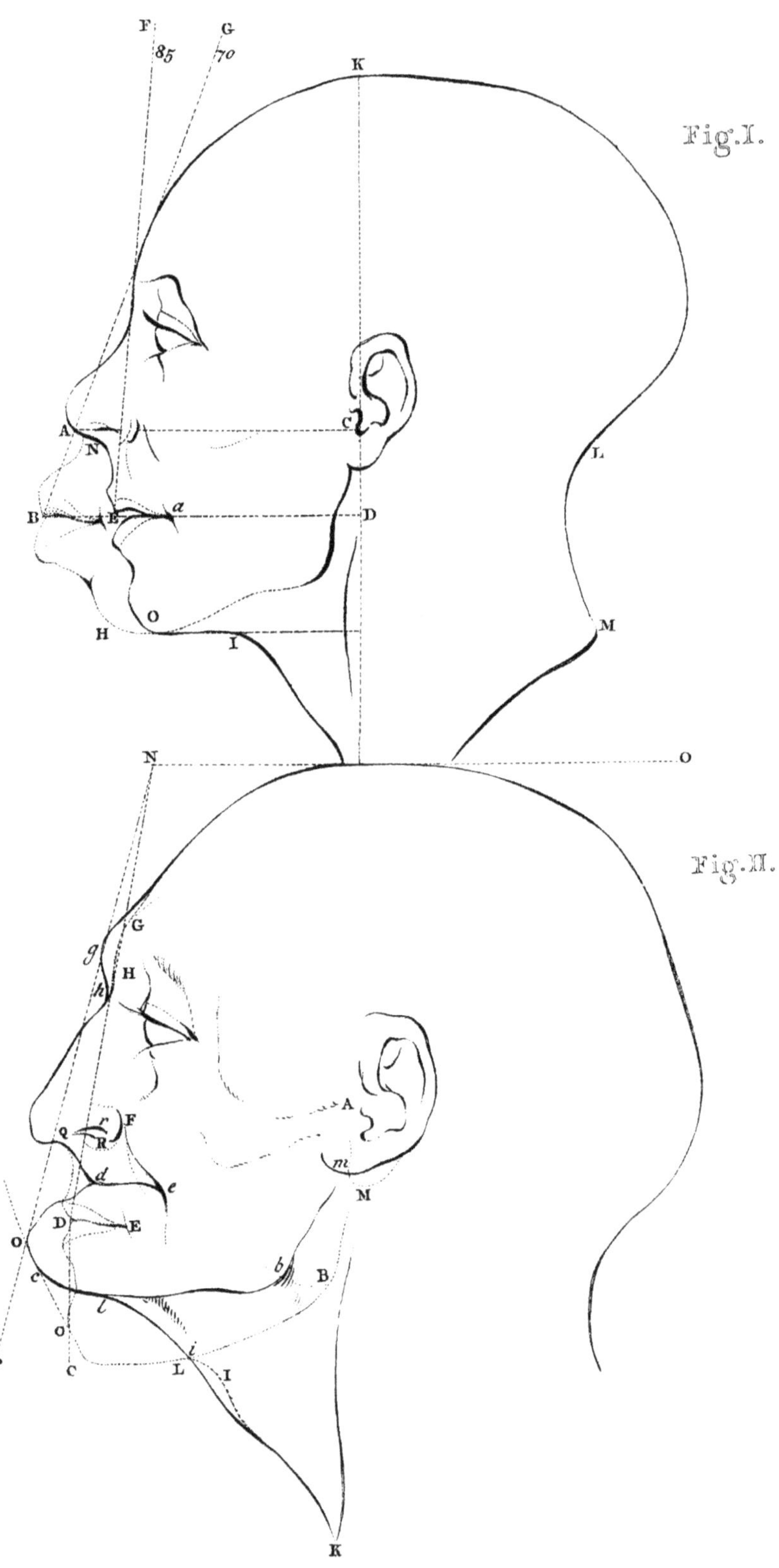
Fig.I.
Fig.II.

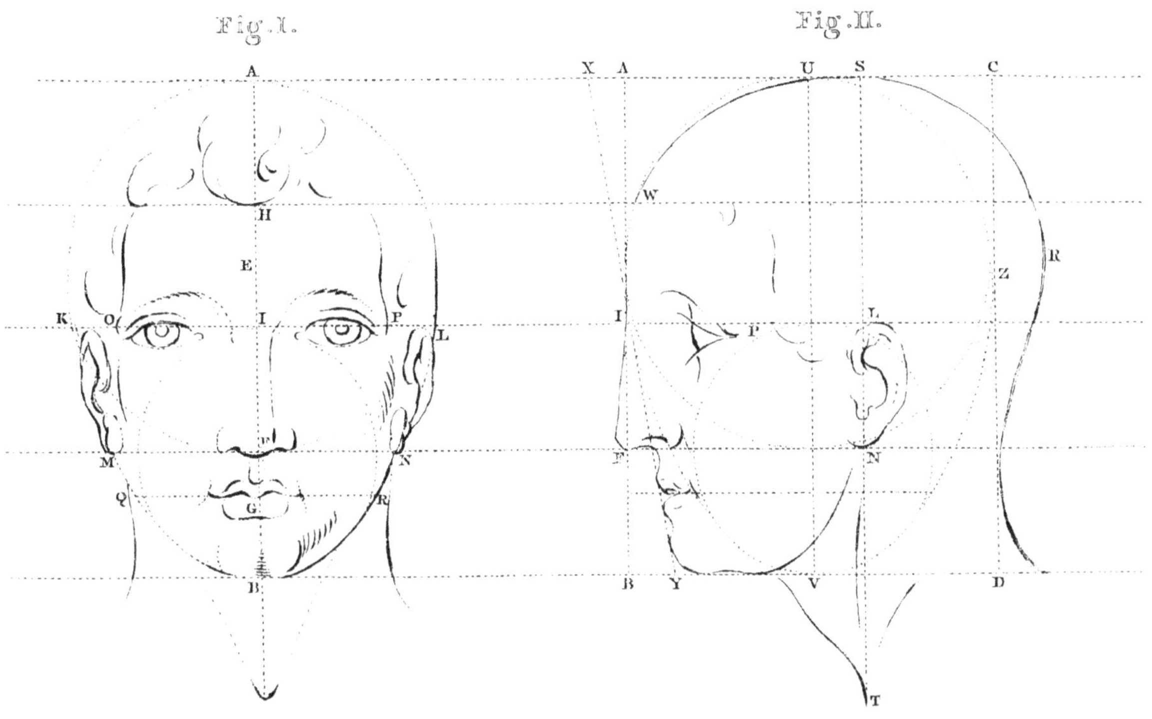

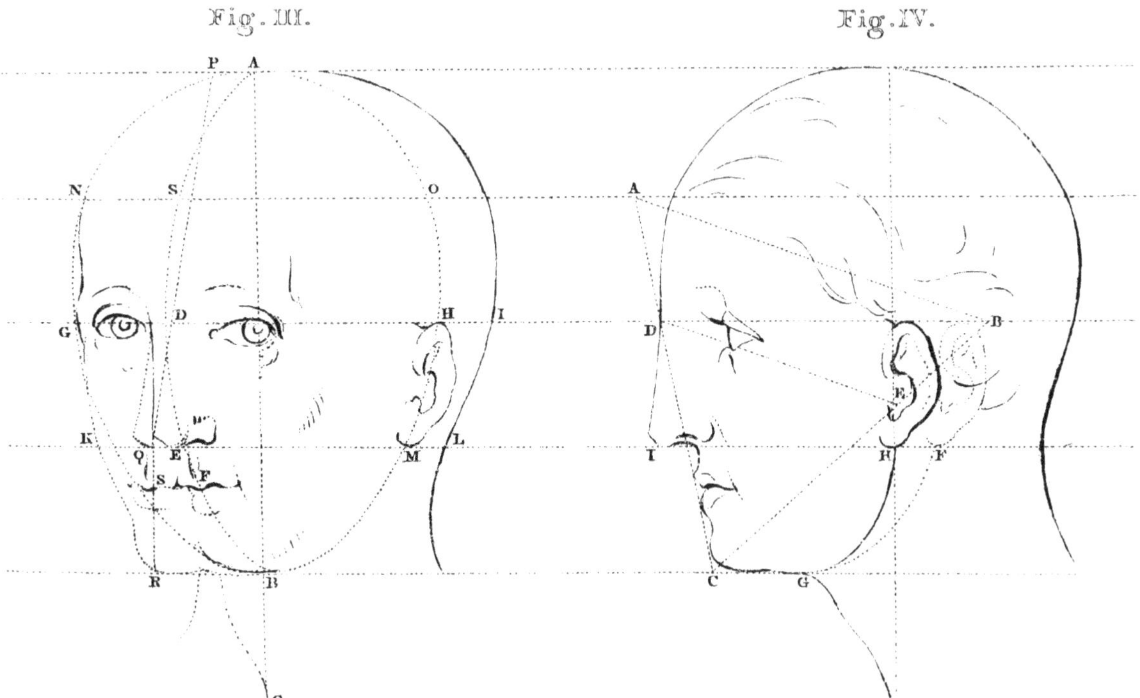

DRAWING THE HUMAN FIGURE

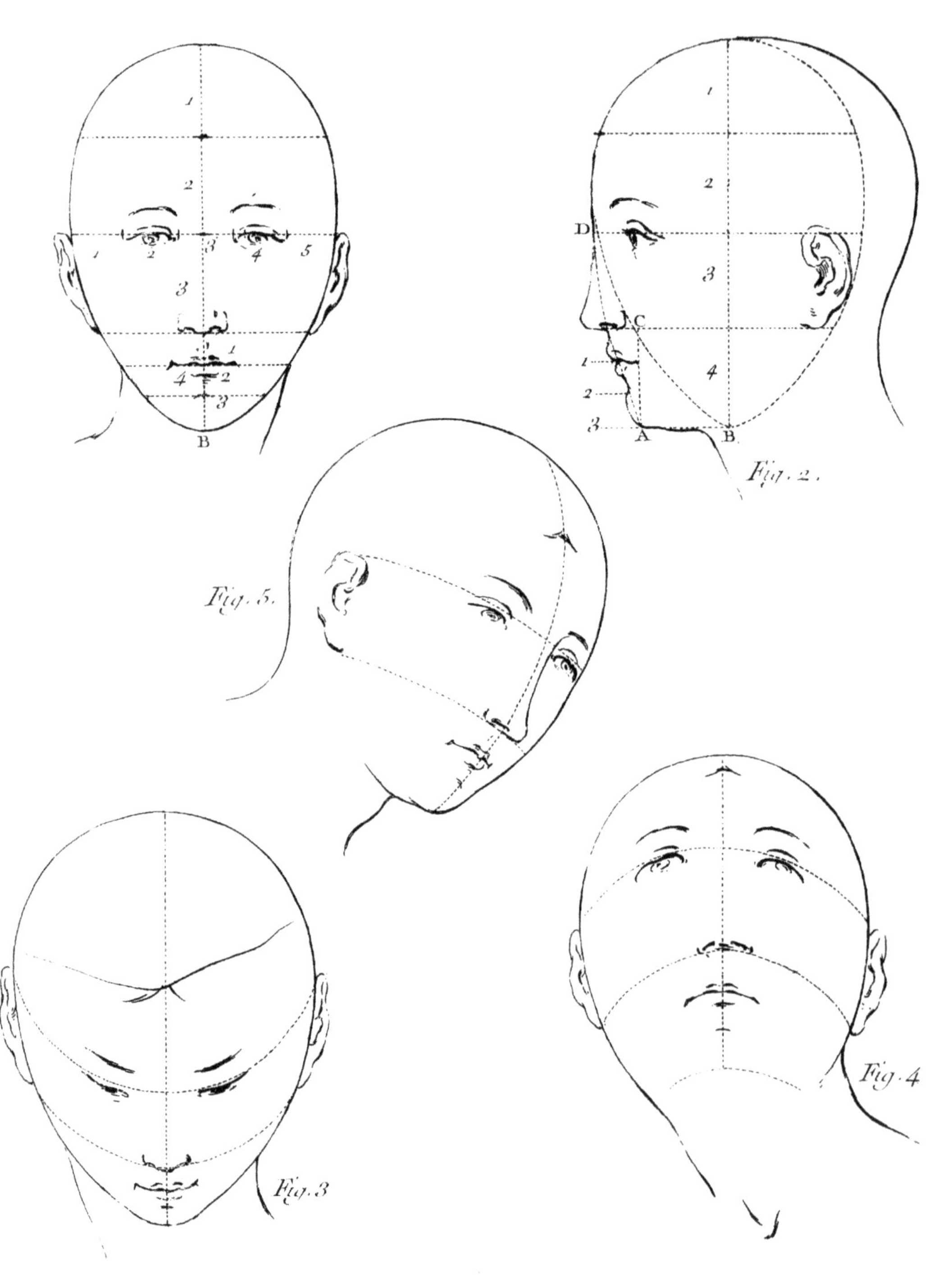
Fig. 2.
Fig. 5.
Fig. 3.
Fig. 4.

14 3/4
7 3/4
4 1/2
7 3/4
14
h
4 3/4
2 1/2
1
2
3
4
5
6
7
8
9
10
11
12
13
14
15
16

69

Fig. I.
Fig. II.
Fig. III.
Fig. IV.
Fig. V.

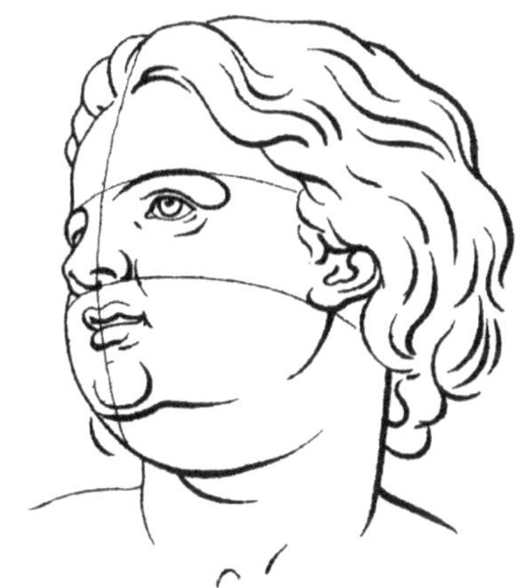

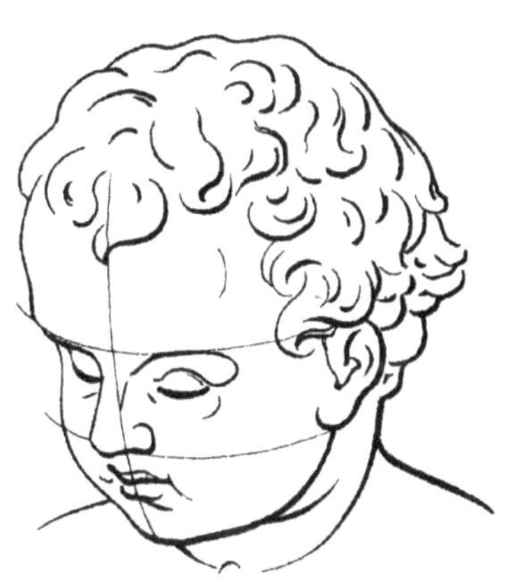

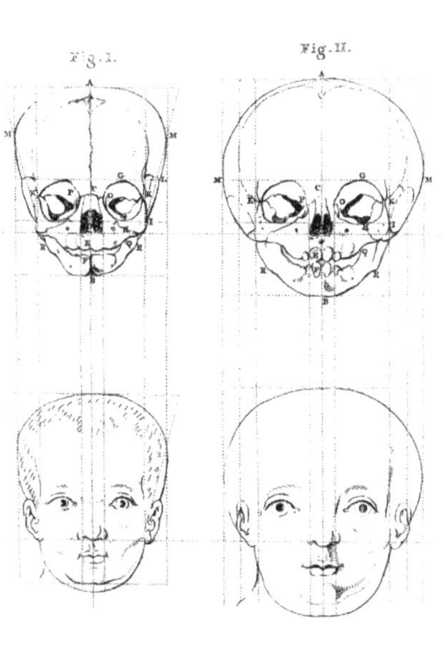

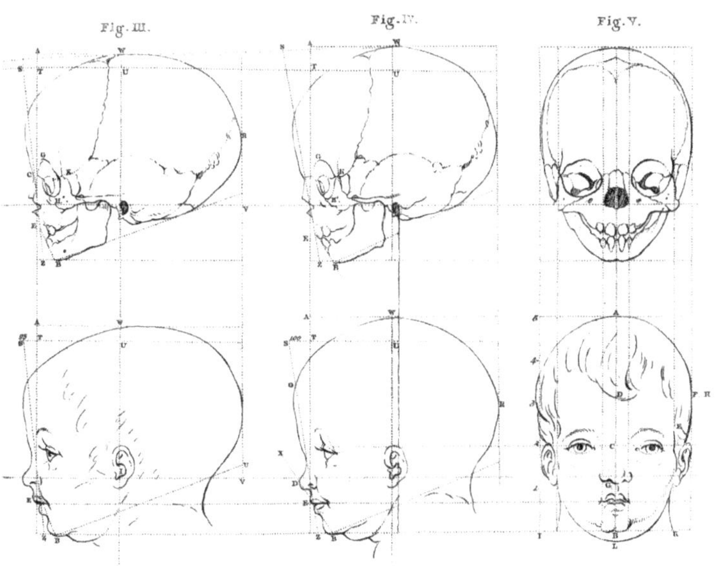

70

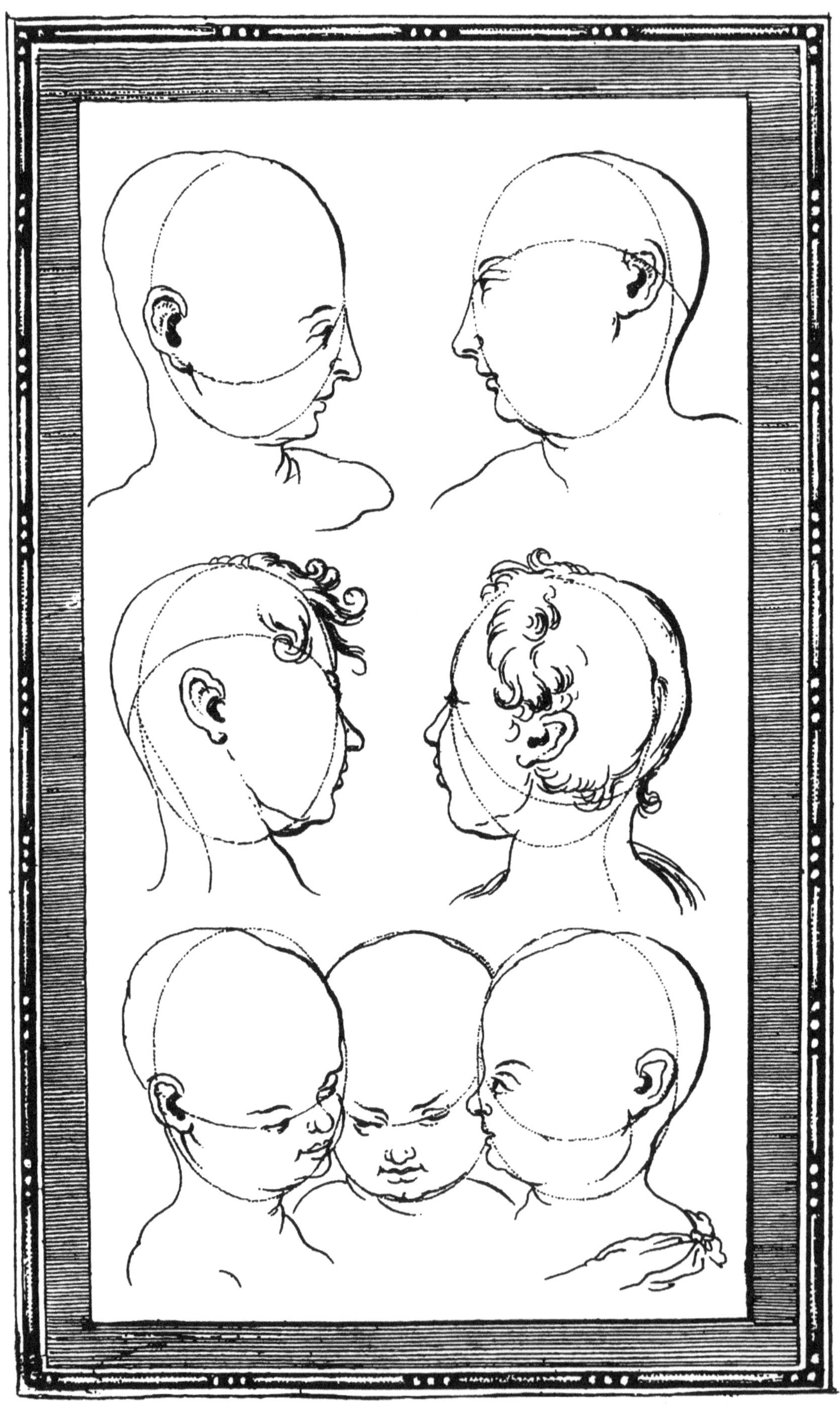

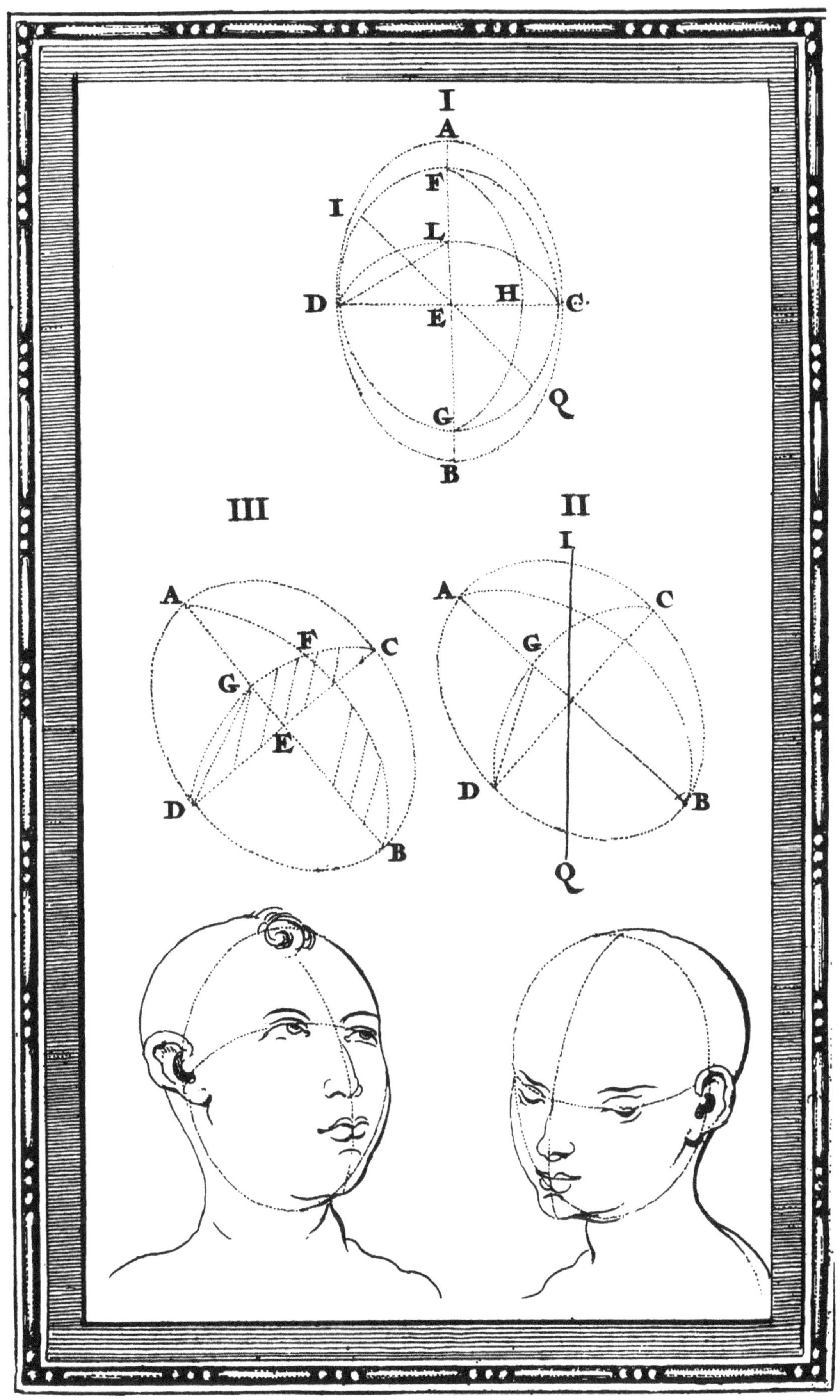

STUDIES OF THE HUMAN FACE

72

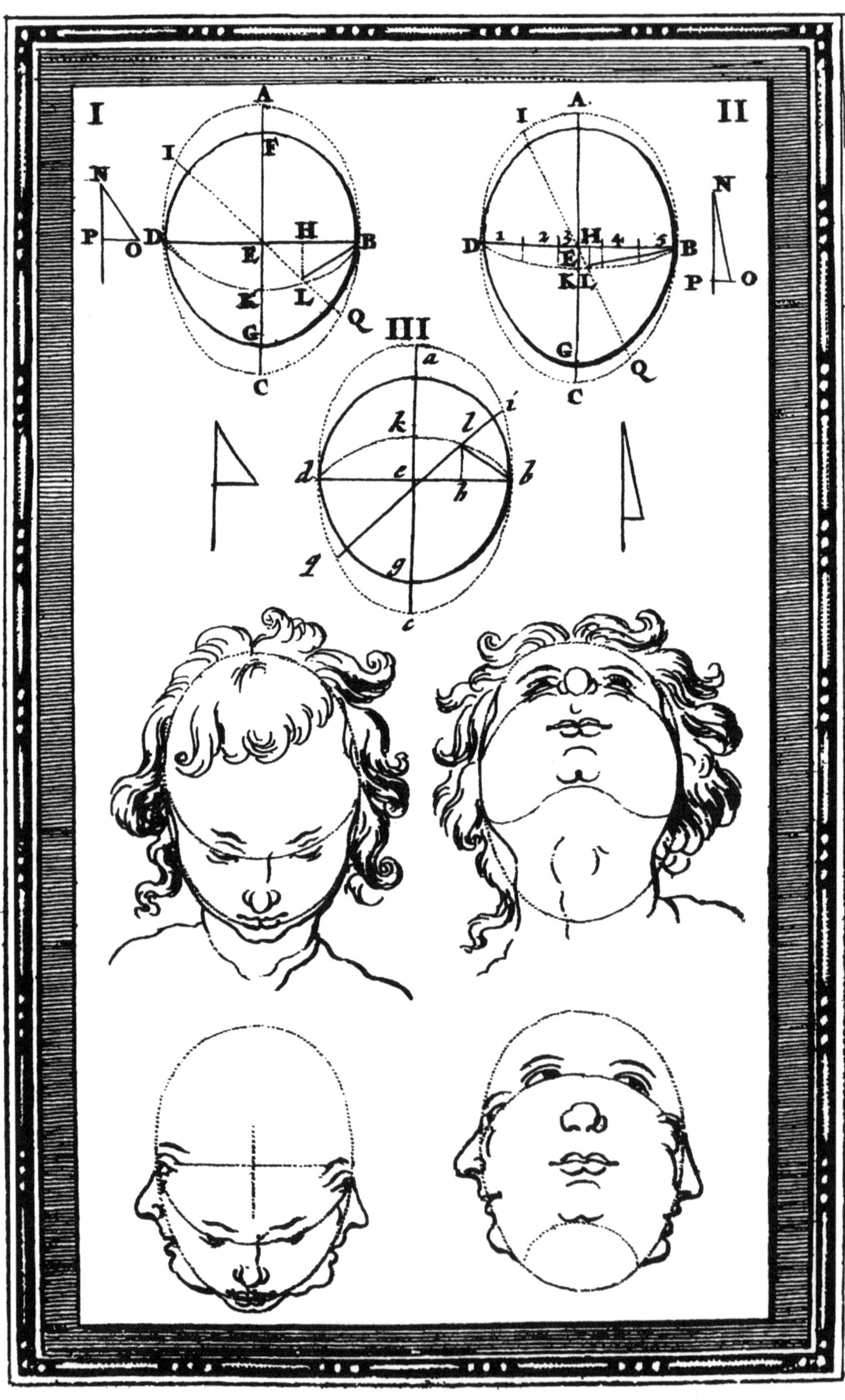

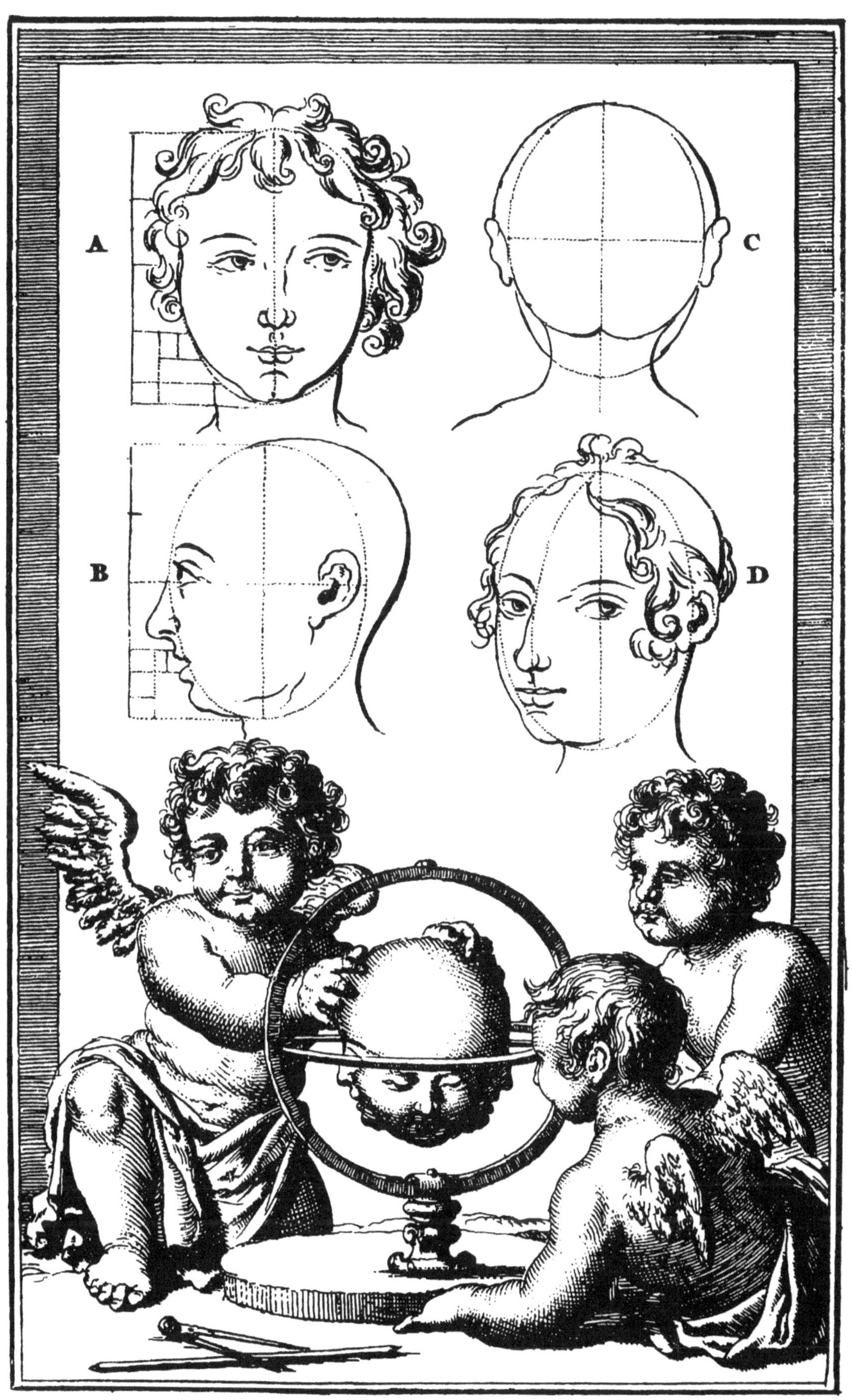

DRAWING THE HUMAN FIGURE

STUDIES OF THE HUMAN FACE

74

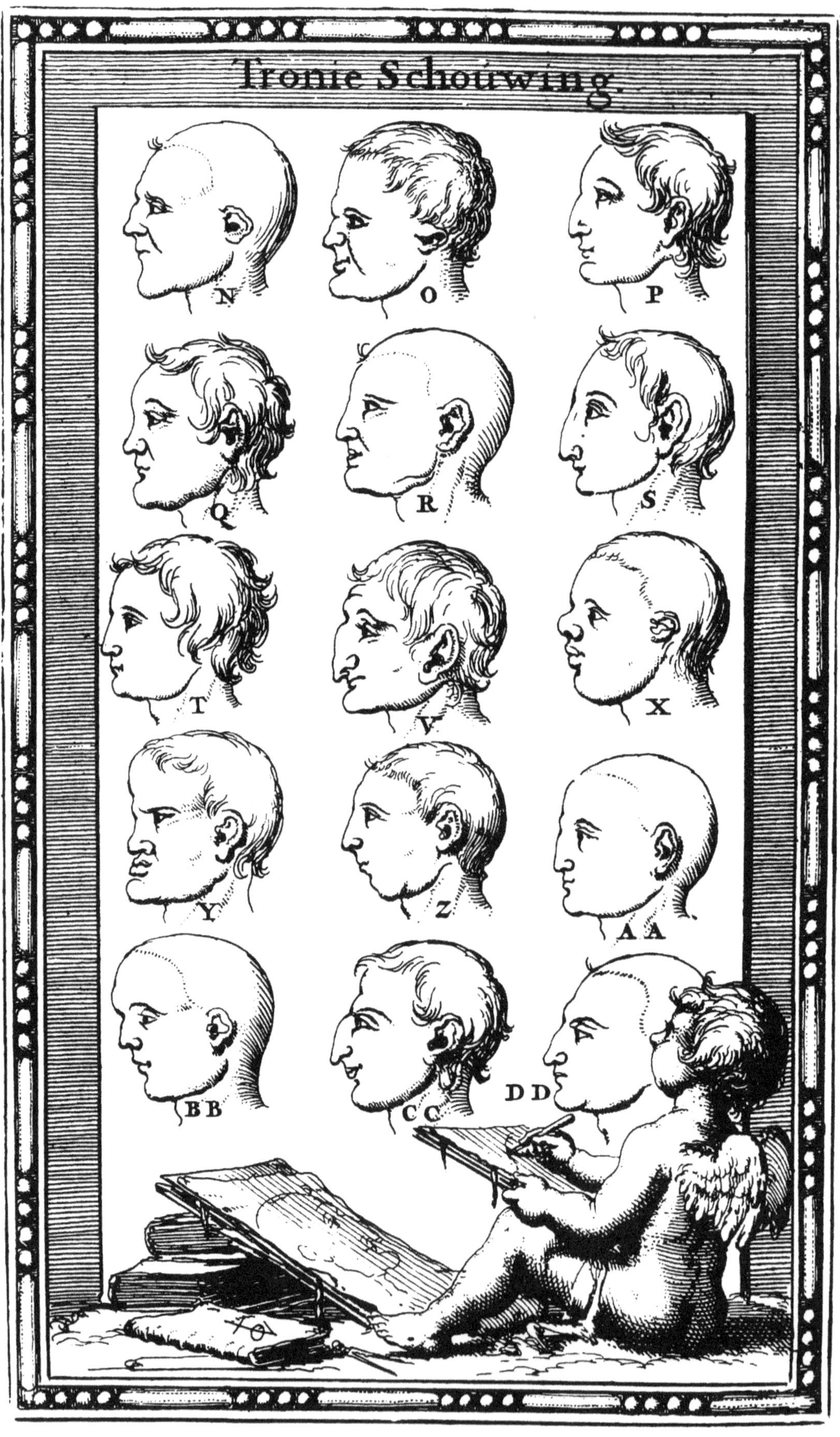

STUDIES OF THE HUMAN FACE

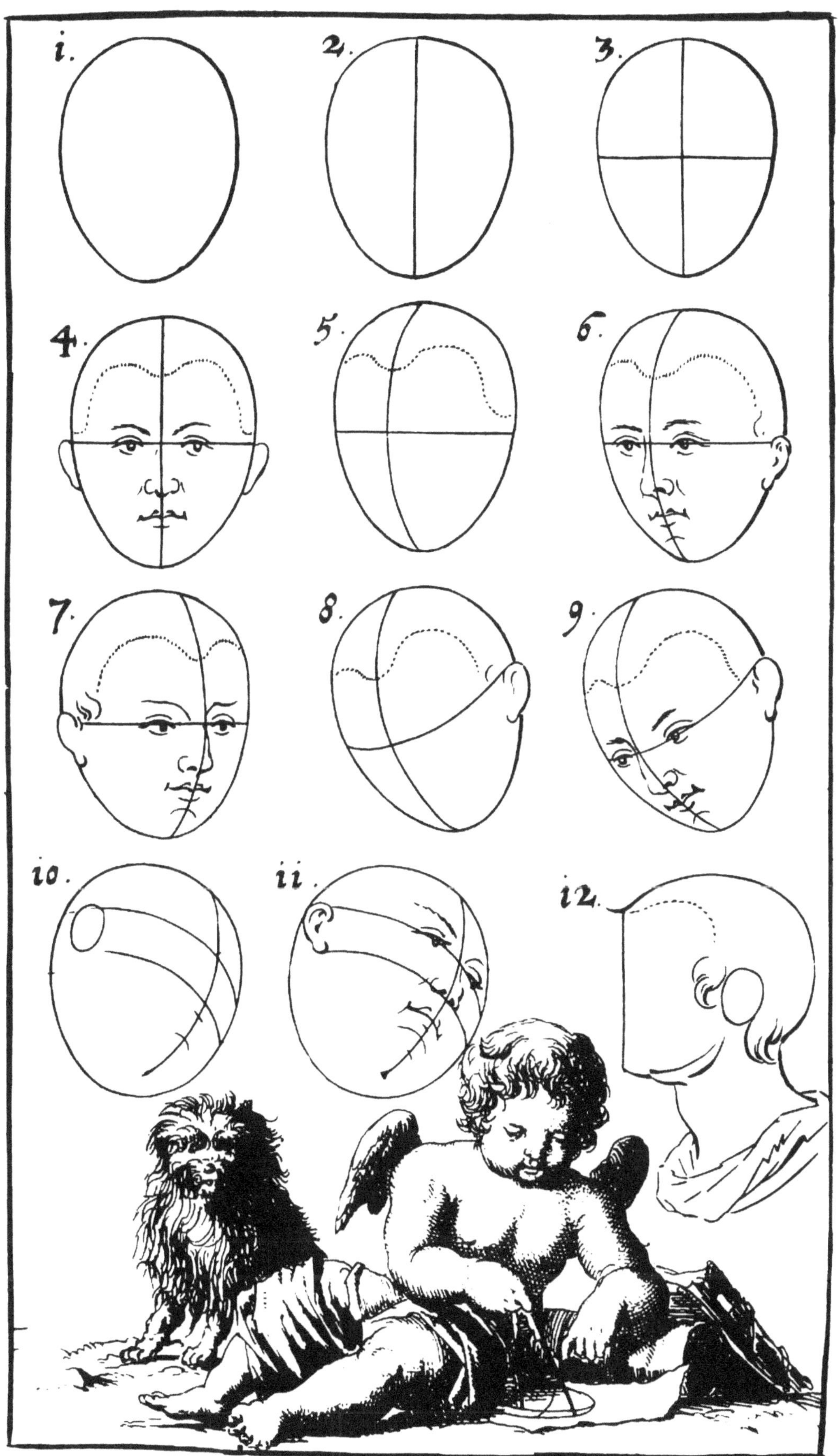

76

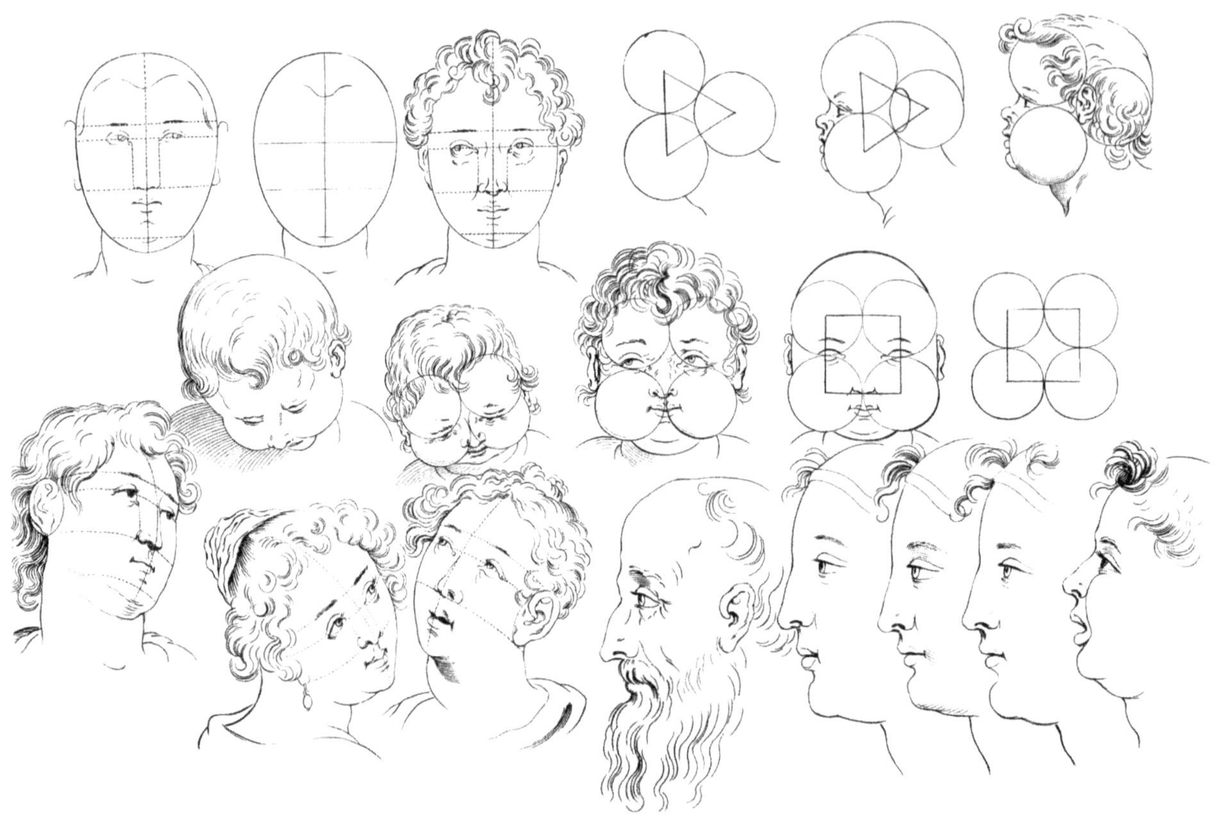

77

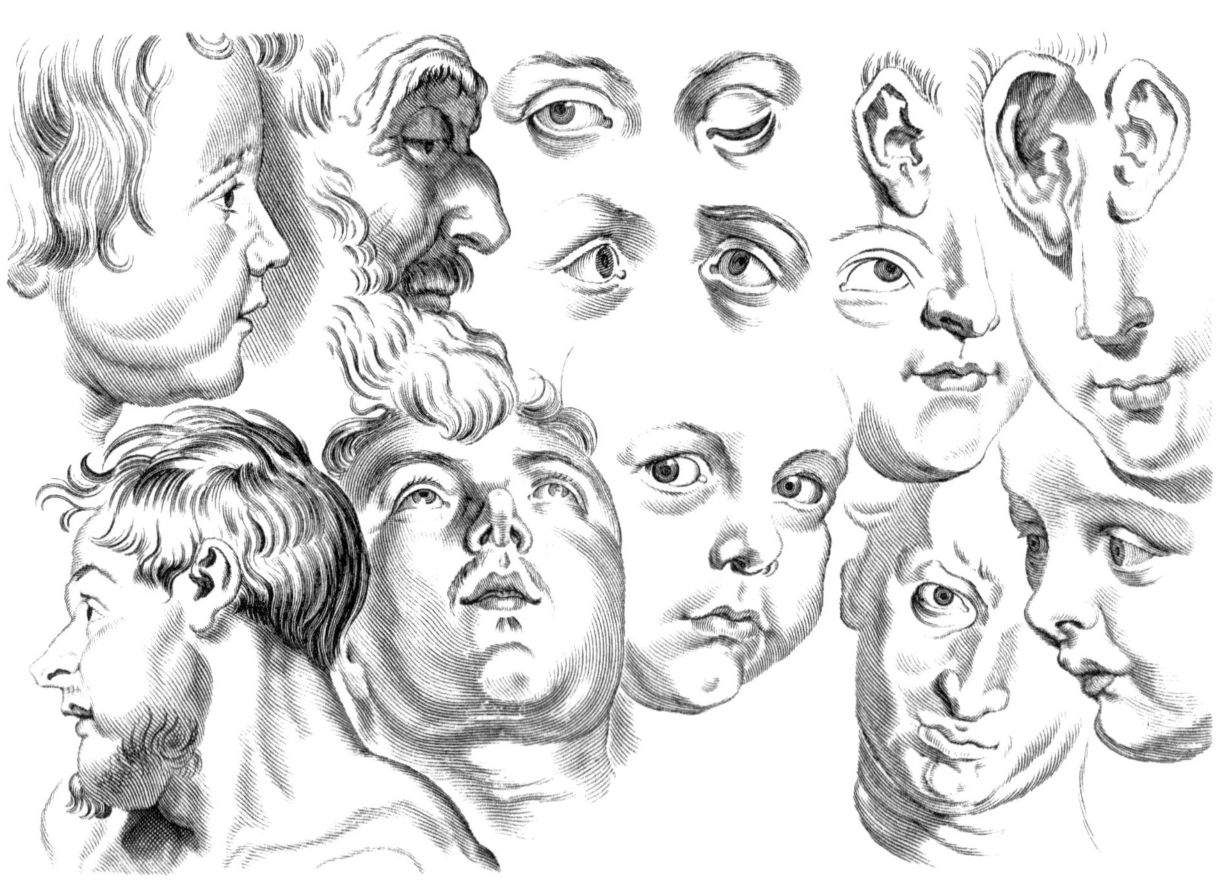

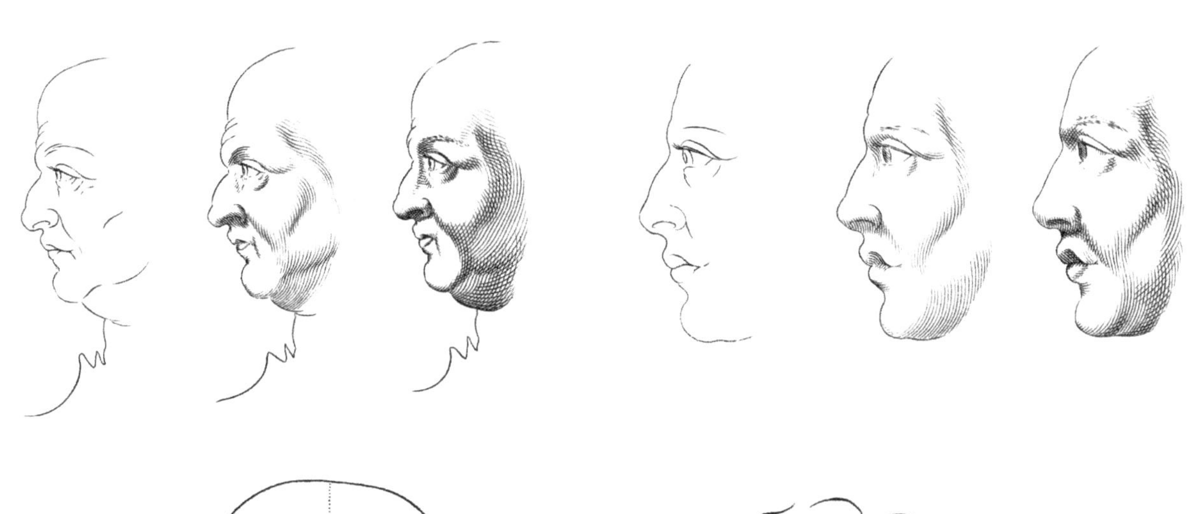

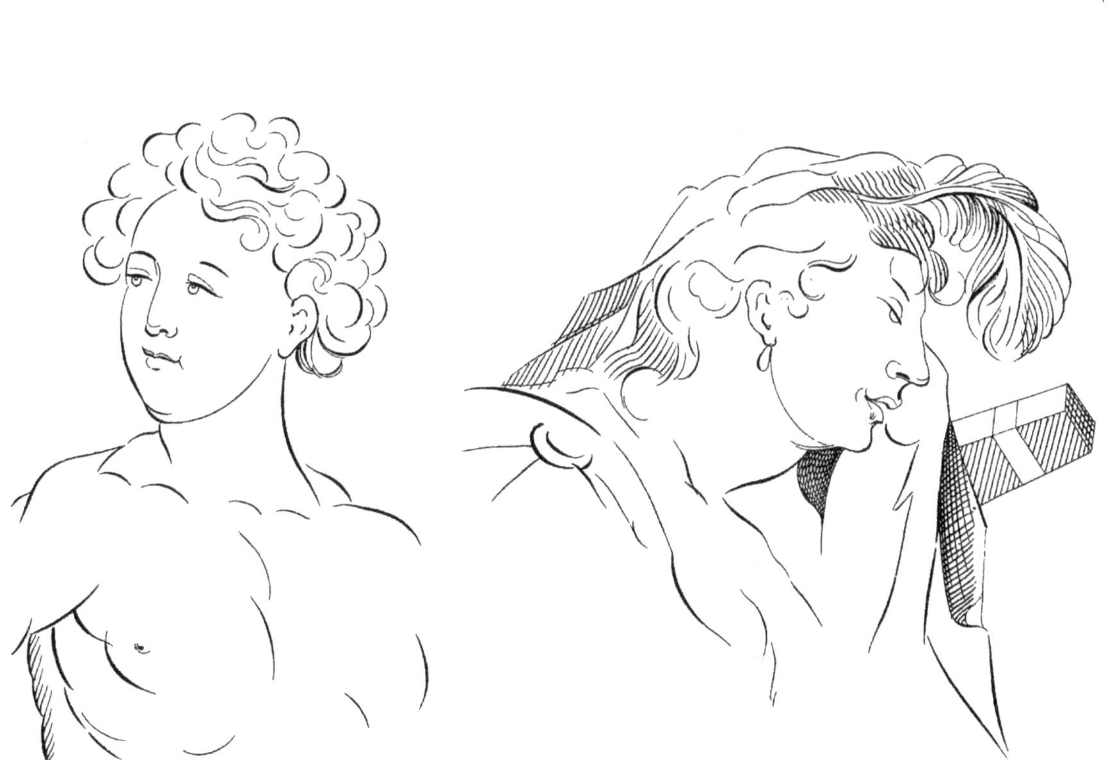

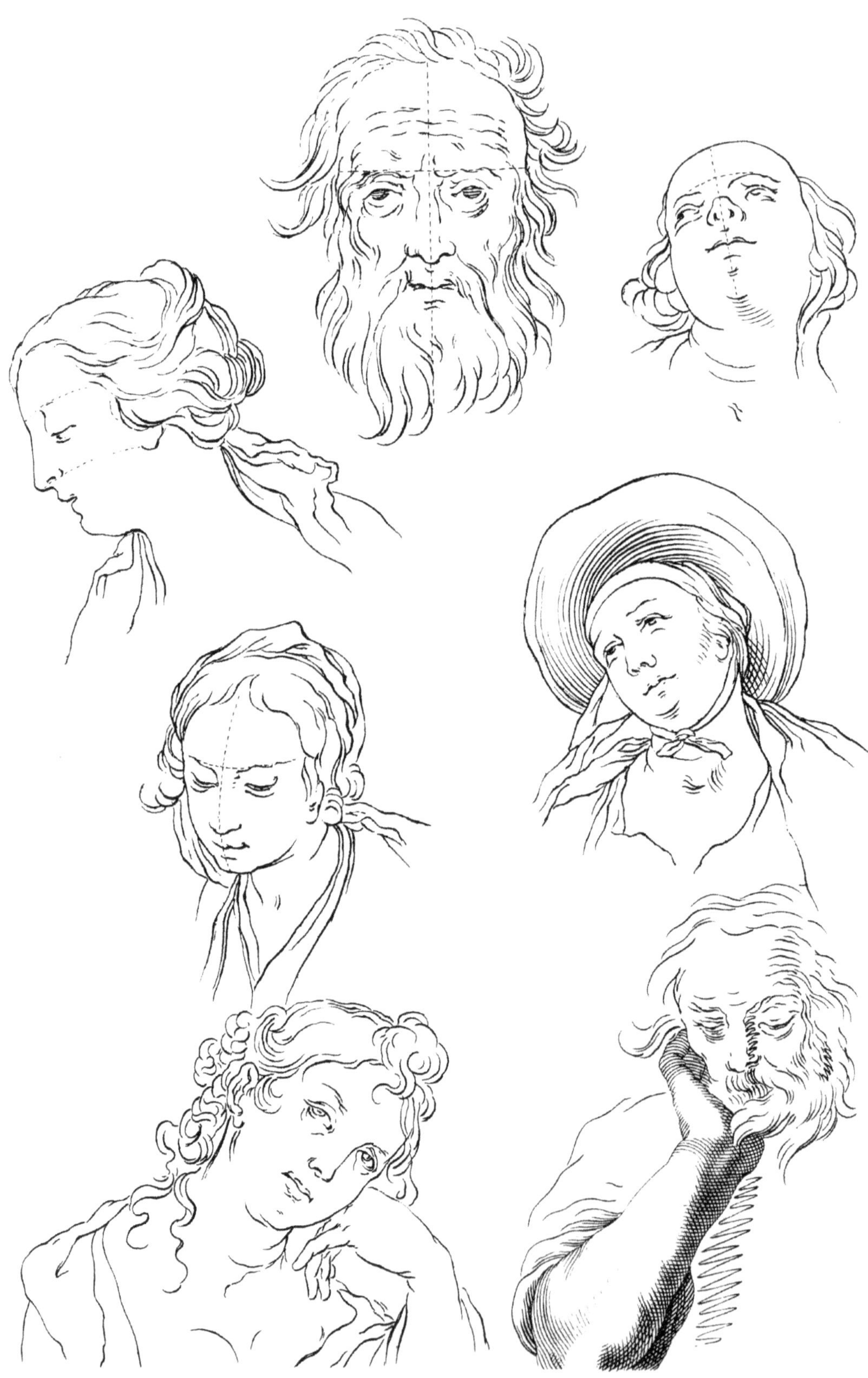

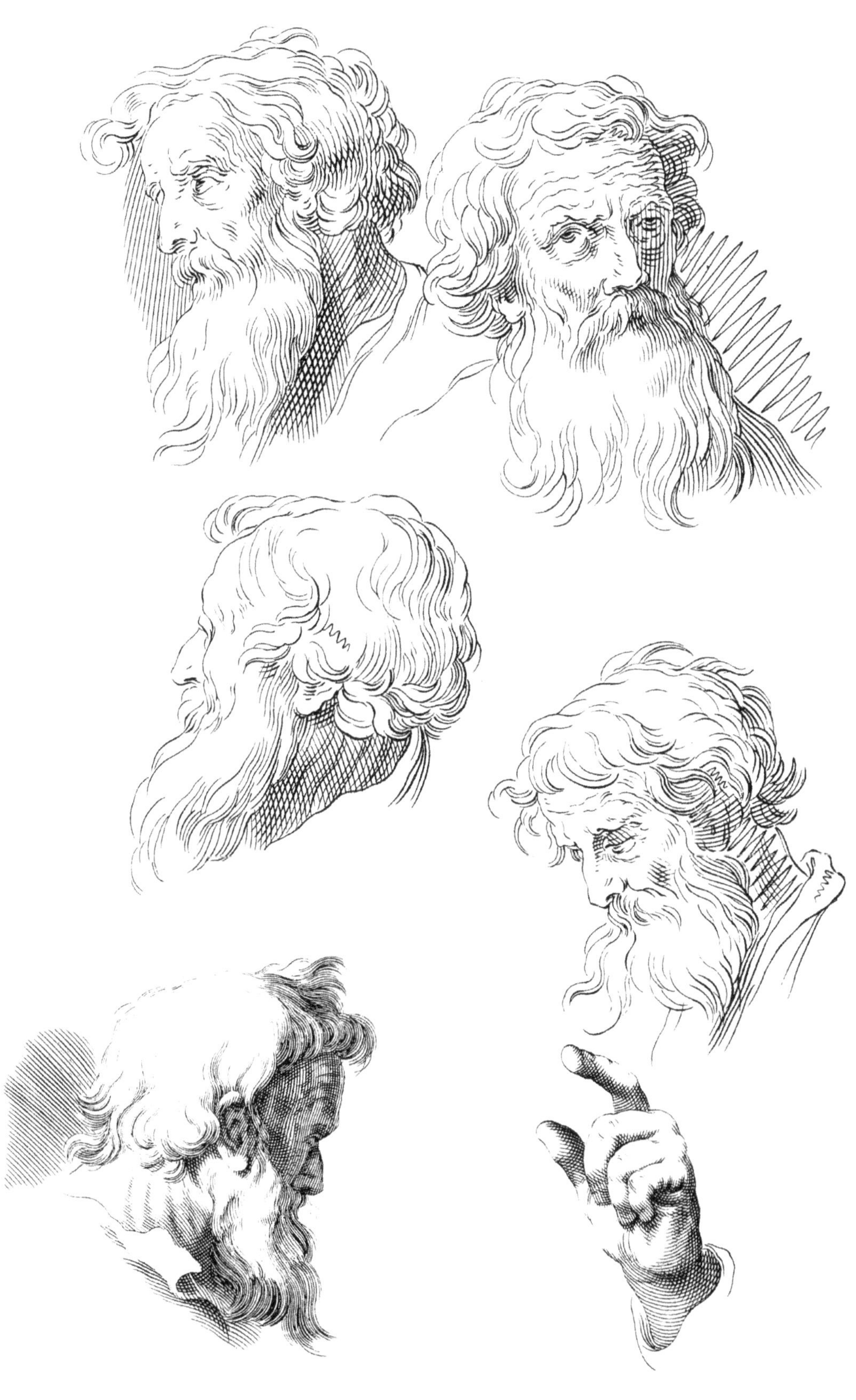

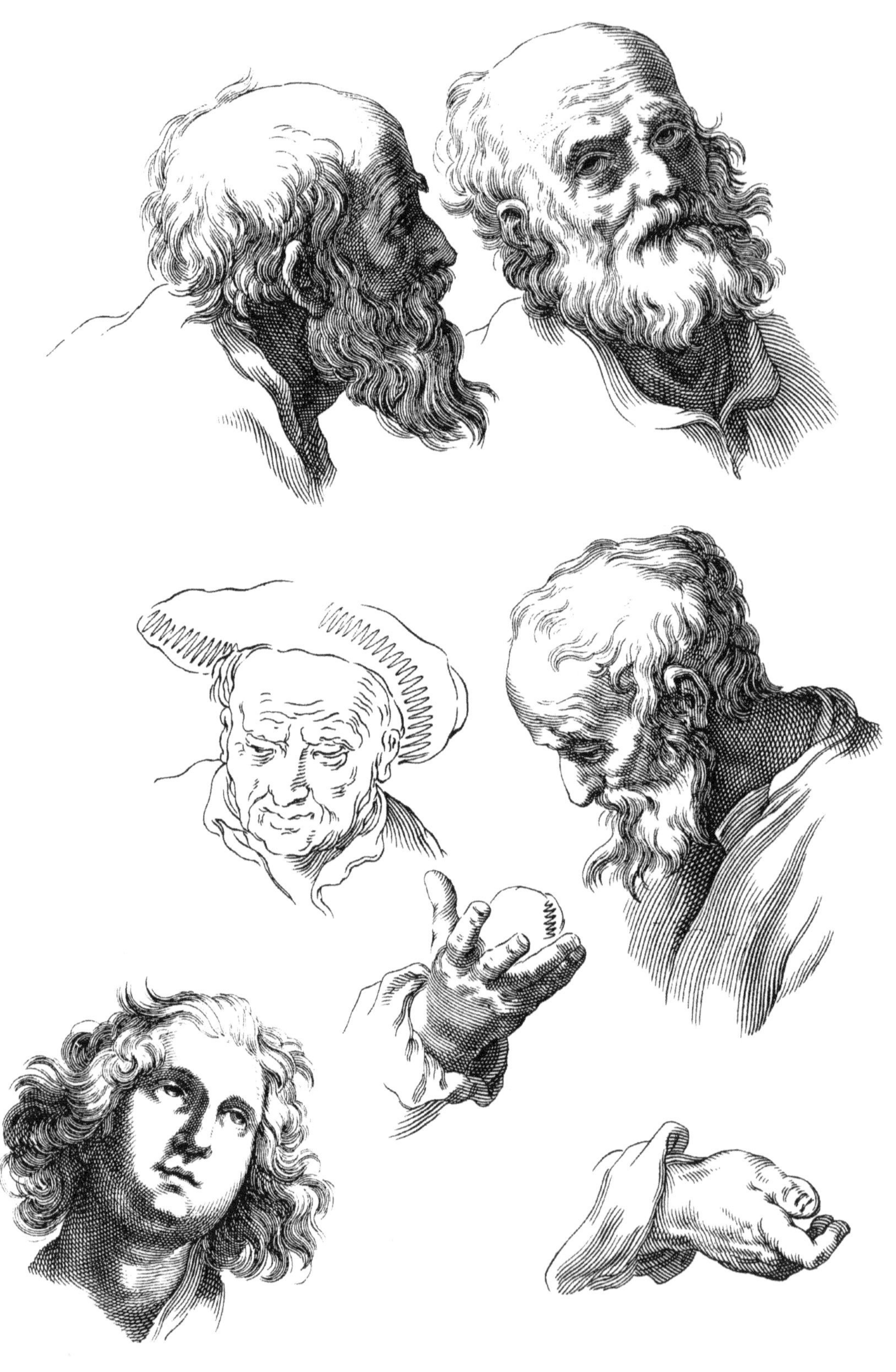

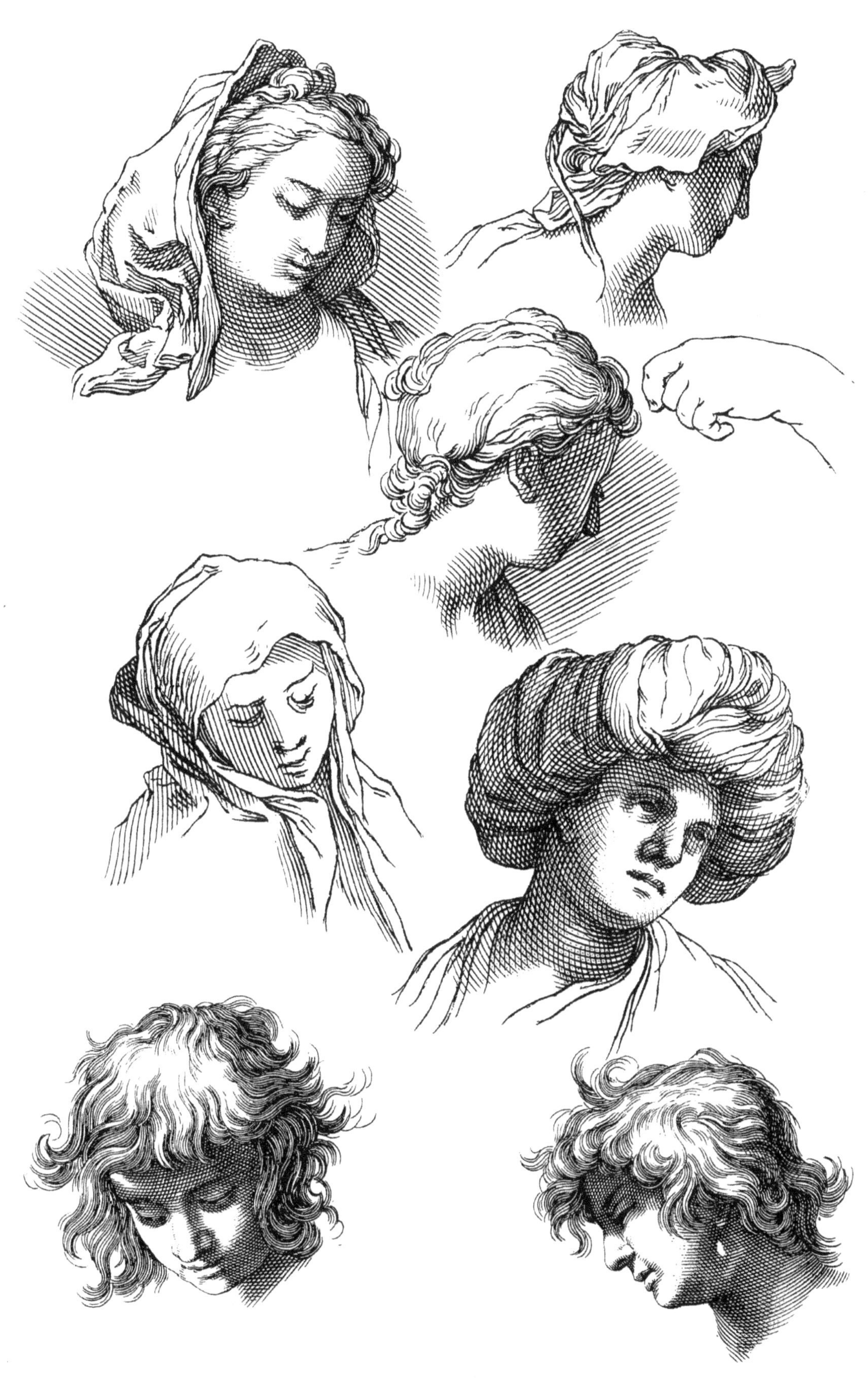

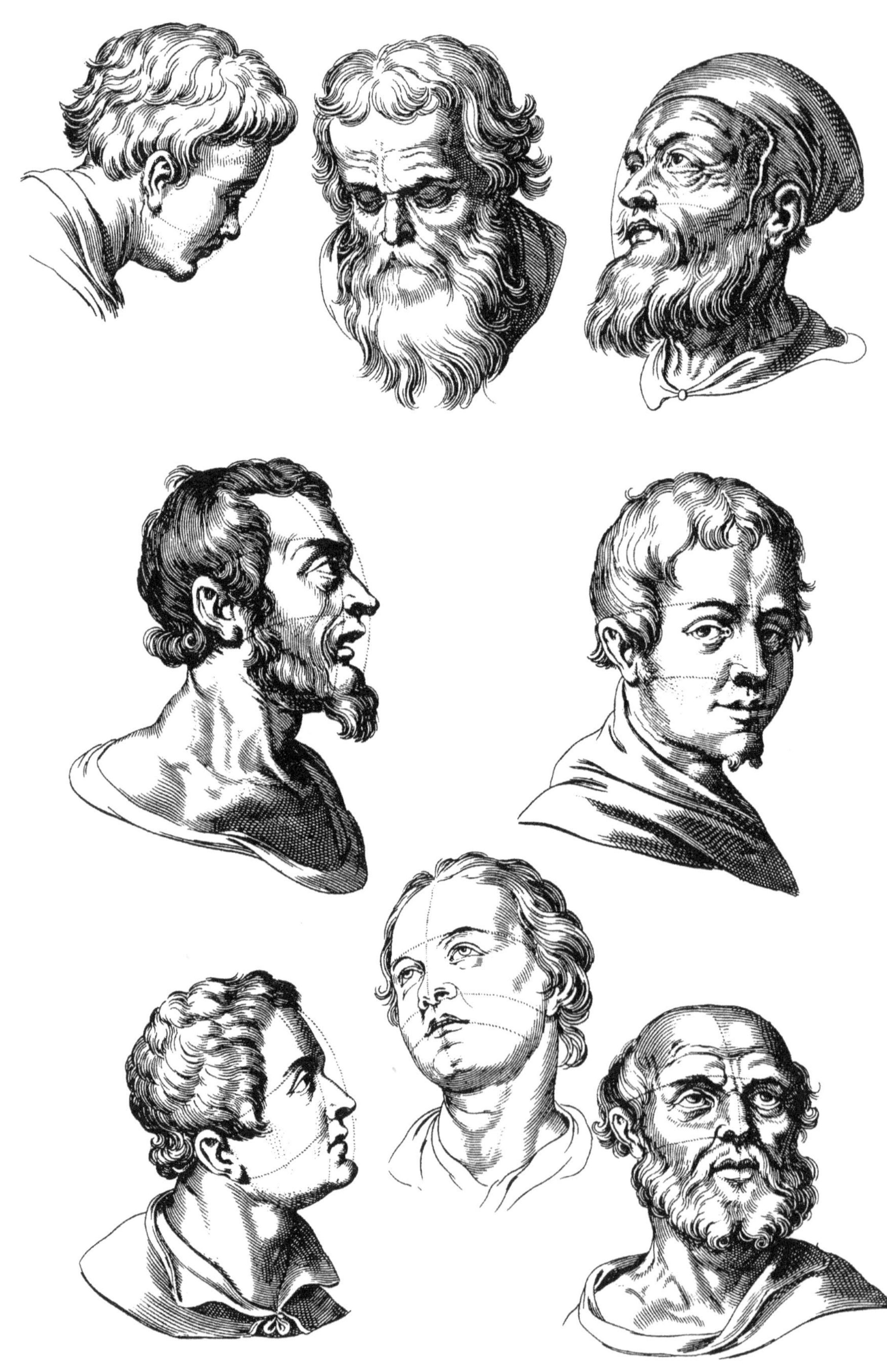

86

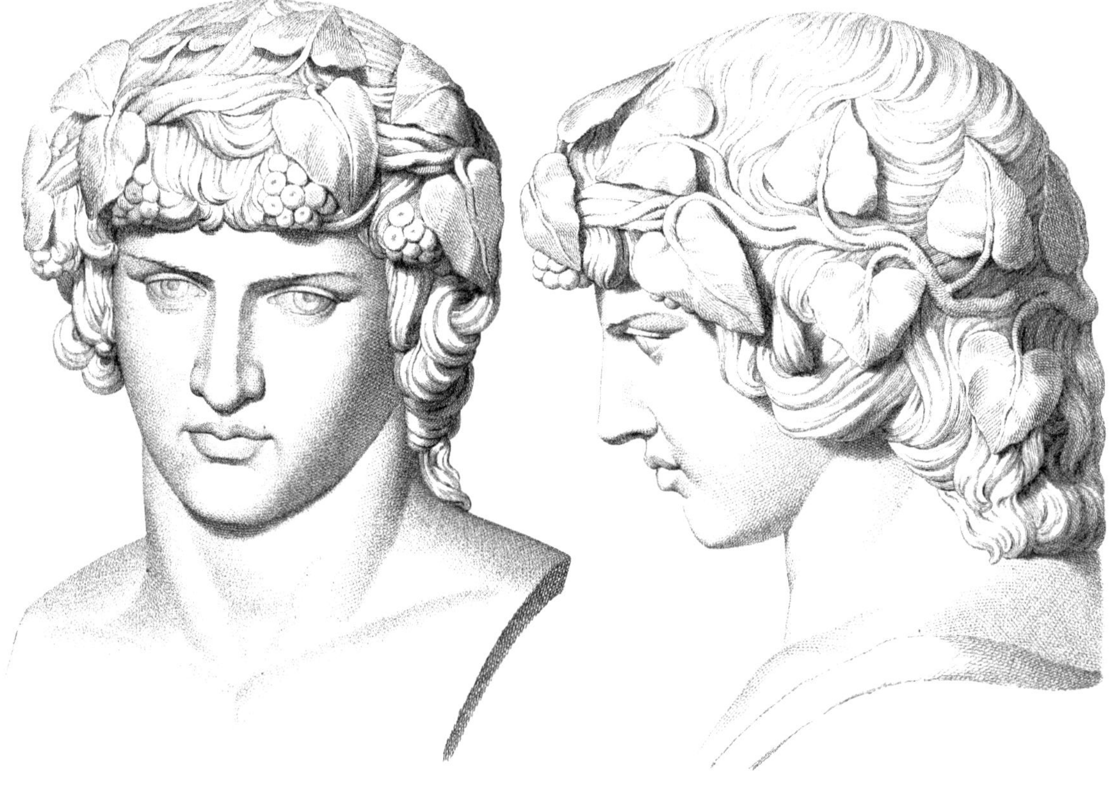

87

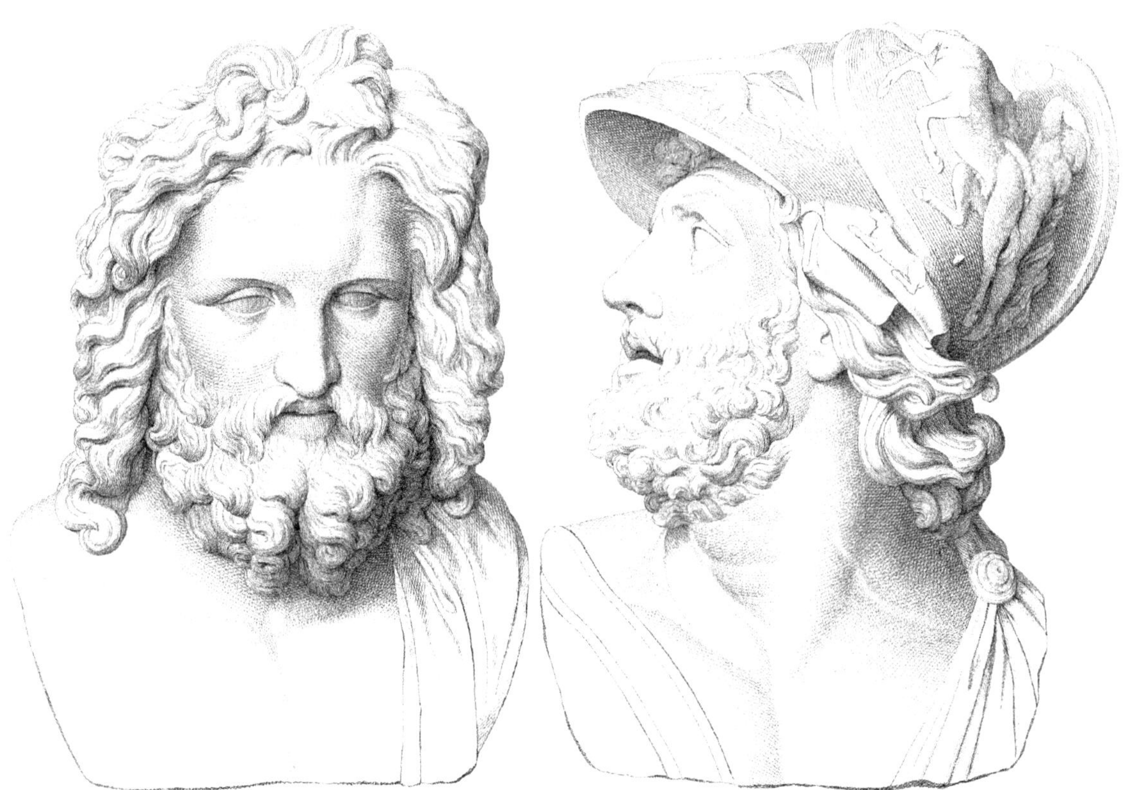

88

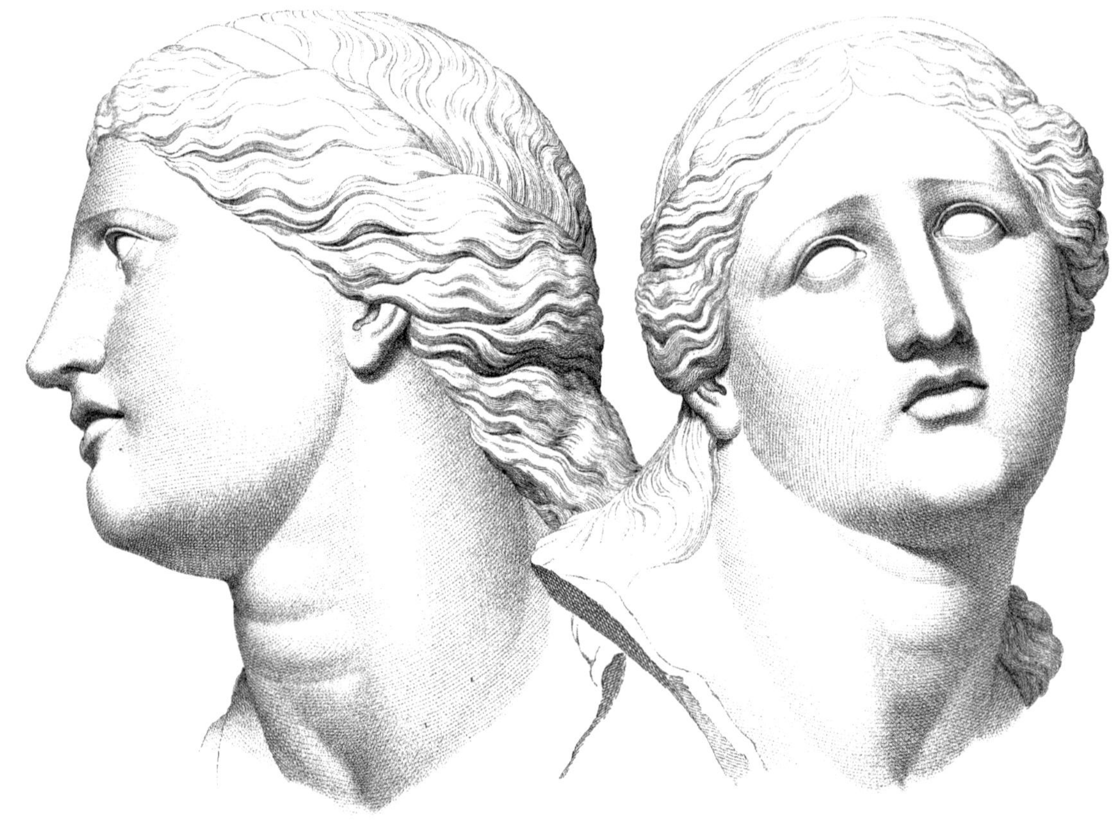

89

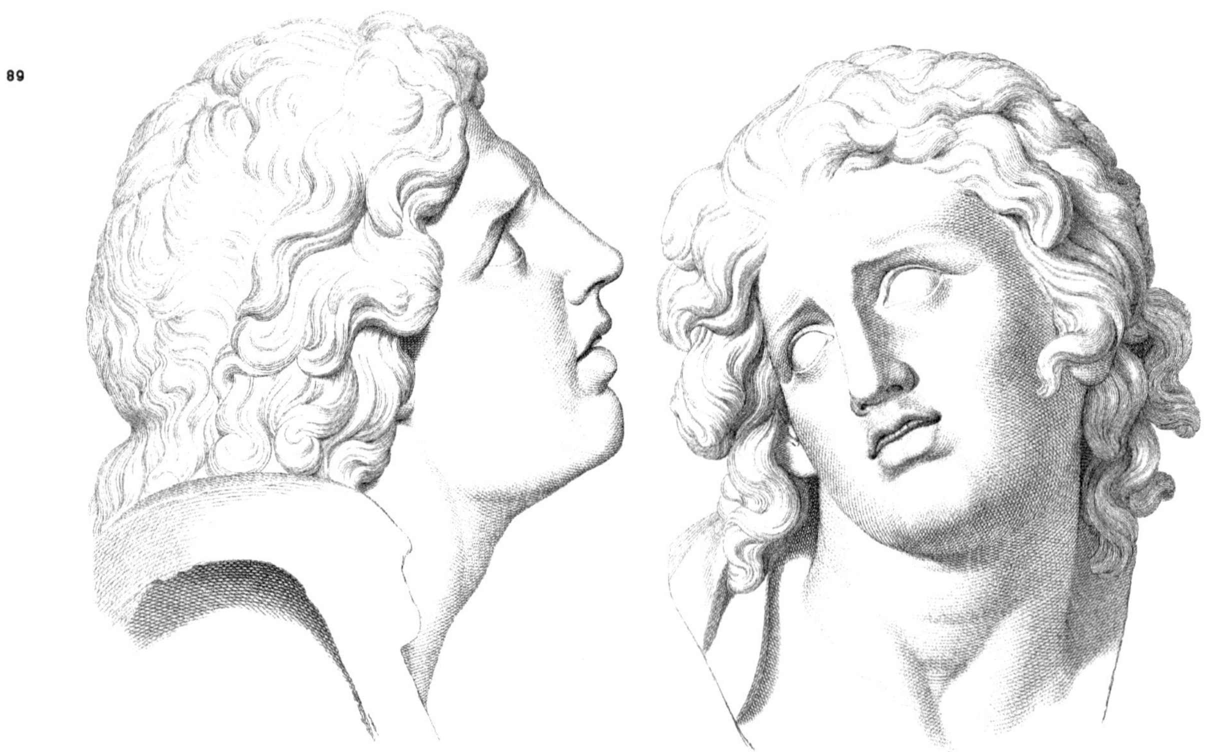

90

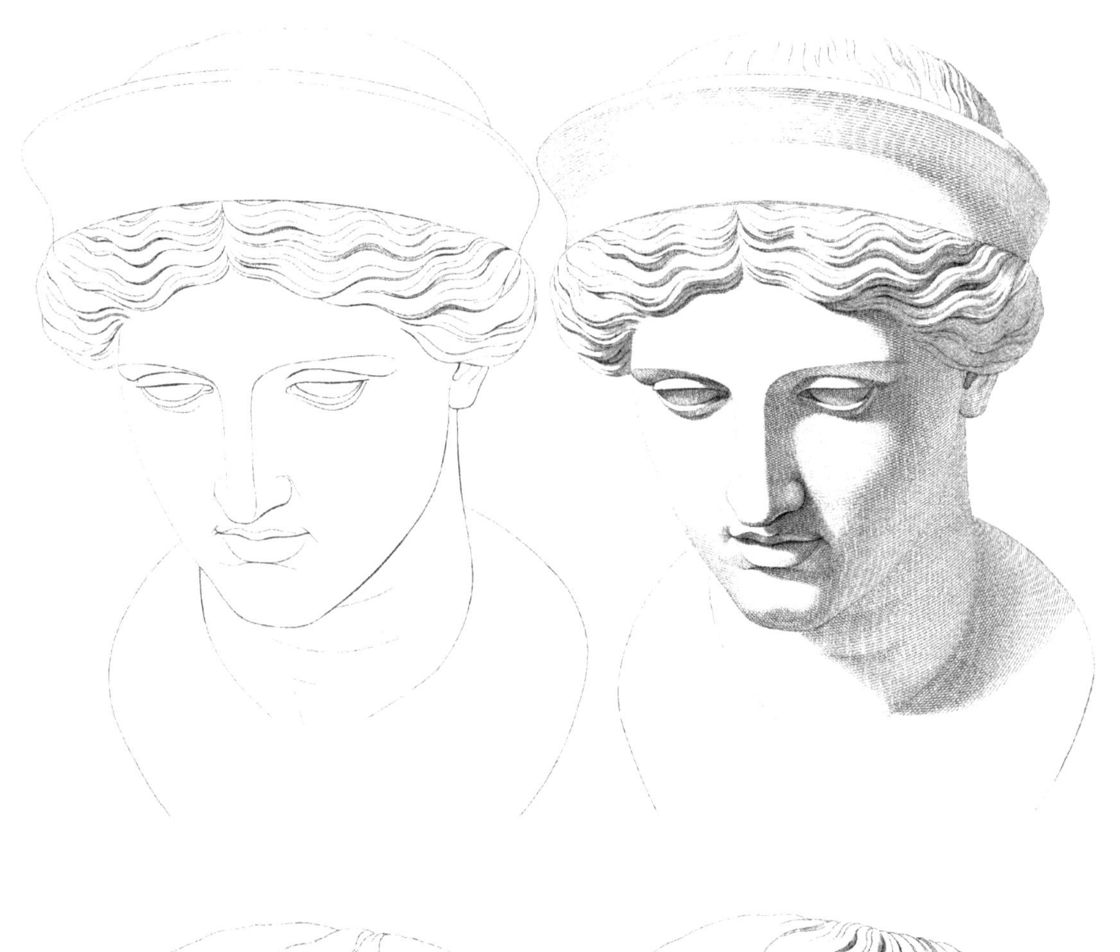

91

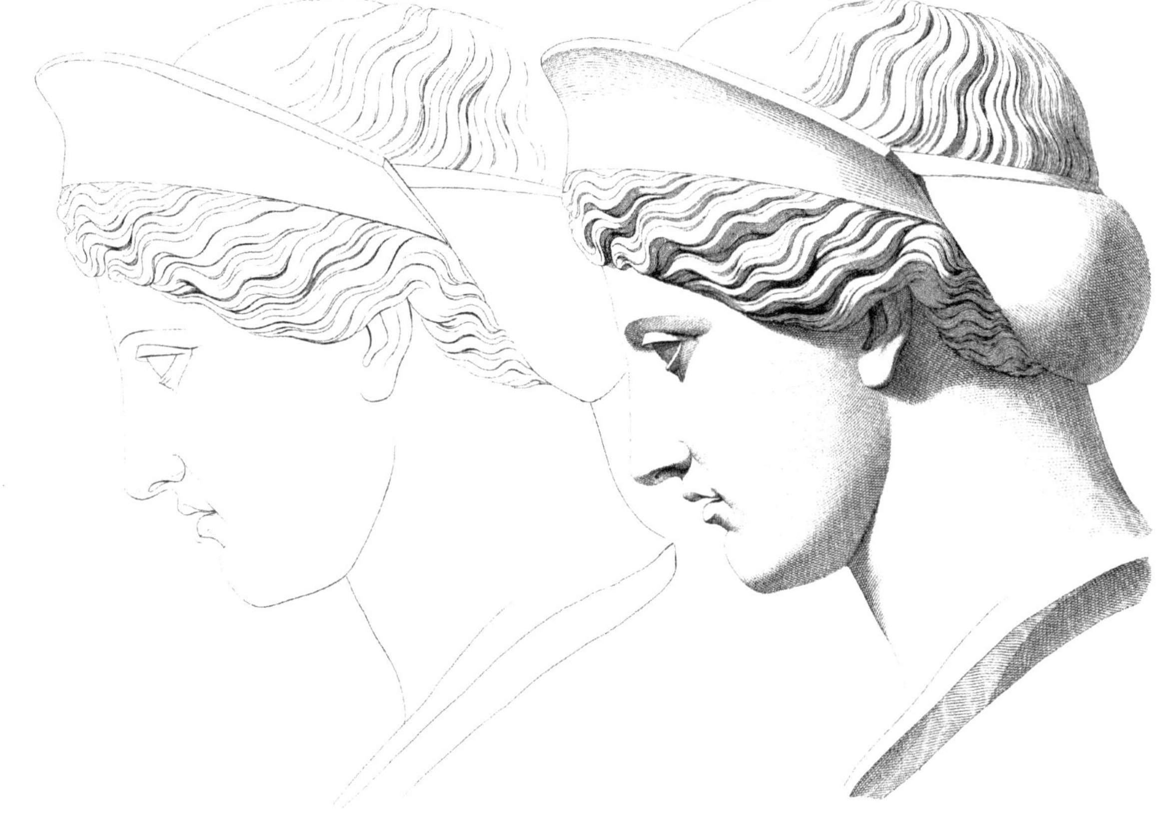

92

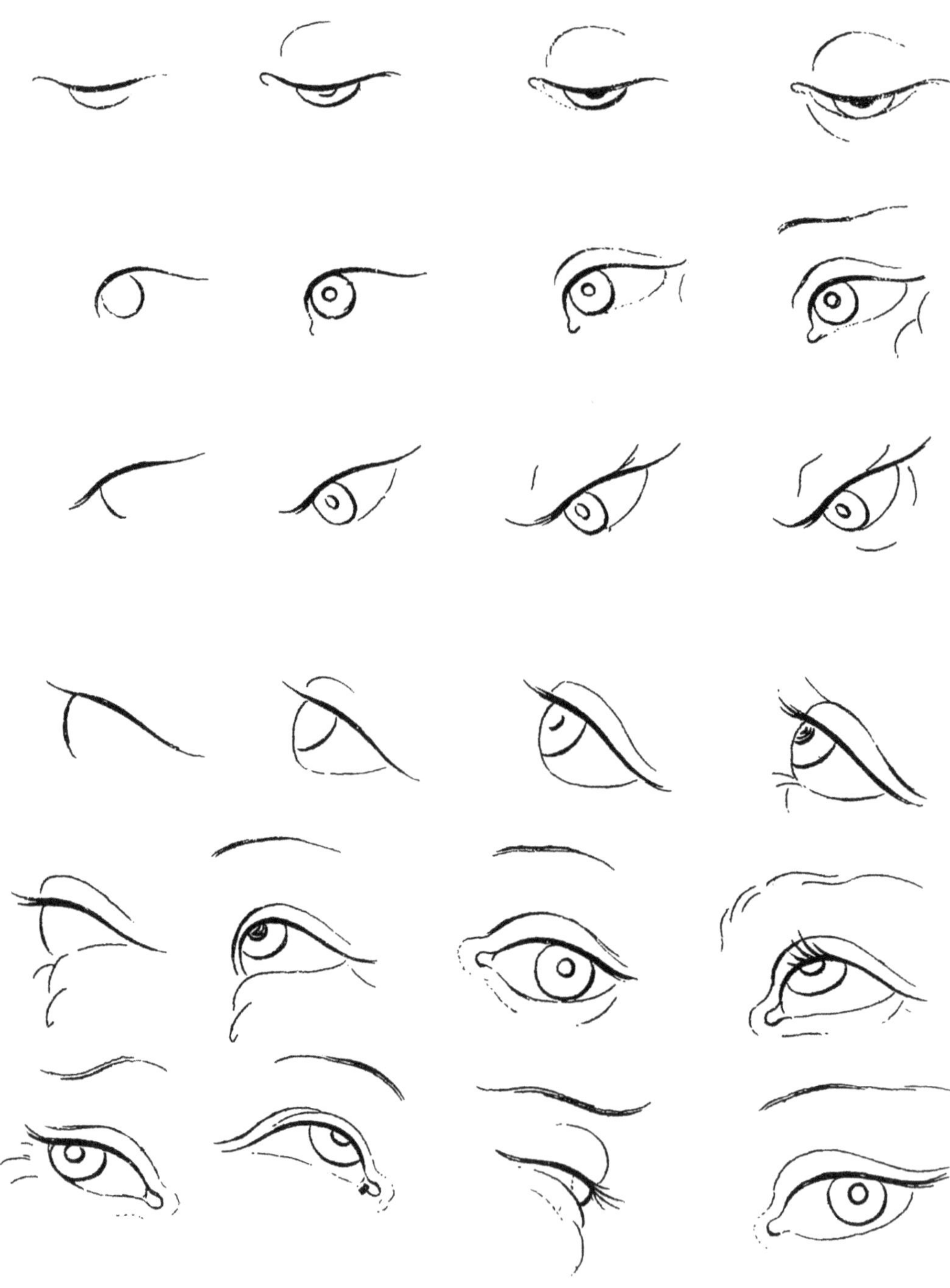

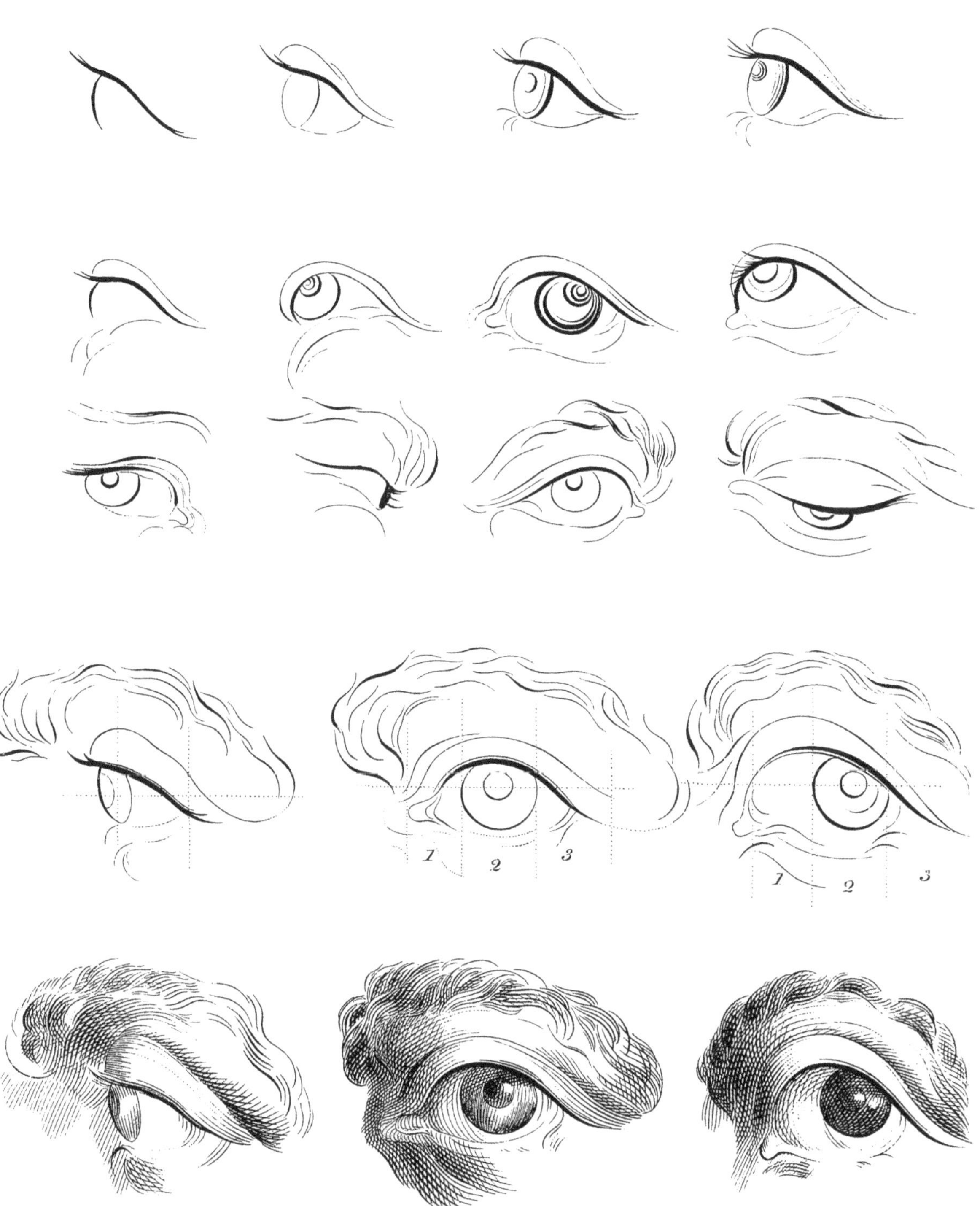

94

95

DRAWING THE HUMAN FIGURE

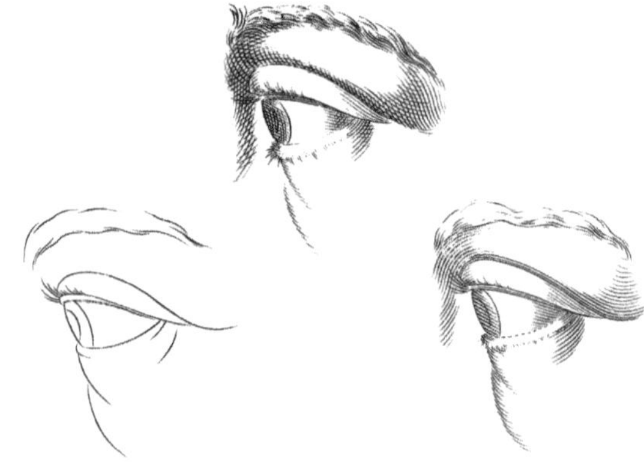

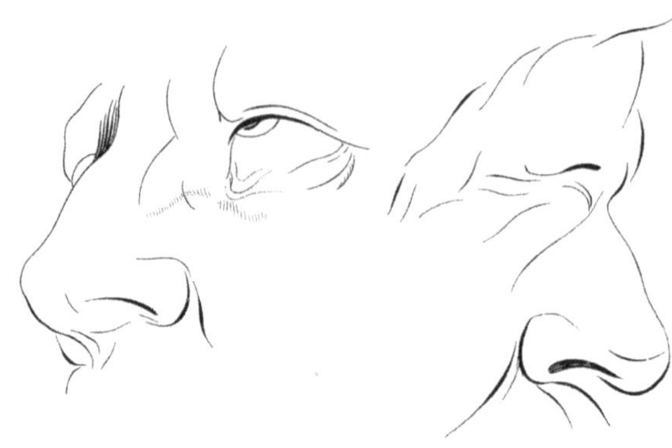

96

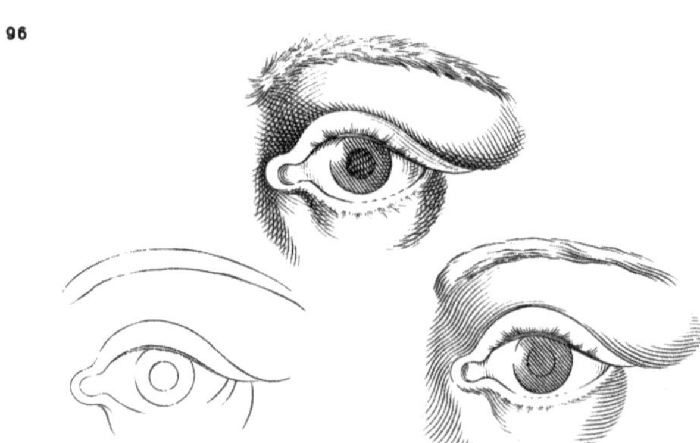

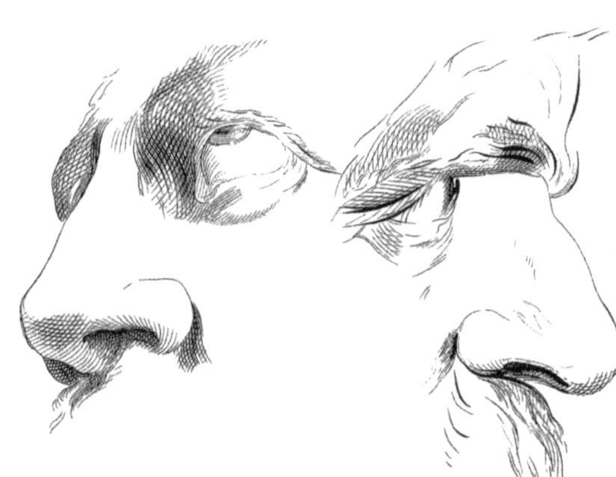

97

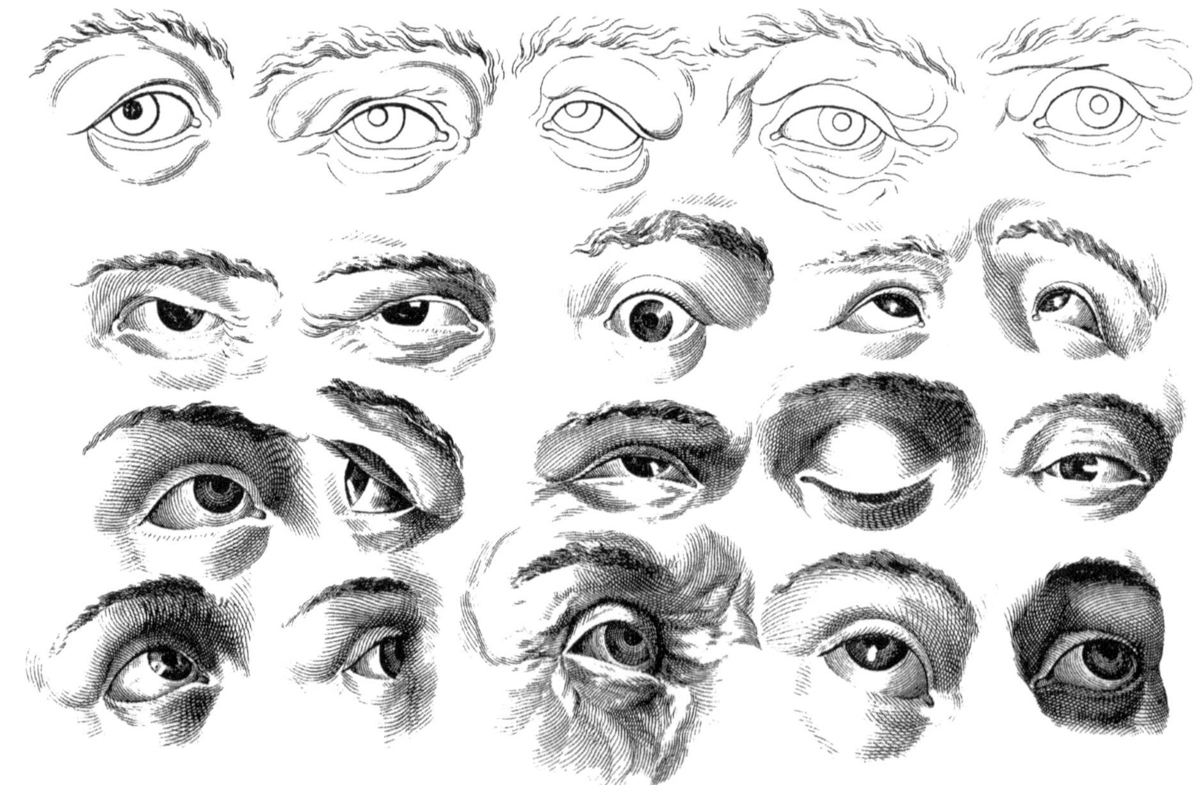

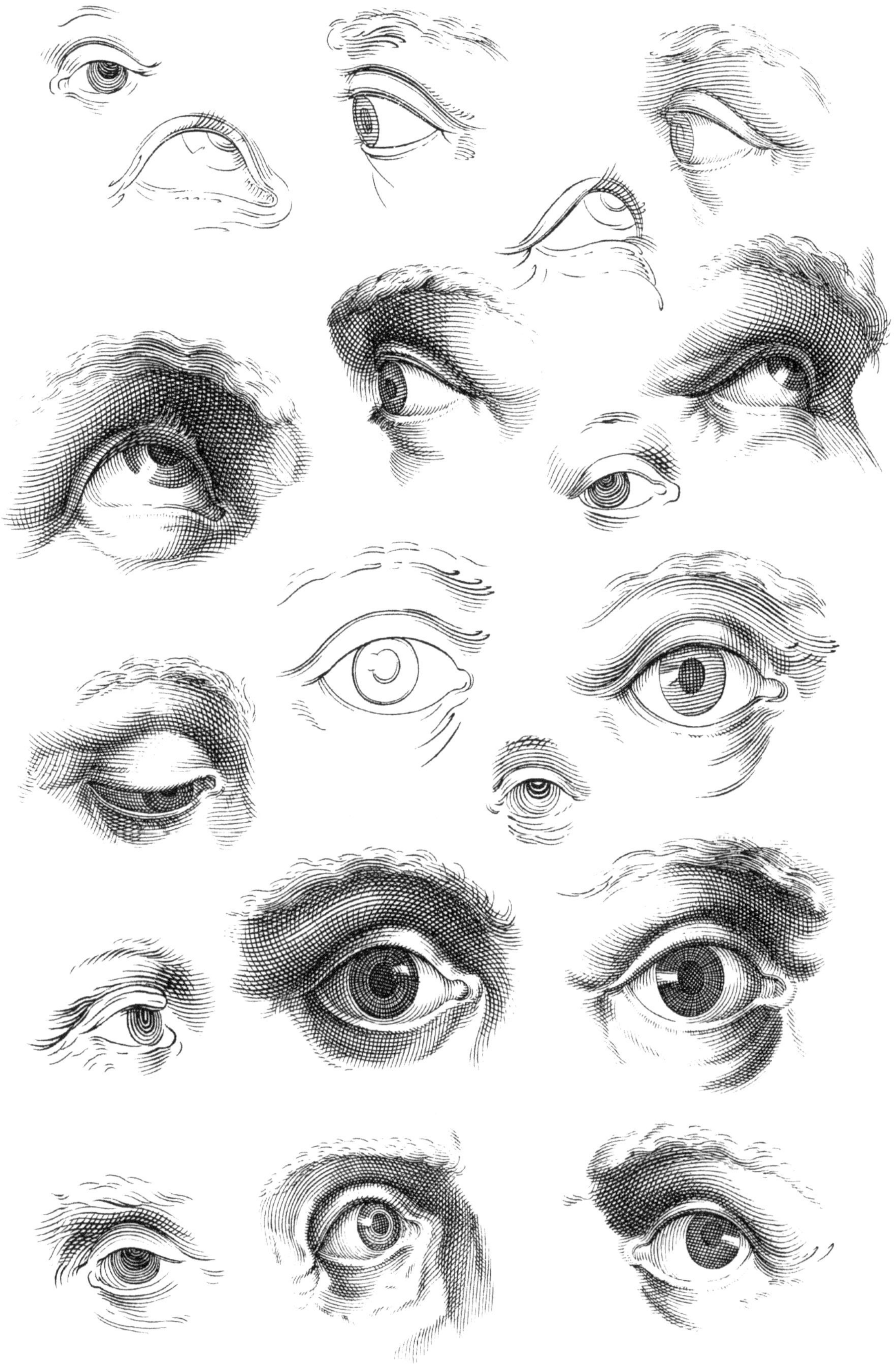

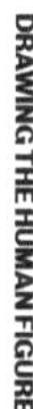

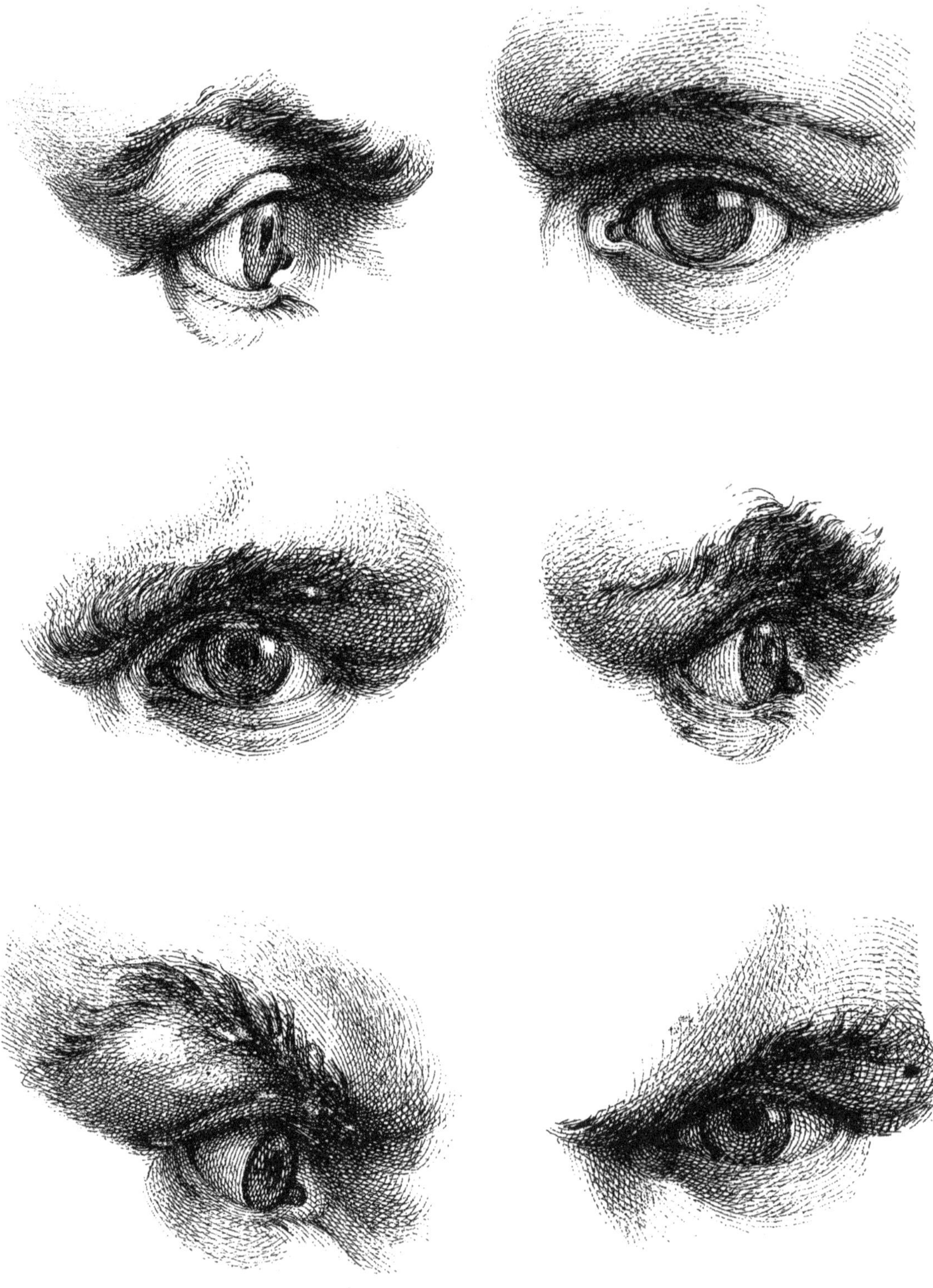

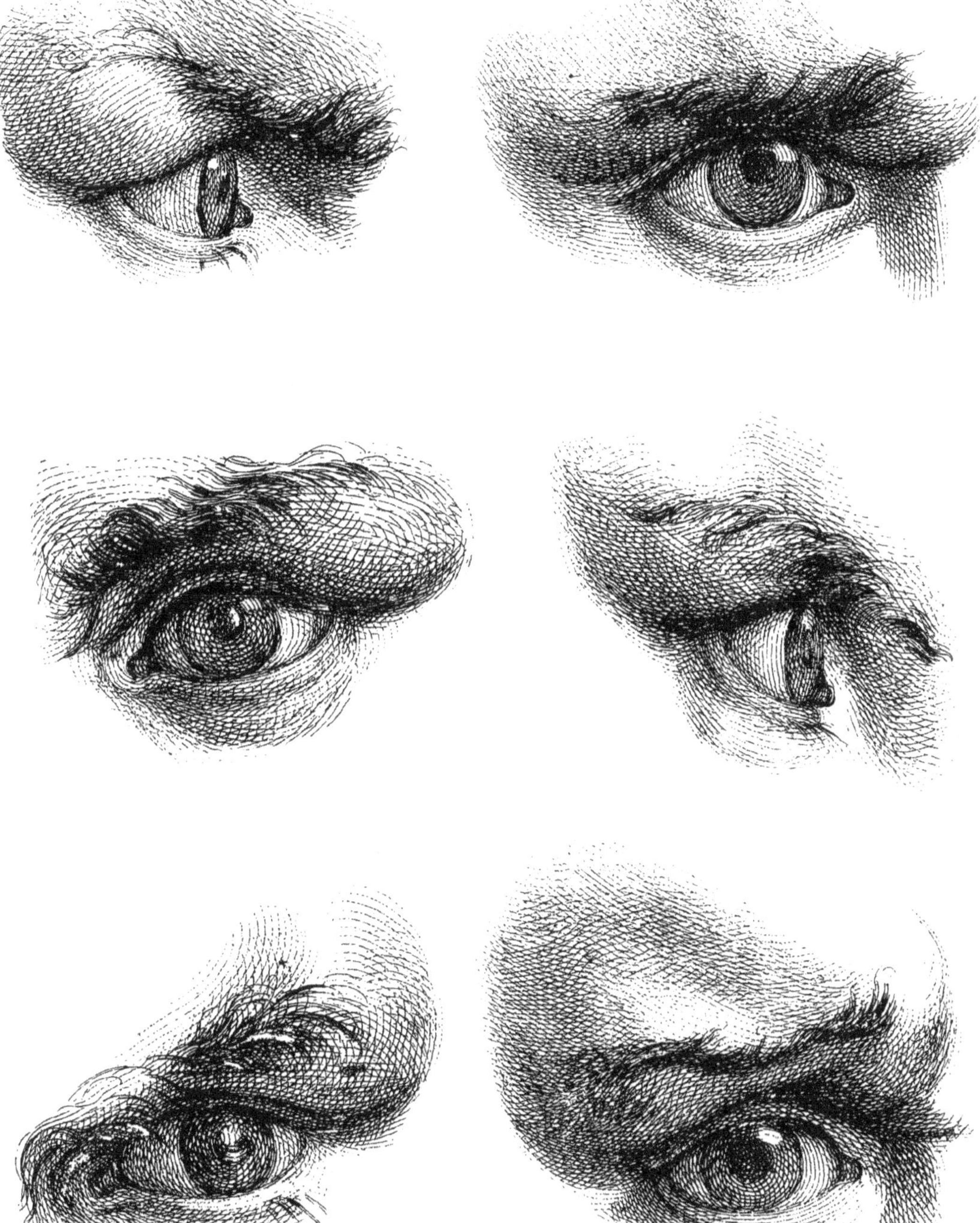

STUDIES OF THE EYE

101

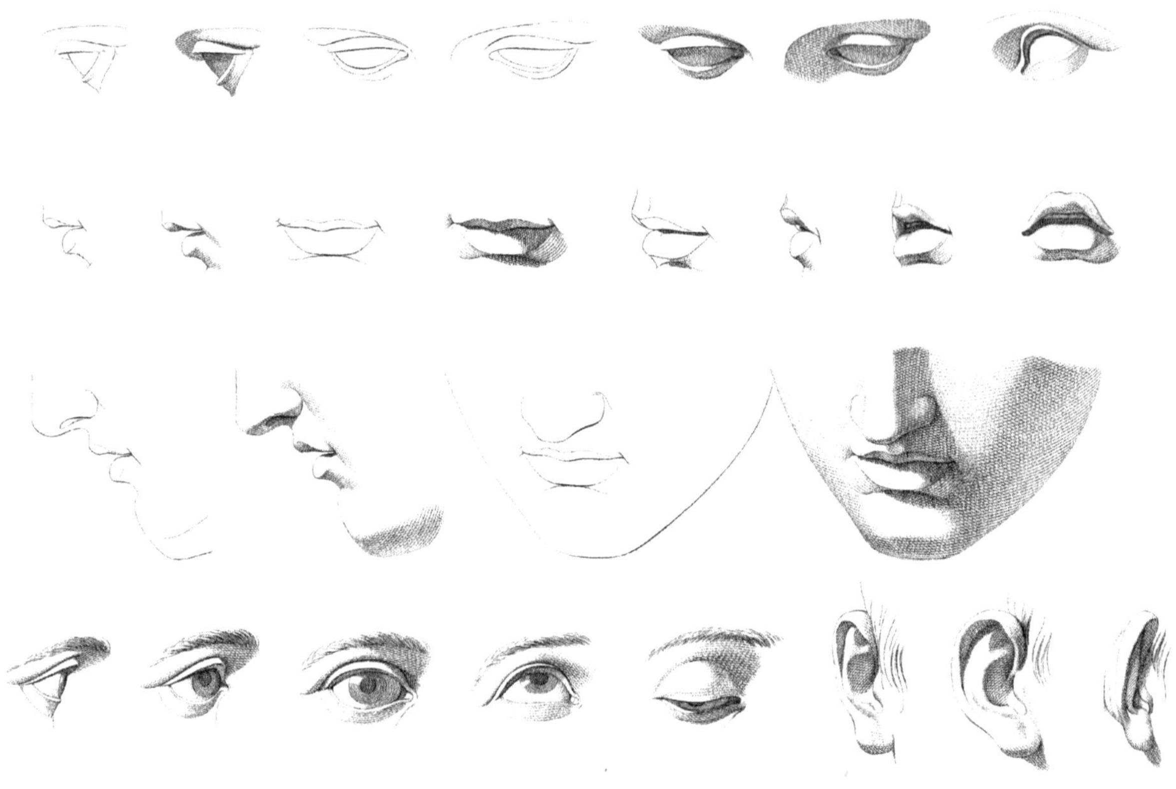

102

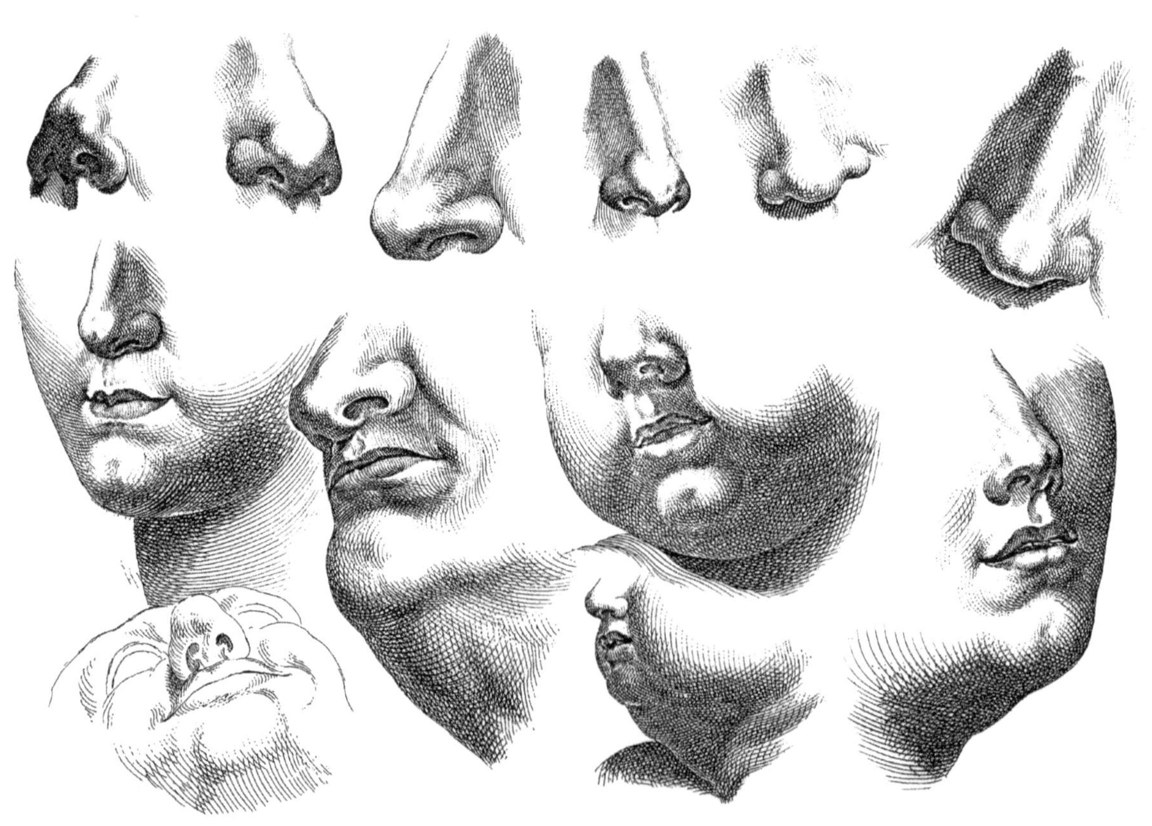

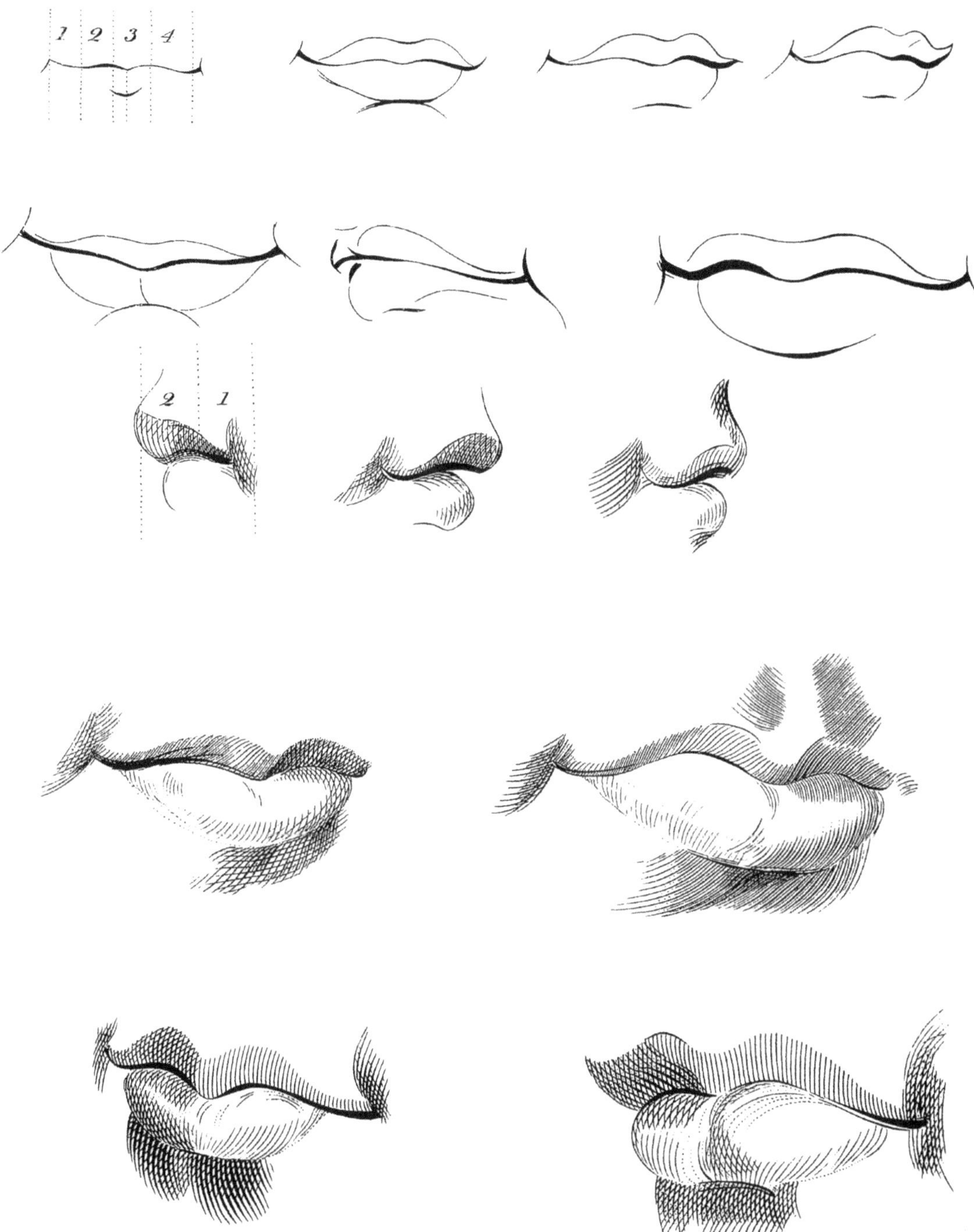

1 2 3 4
2 1

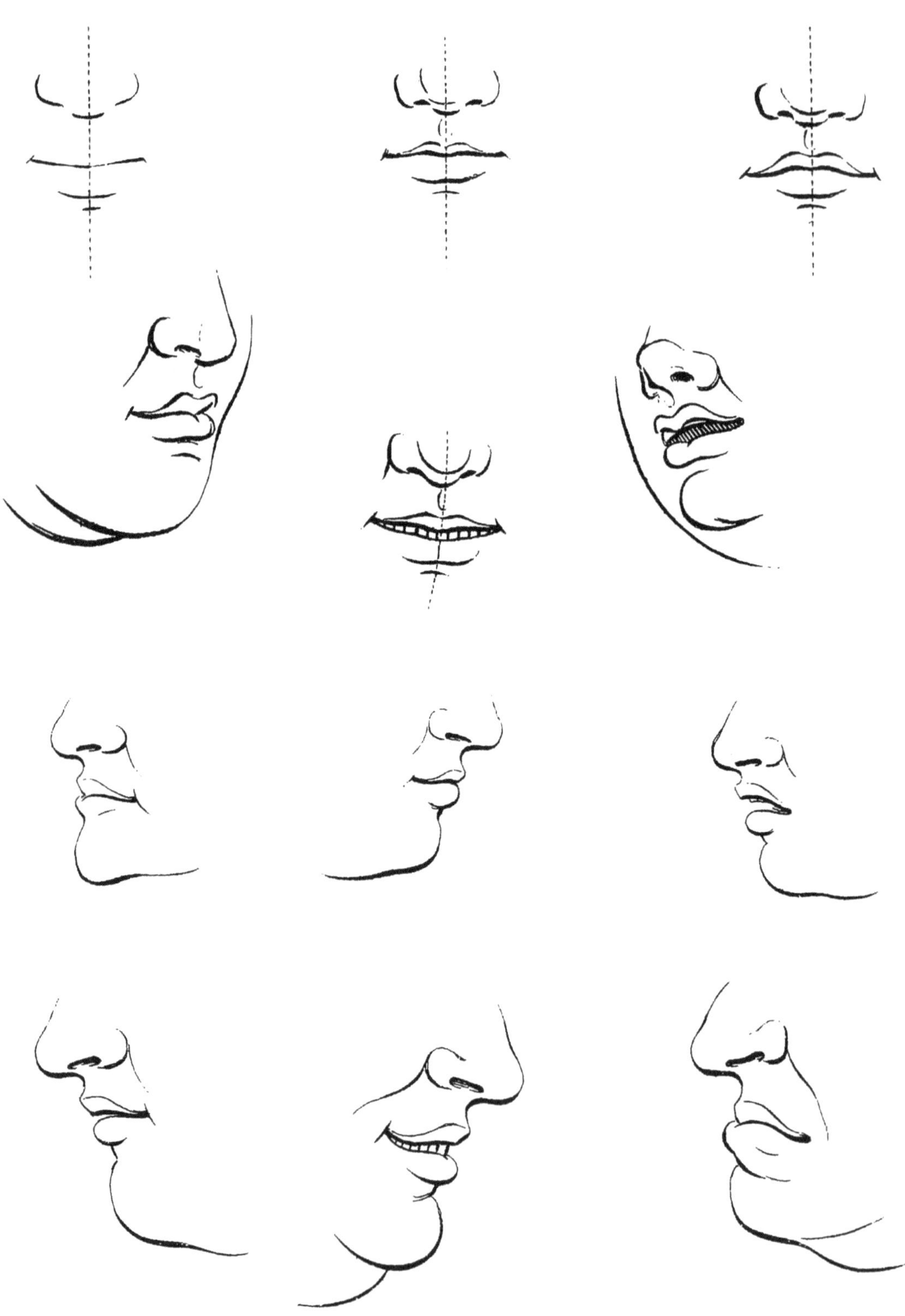

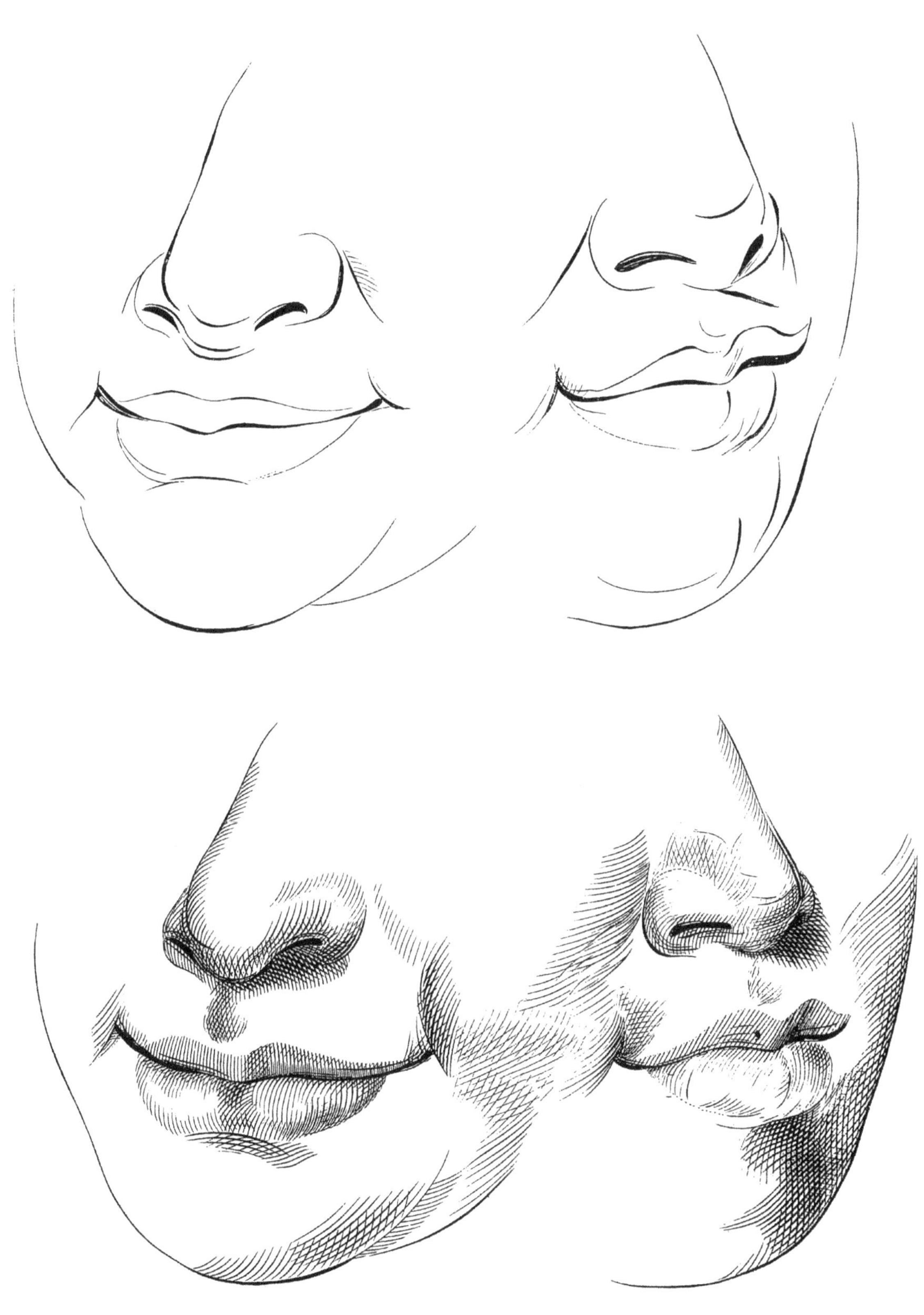

STUDIES OF THE NOSE AND MOUTH

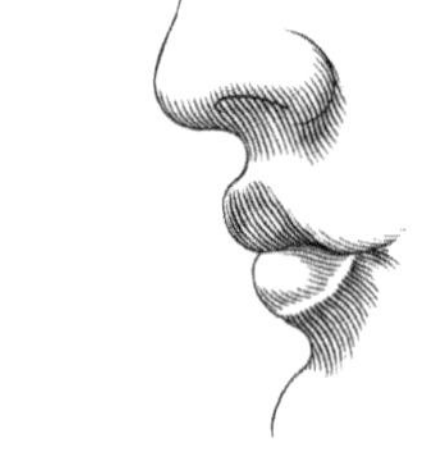
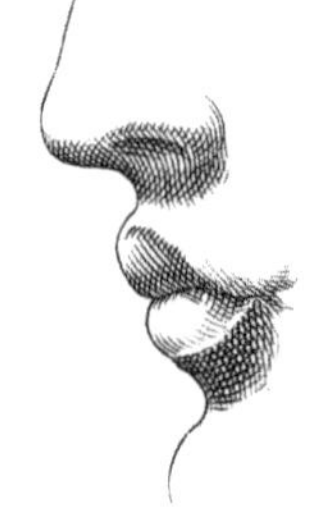
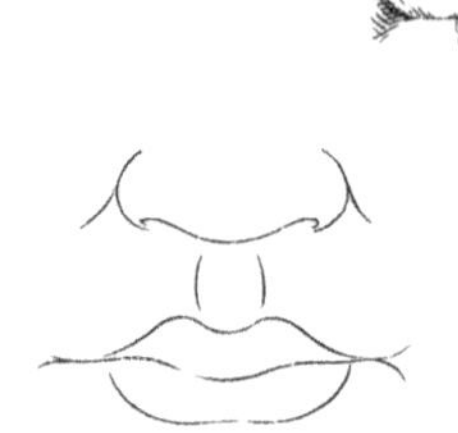
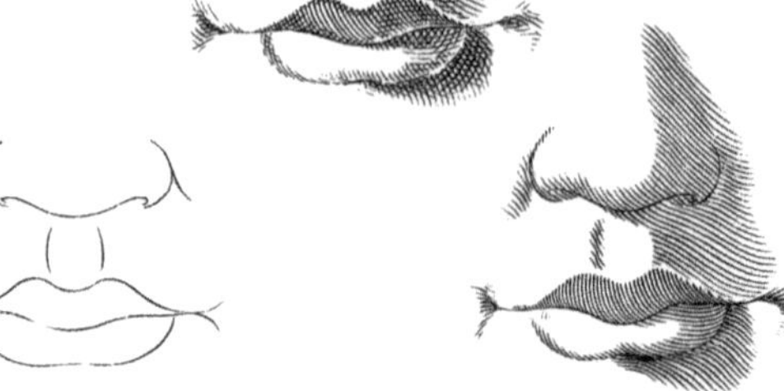

108

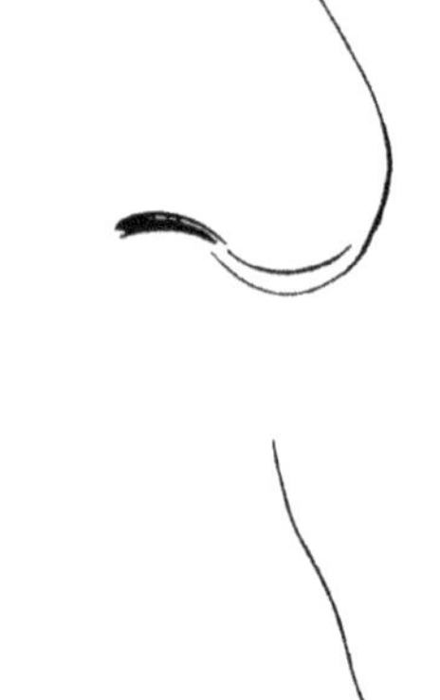
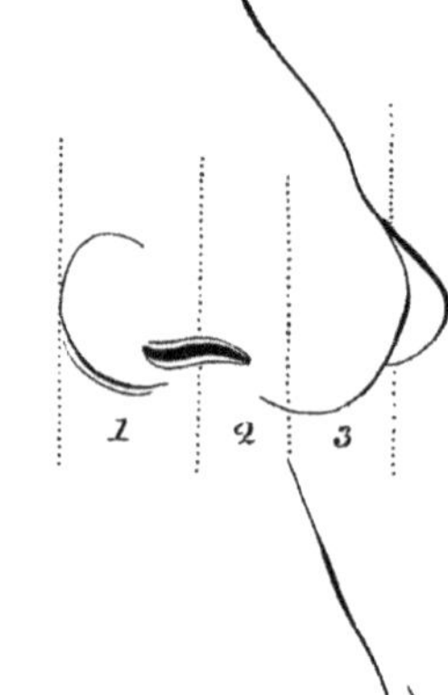
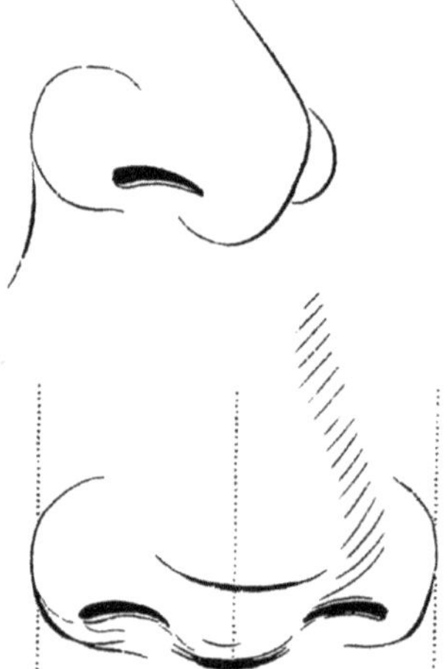
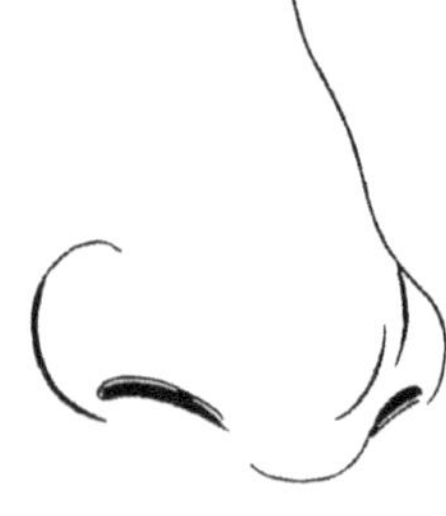
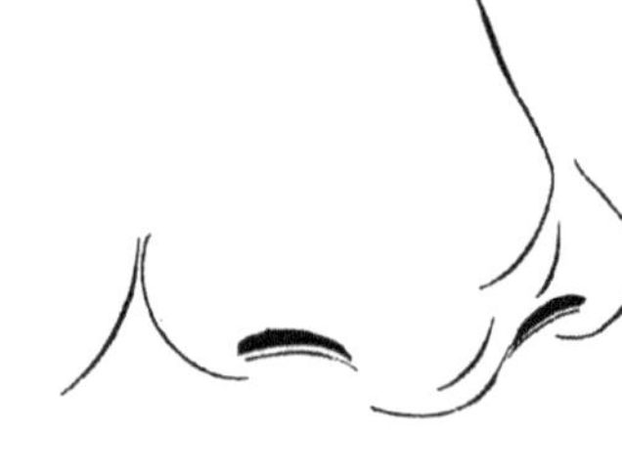

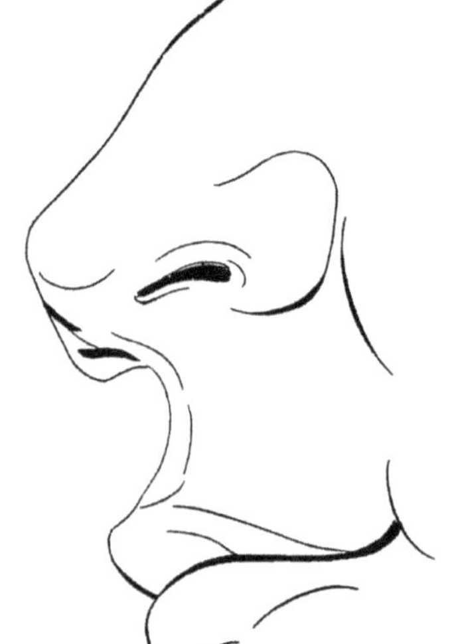
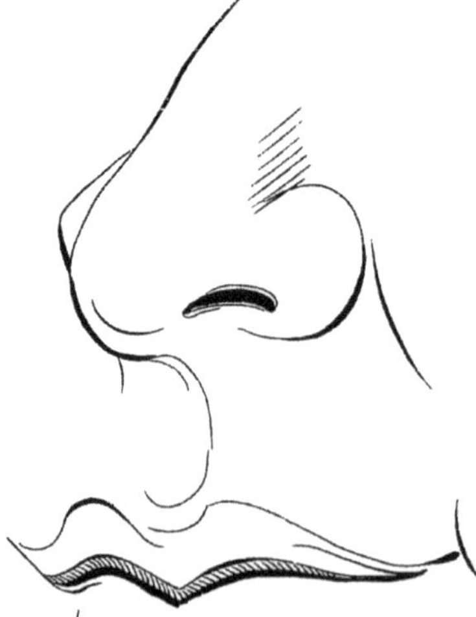
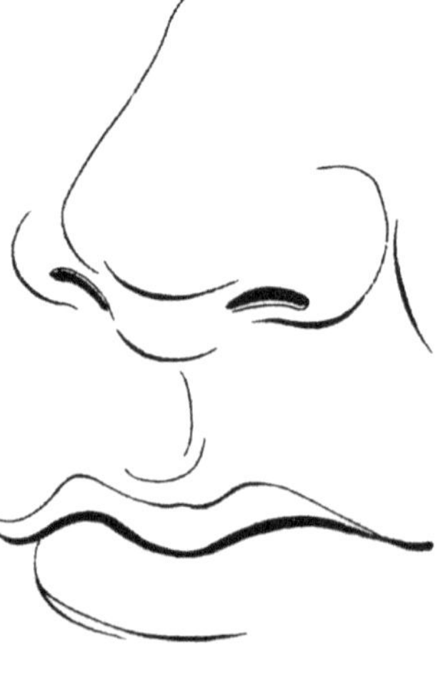

DRAWING THE HUMAN FIGURE

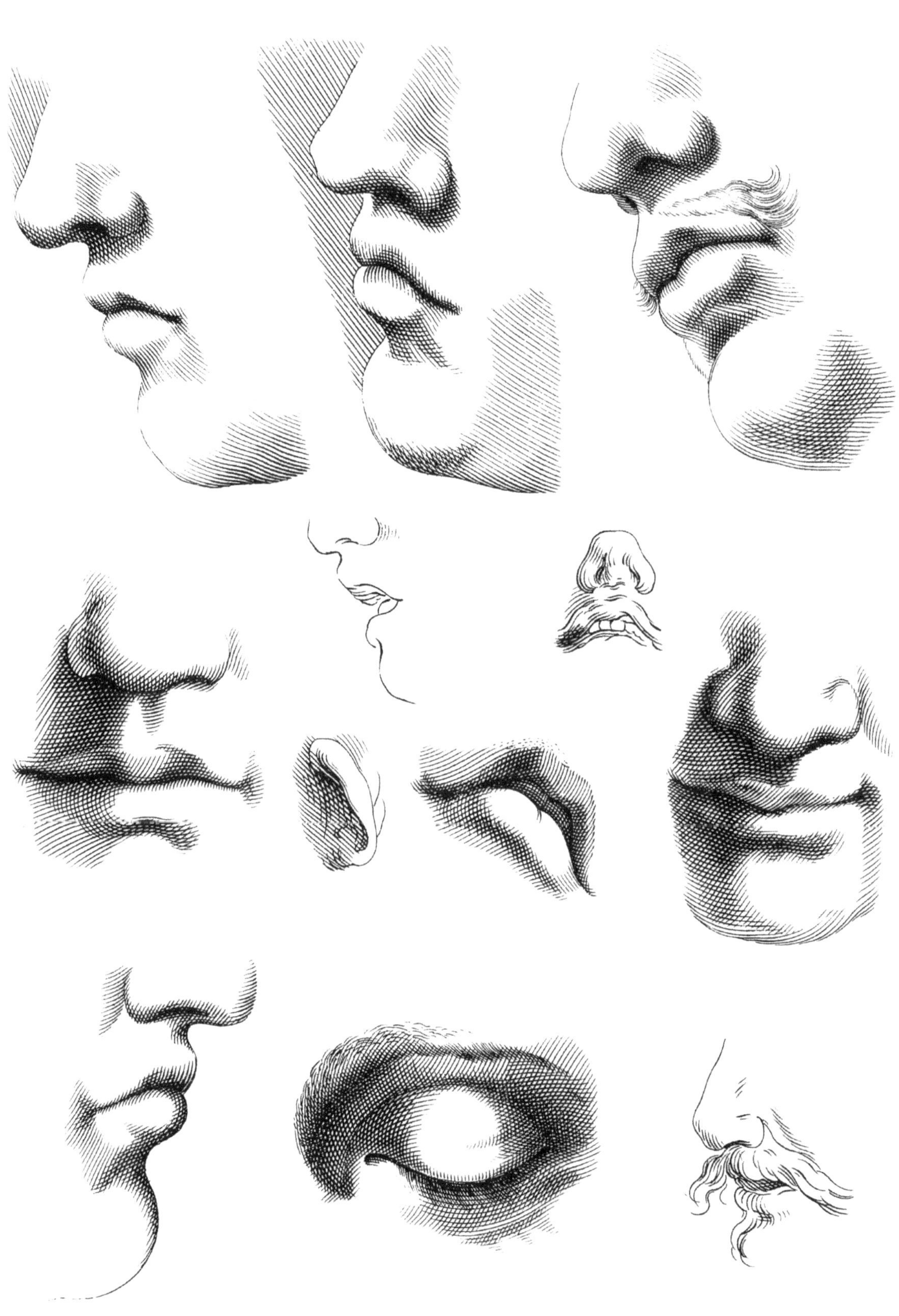

STUDIES OF THE NOSE AND MOUTH

110

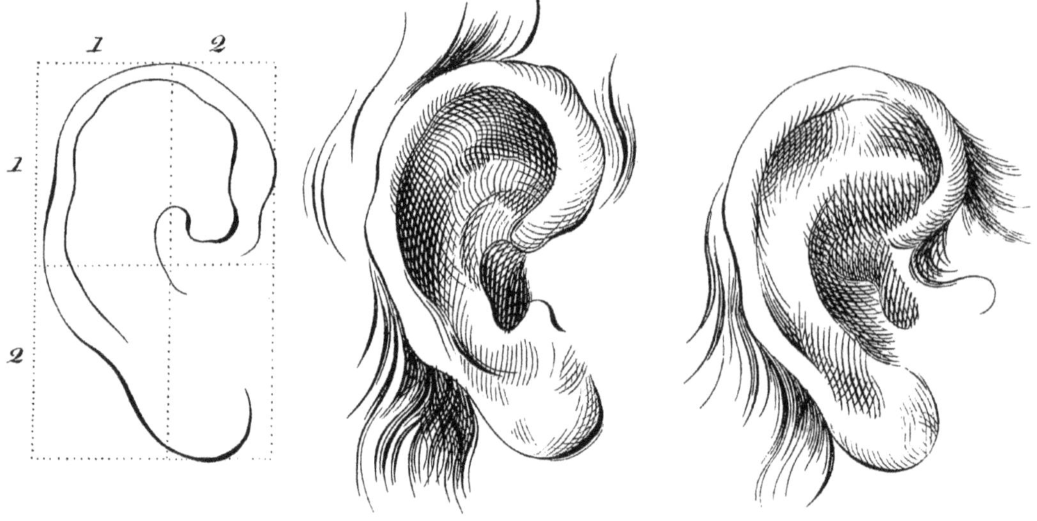

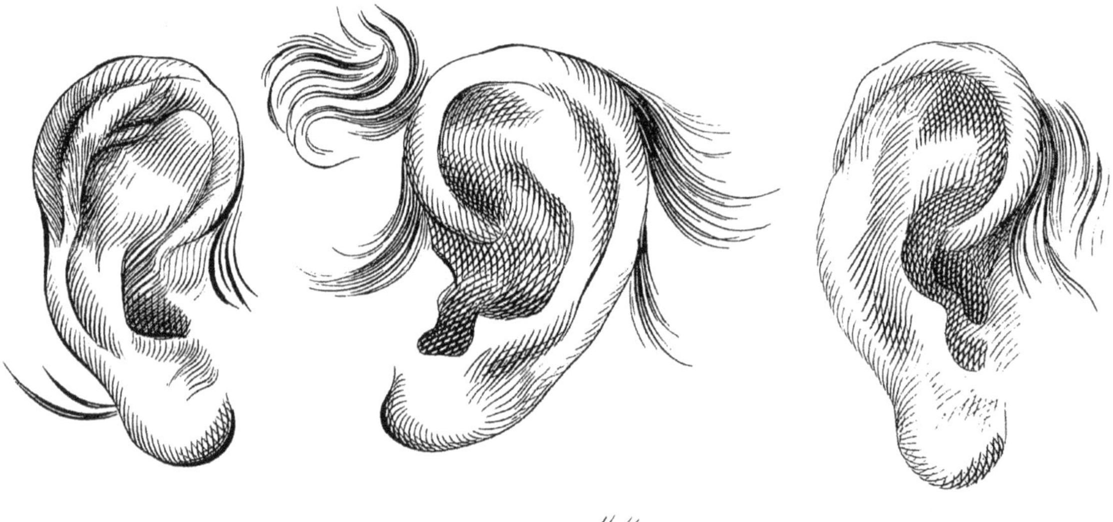

111

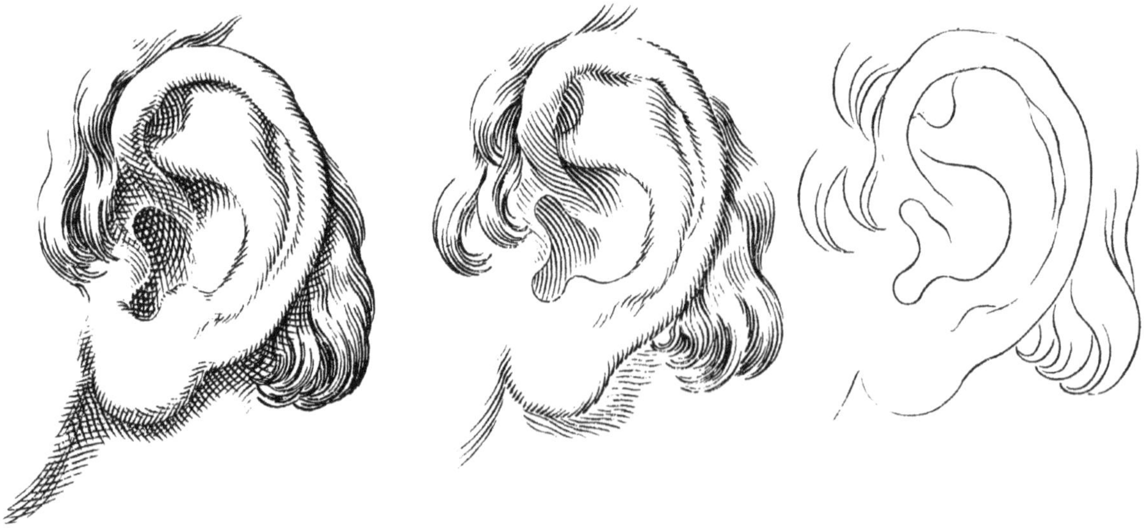

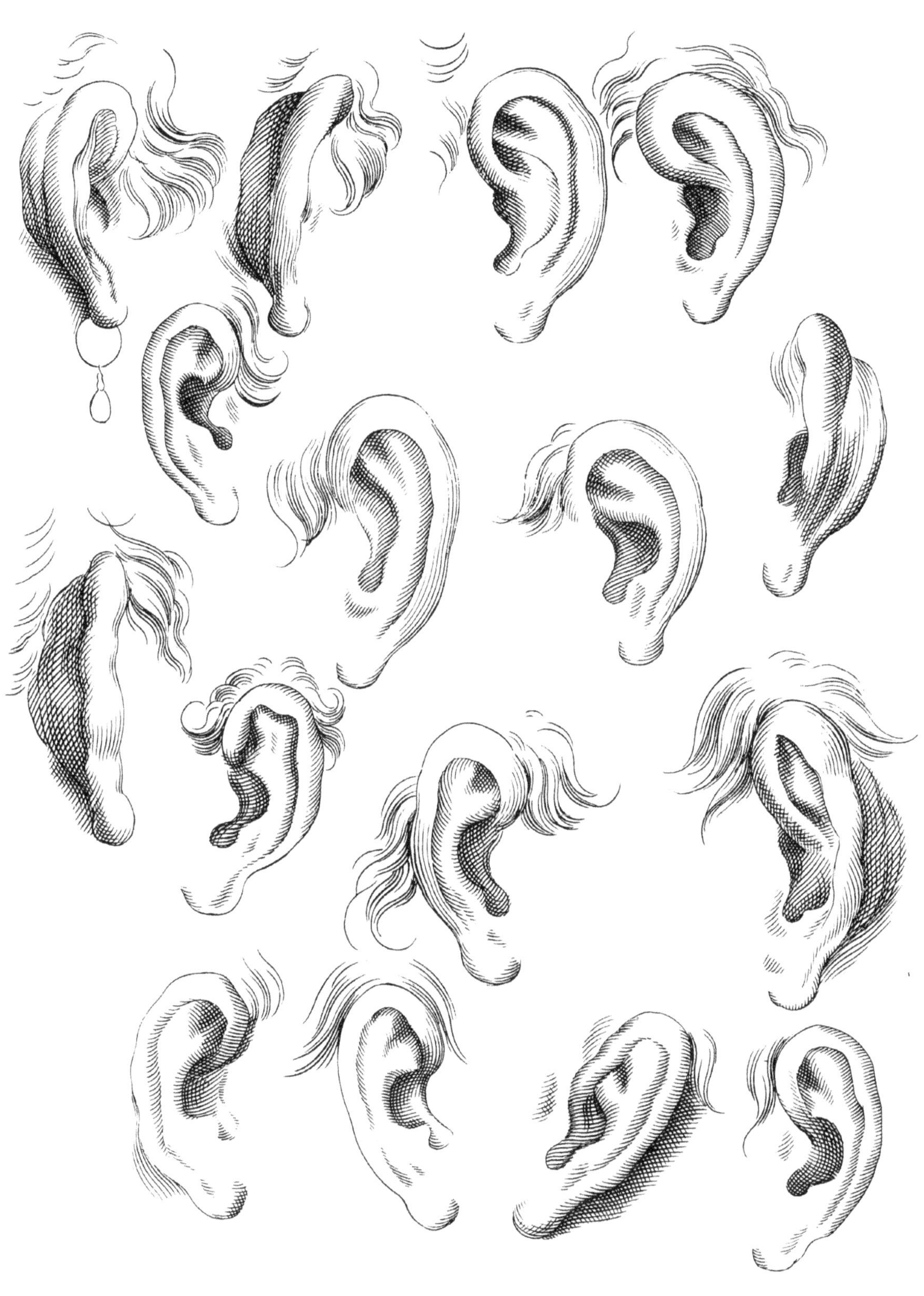

113

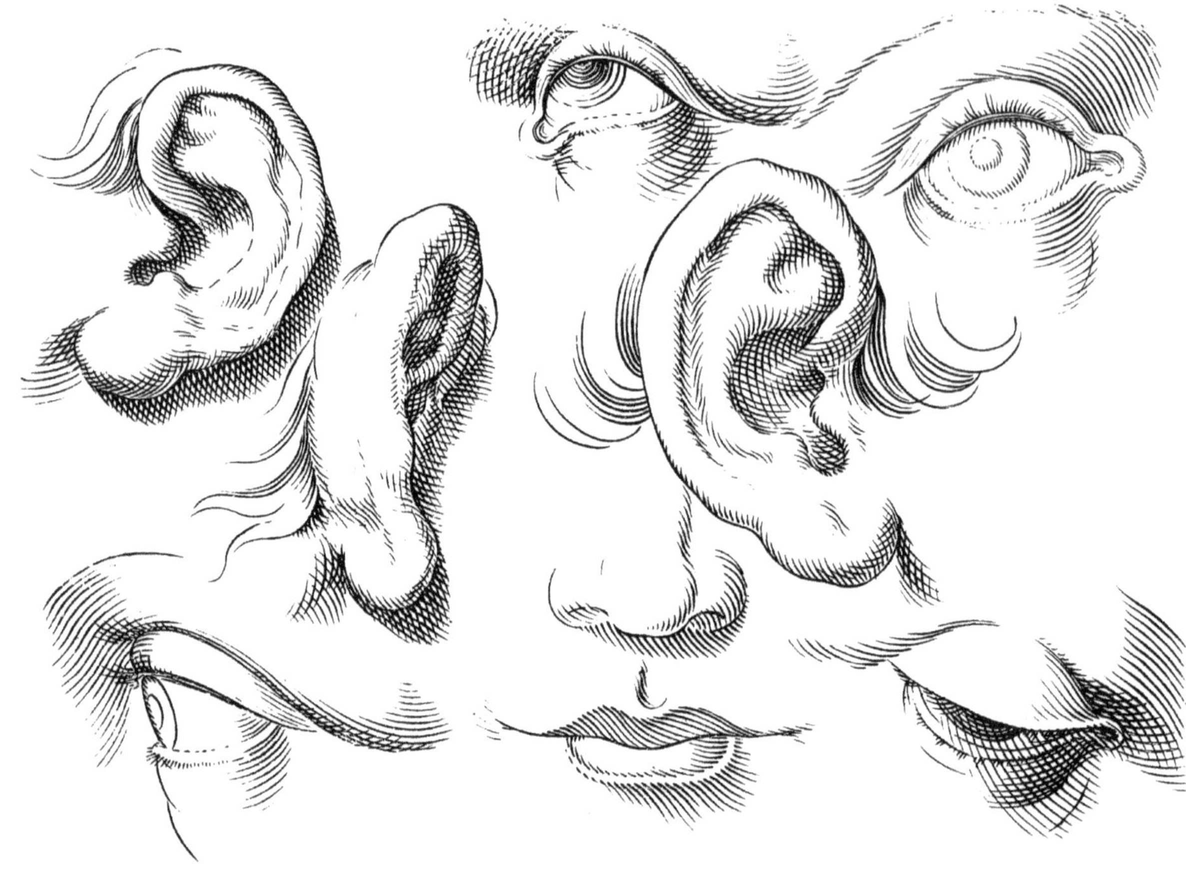

114

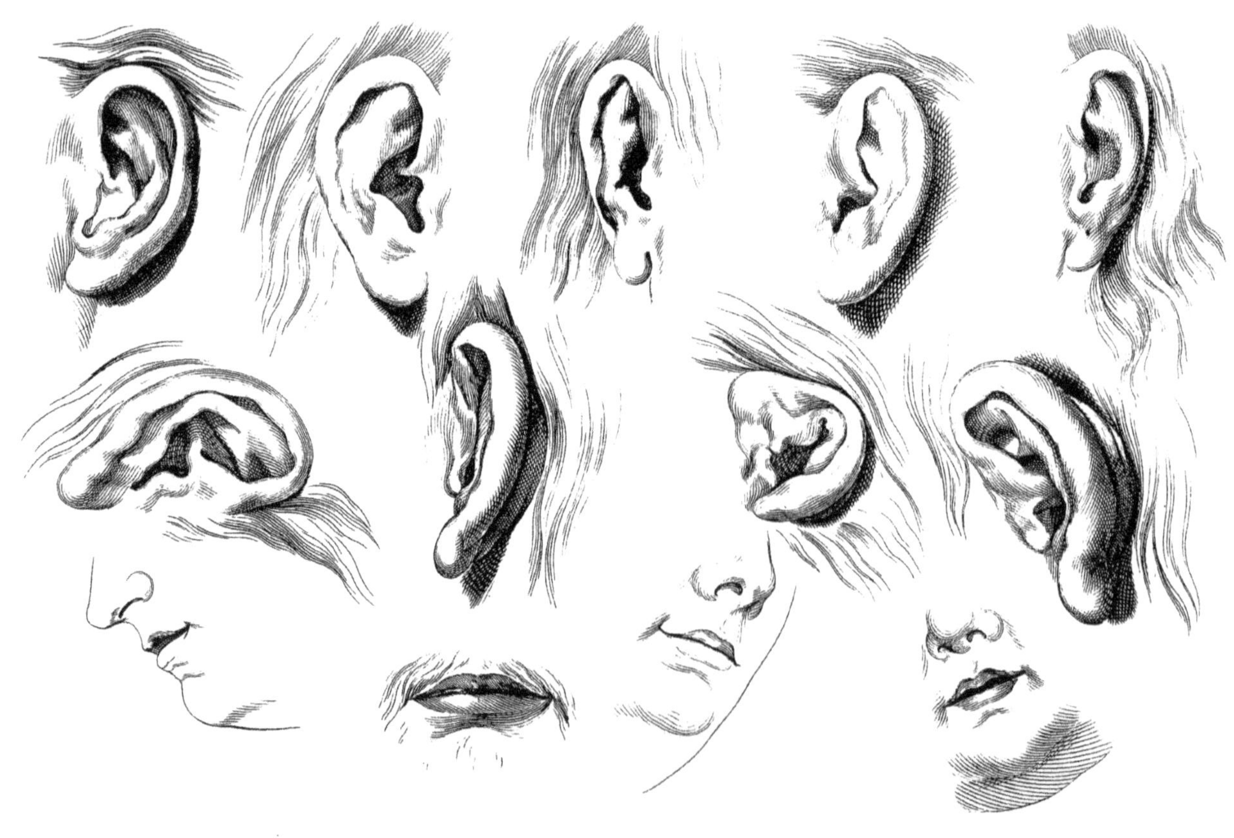

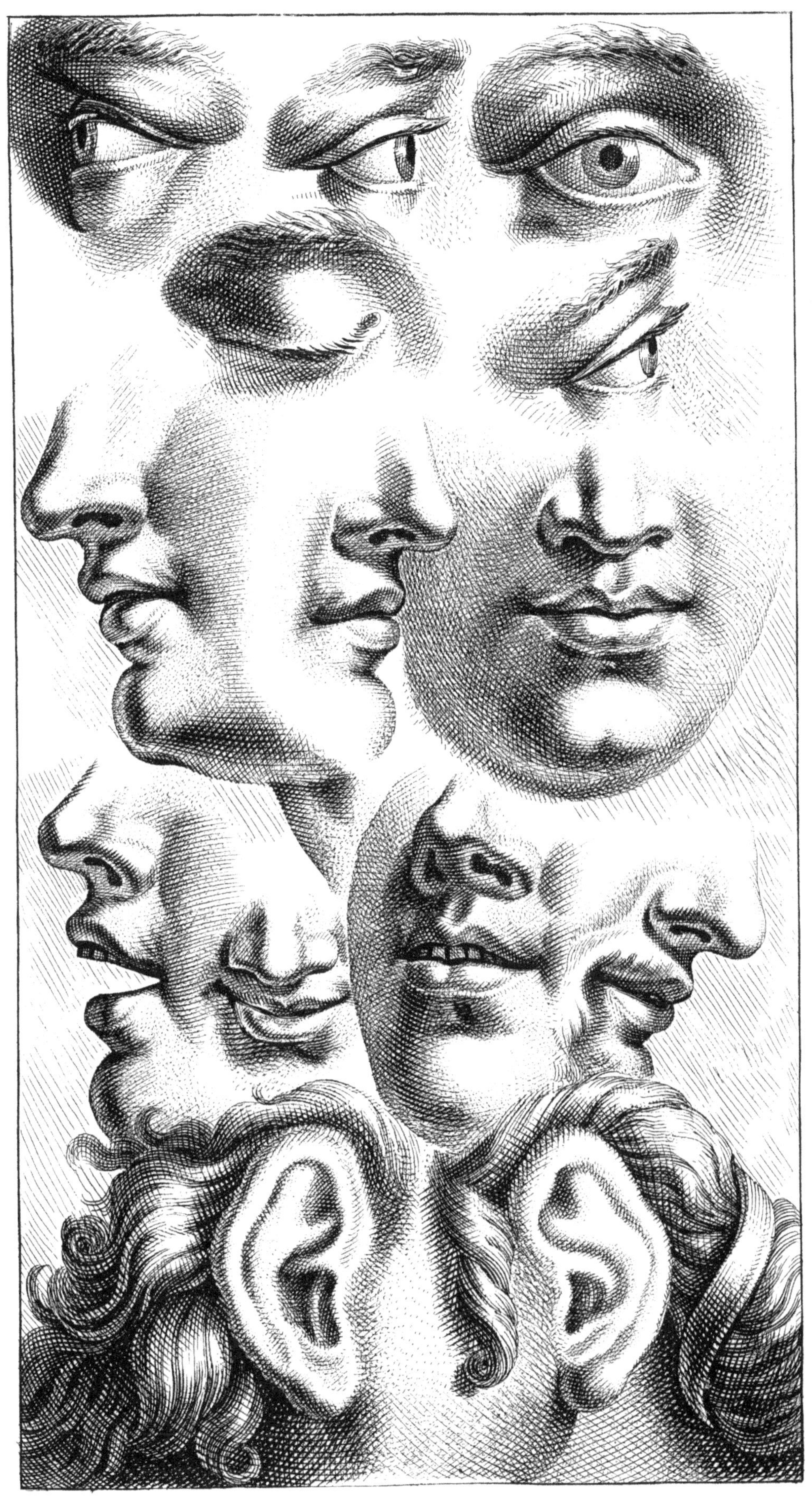

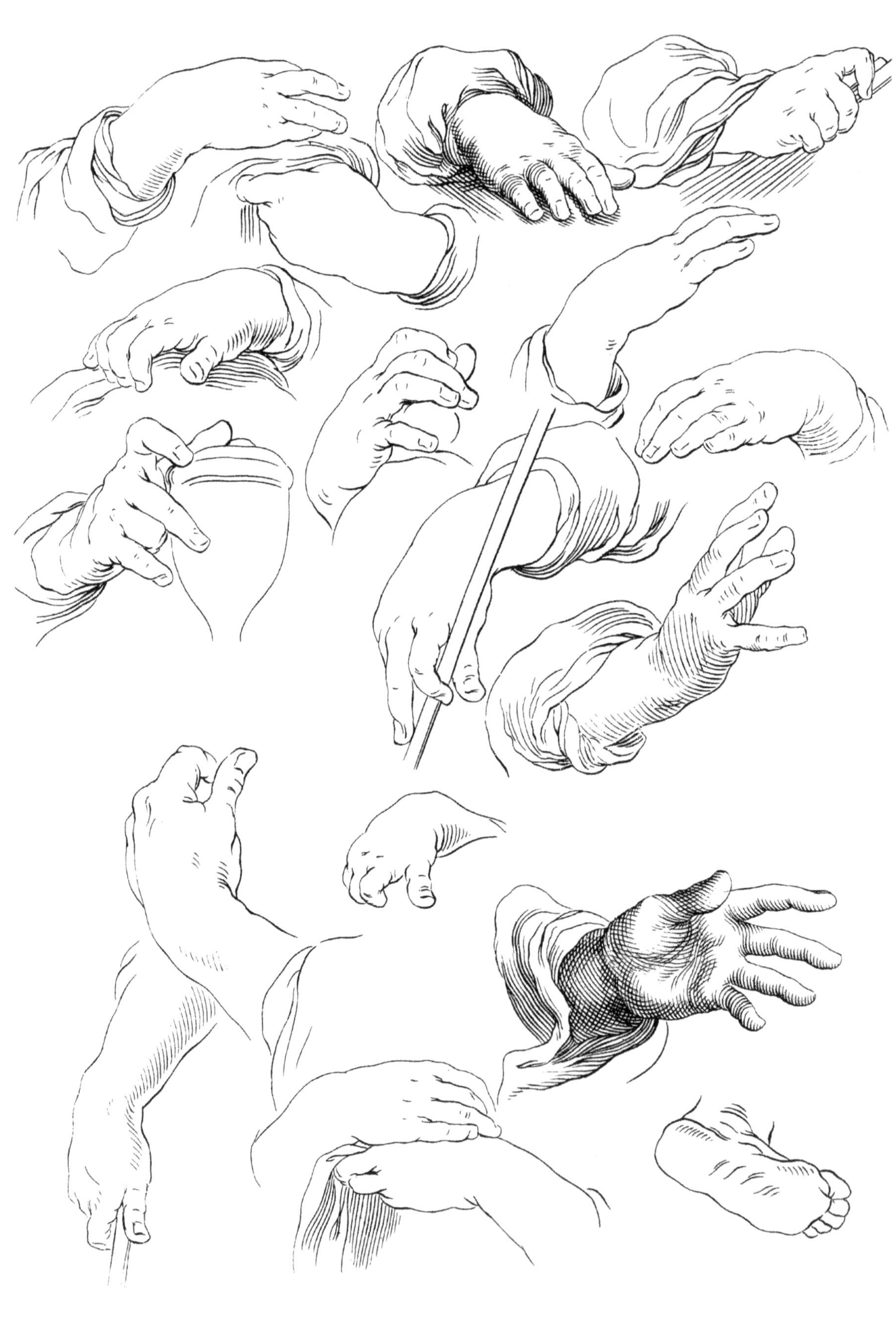

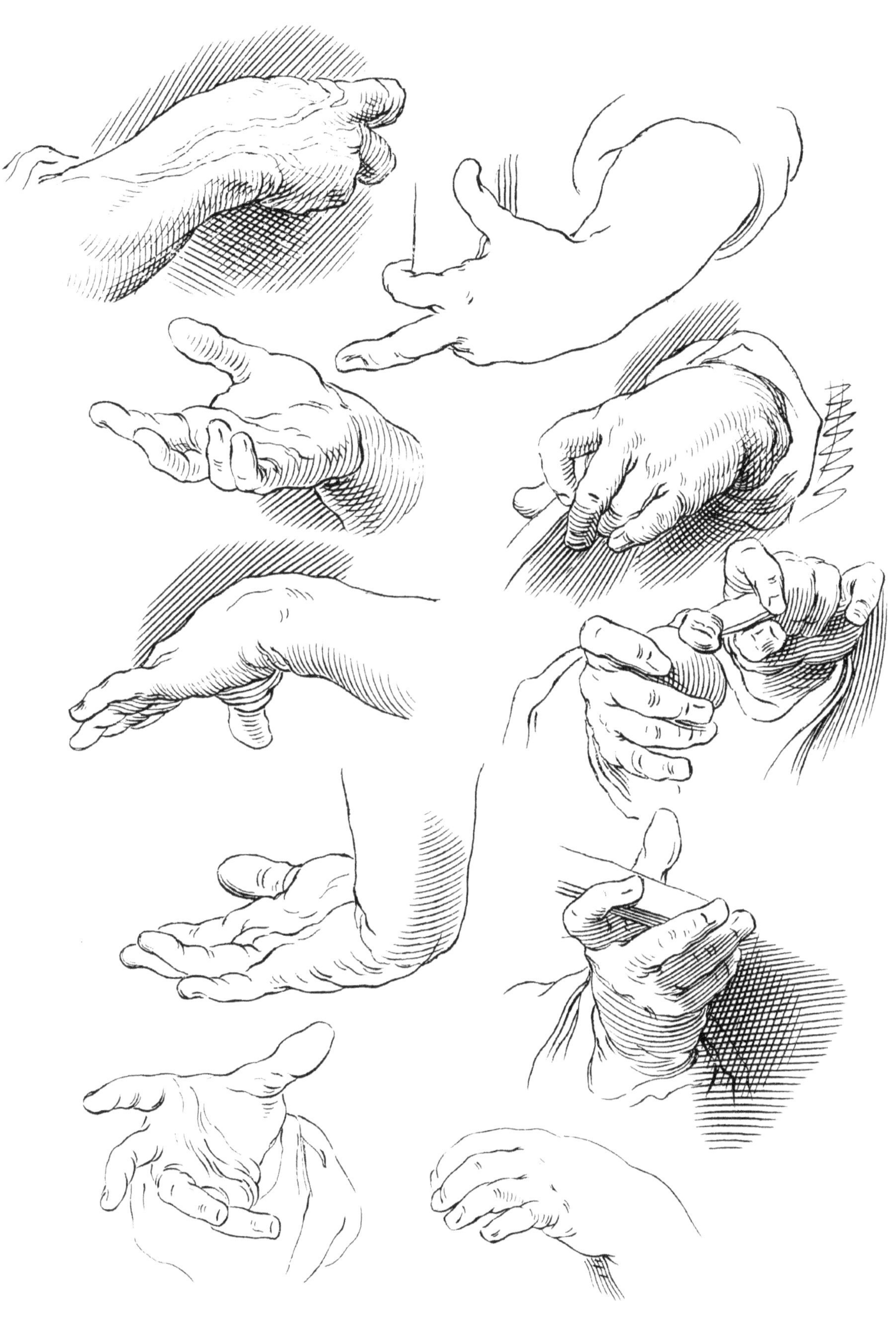

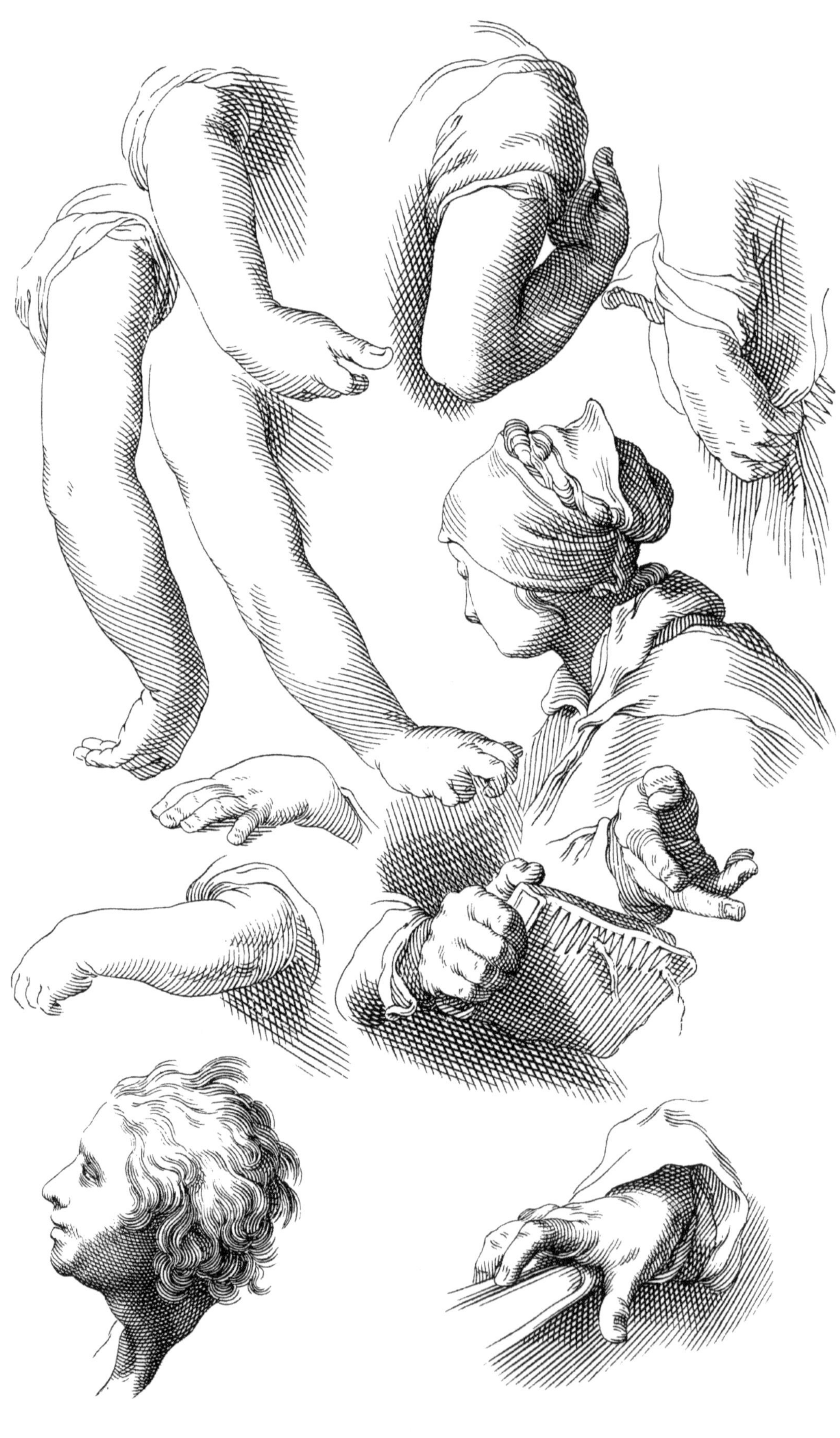

STUDIES OF THE ARM, HAND AND EXTREMITIES

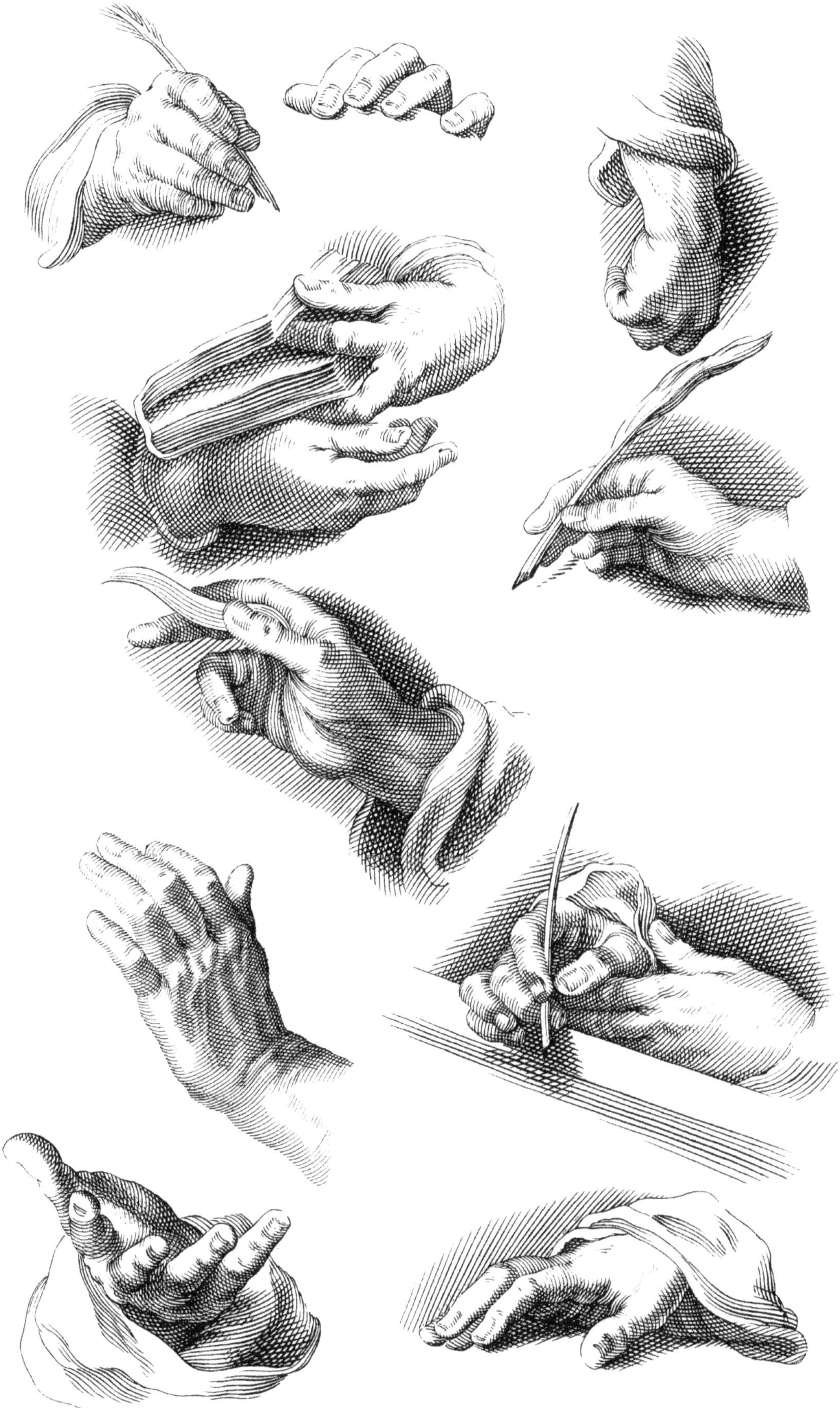

DRAWING THE HUMAN FIGURE

120

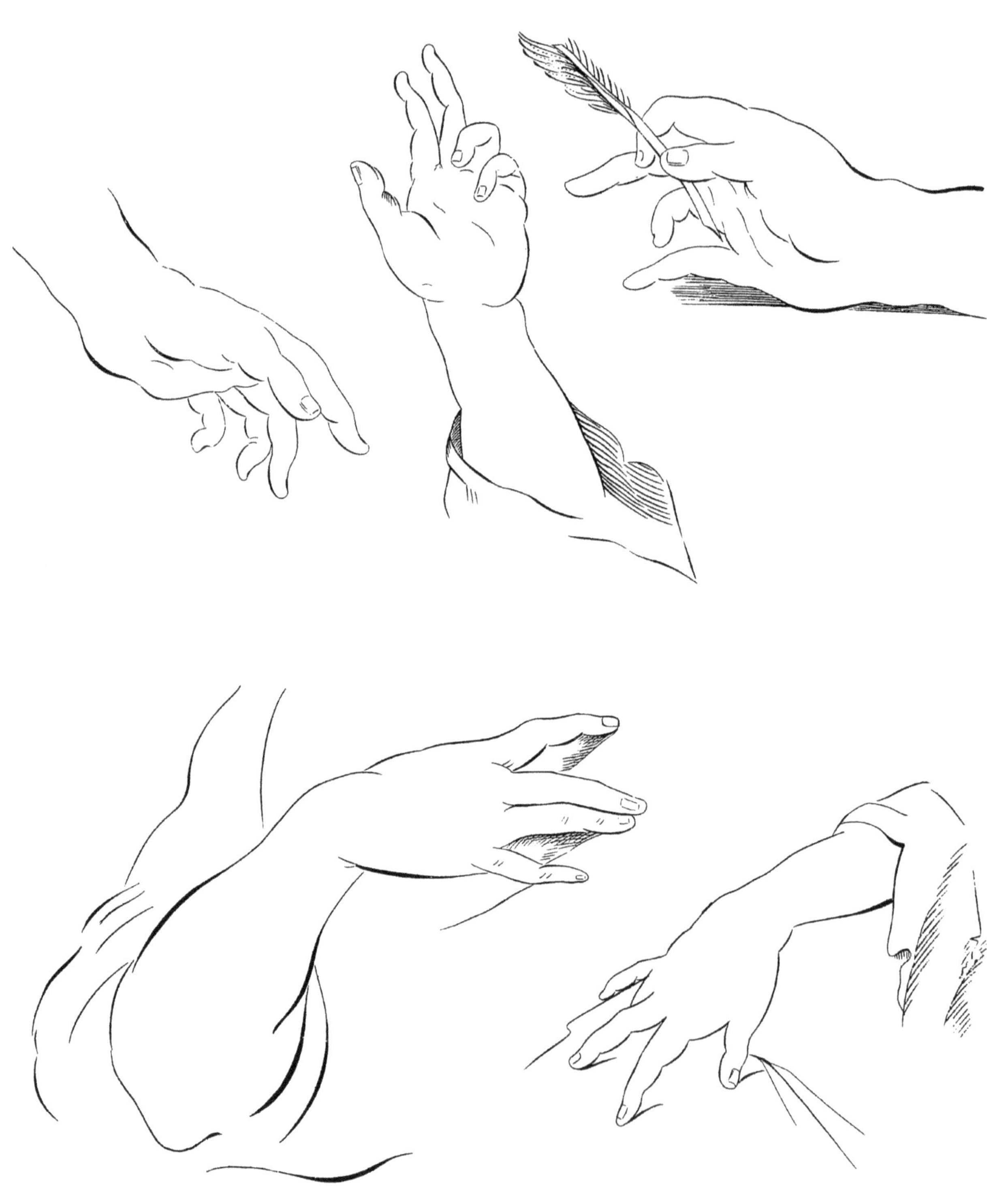

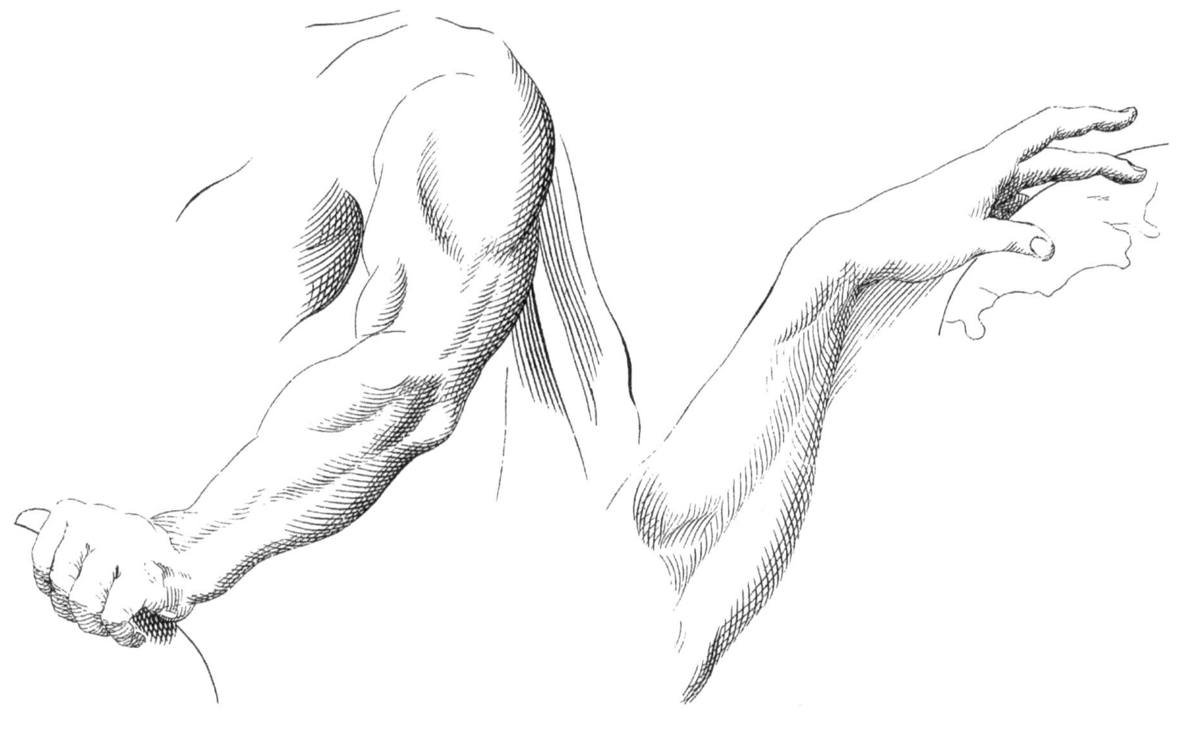

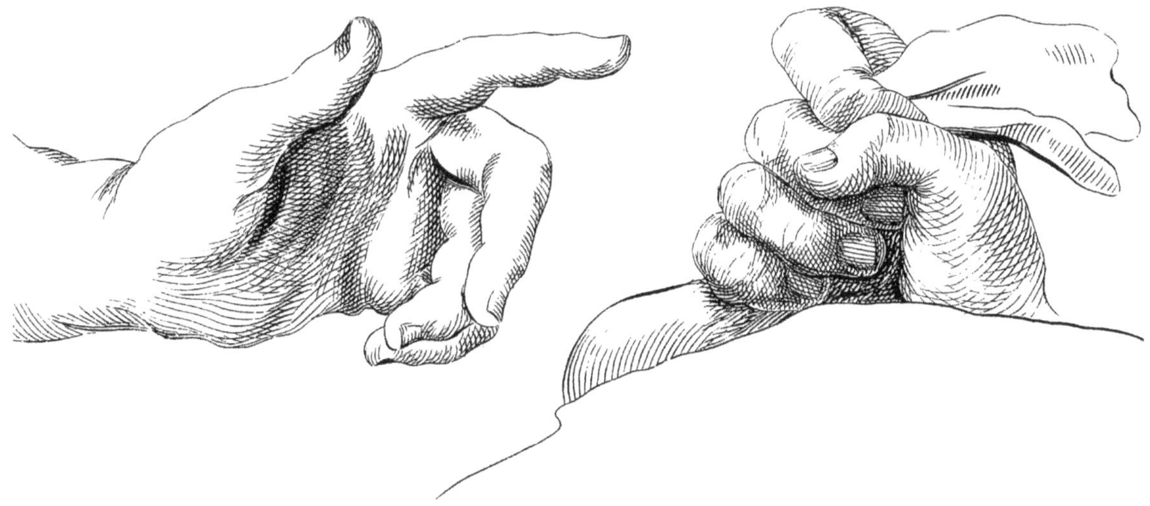

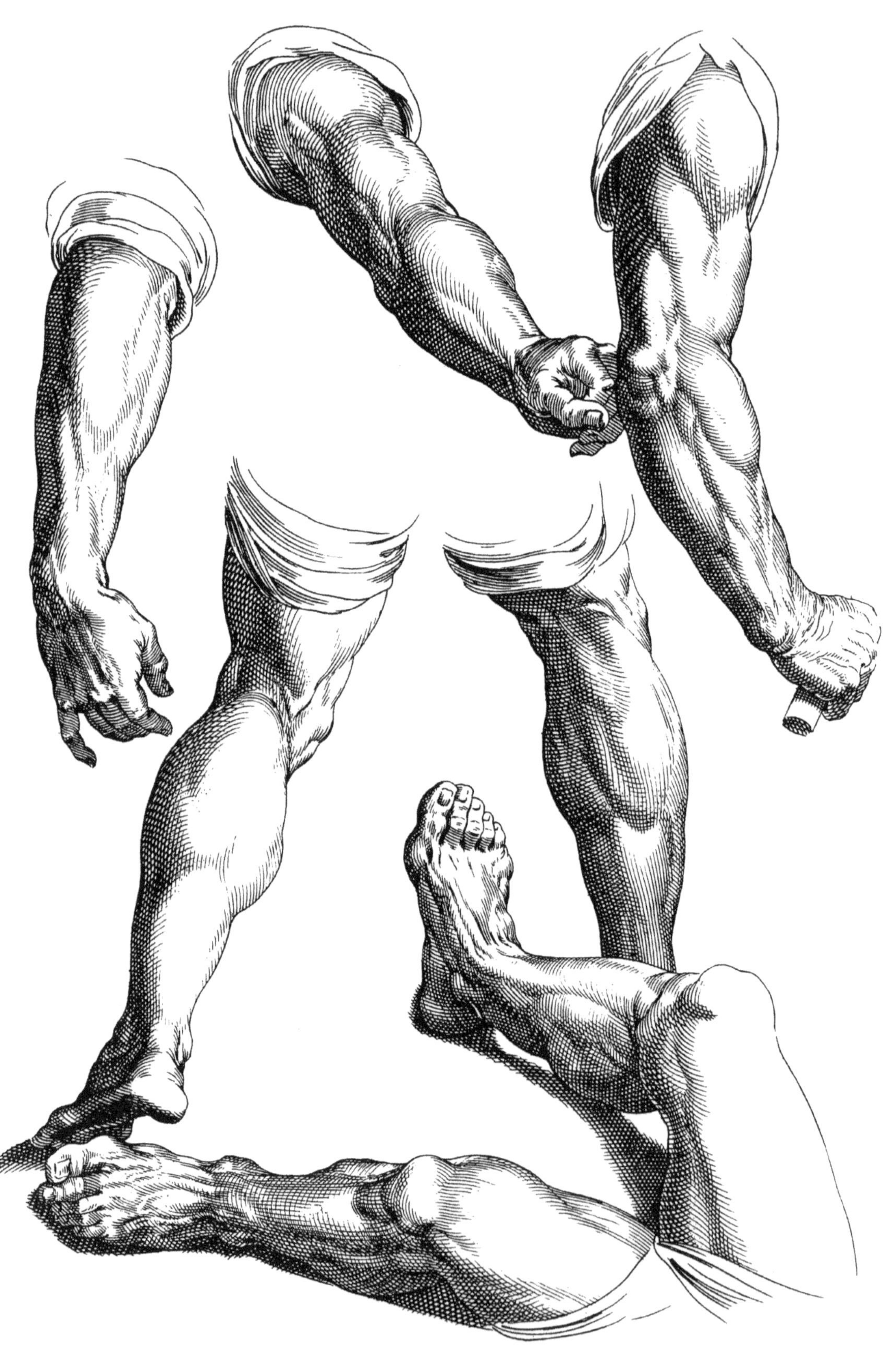

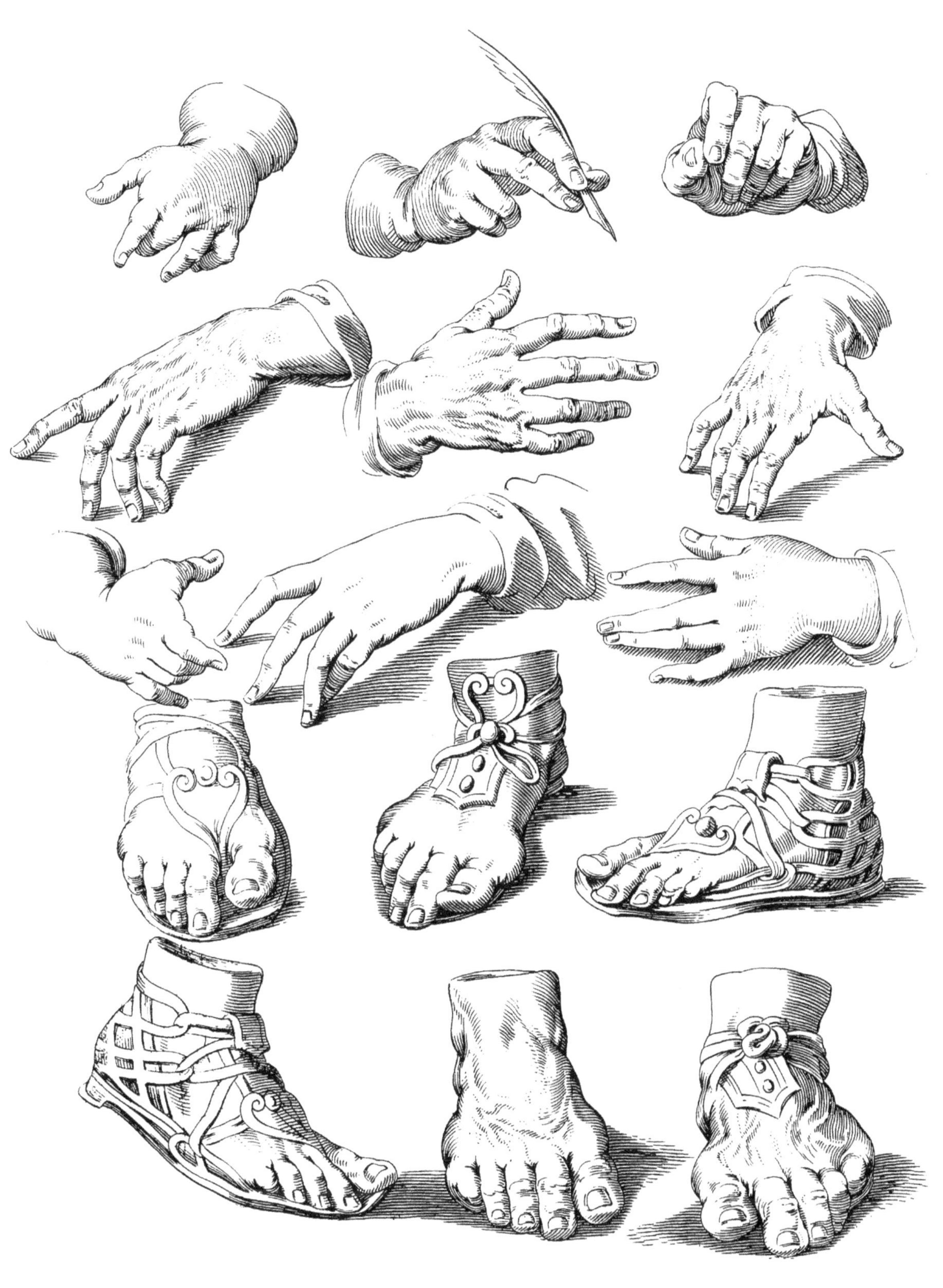

124

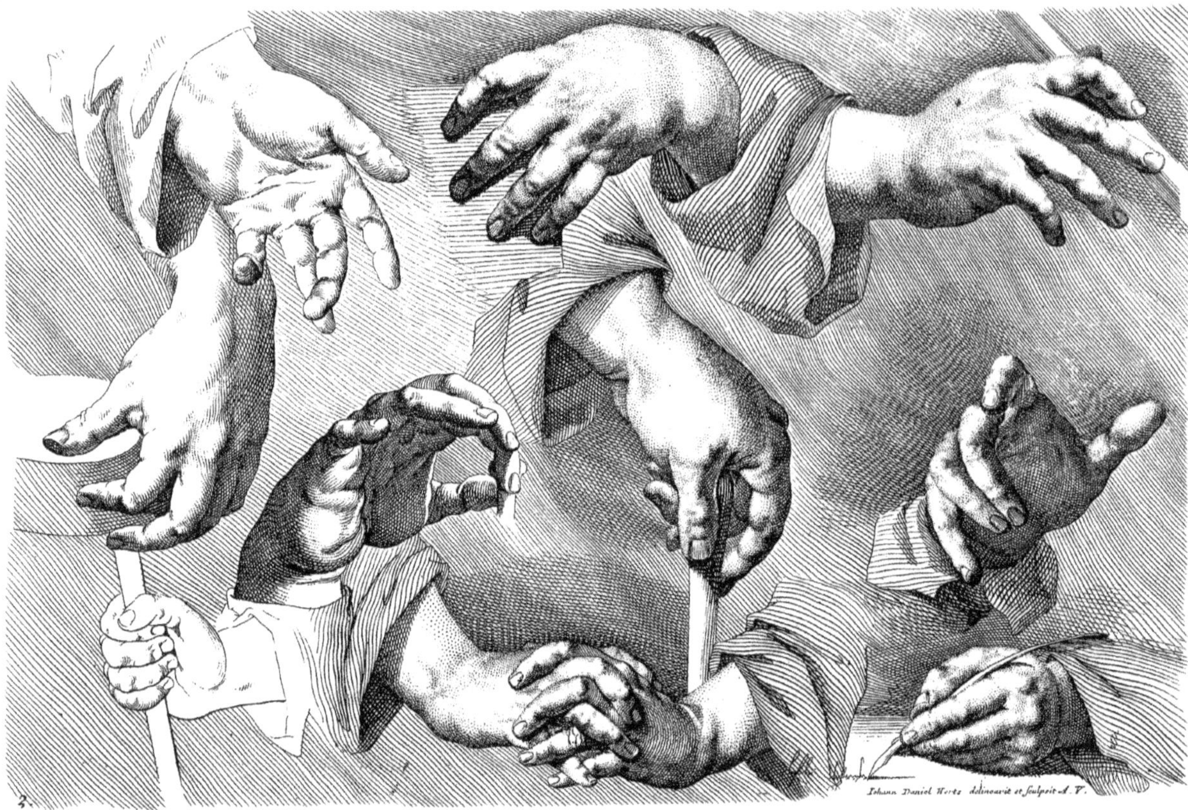

125

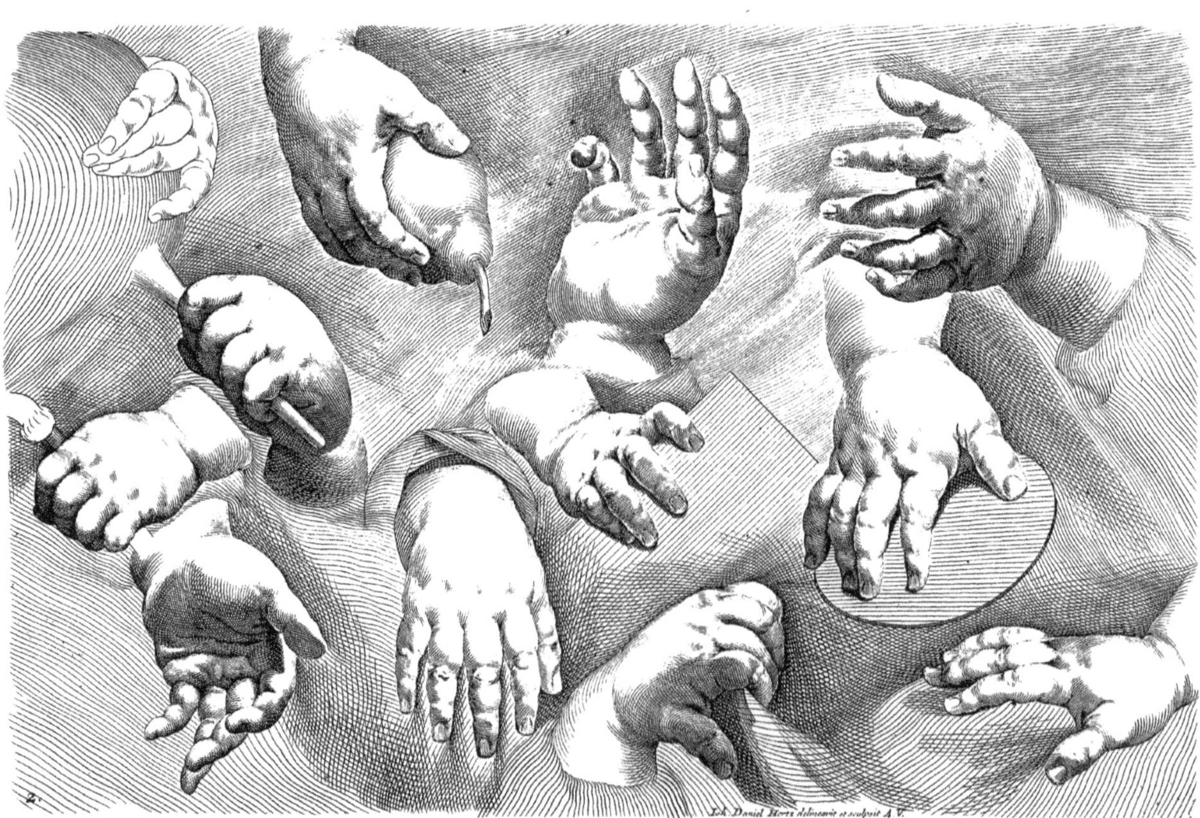

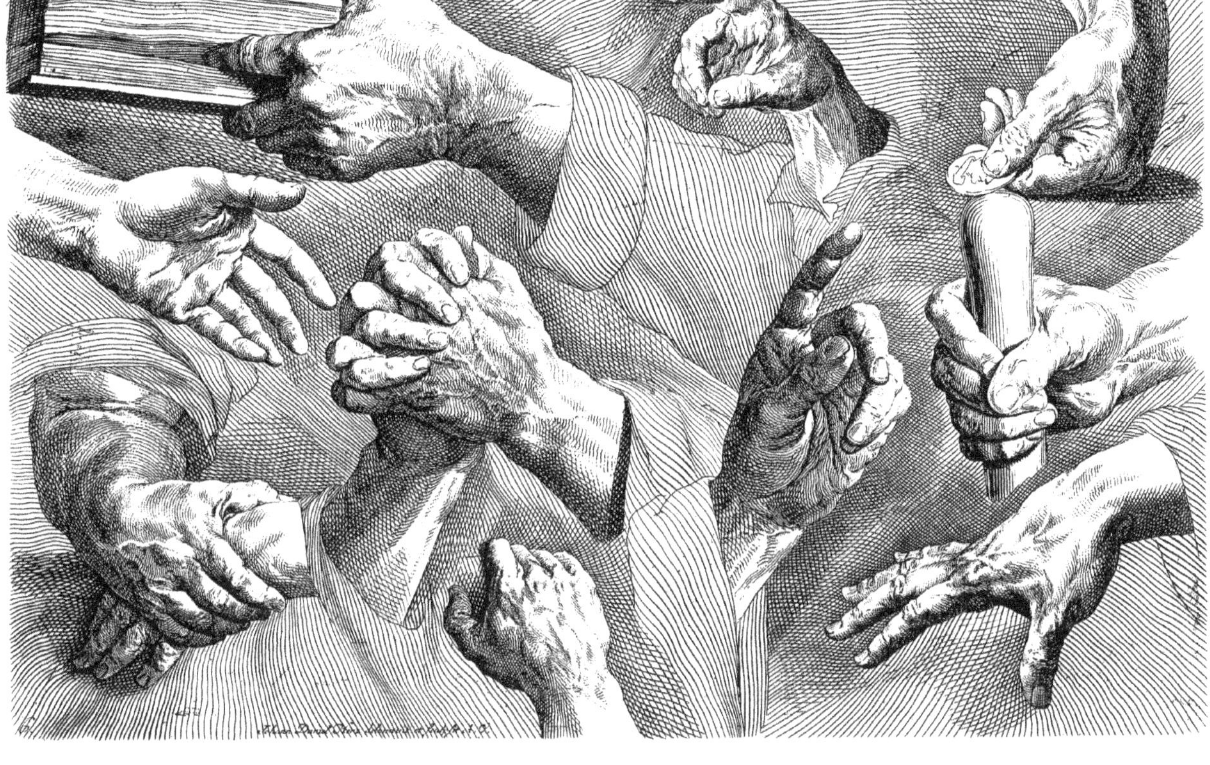

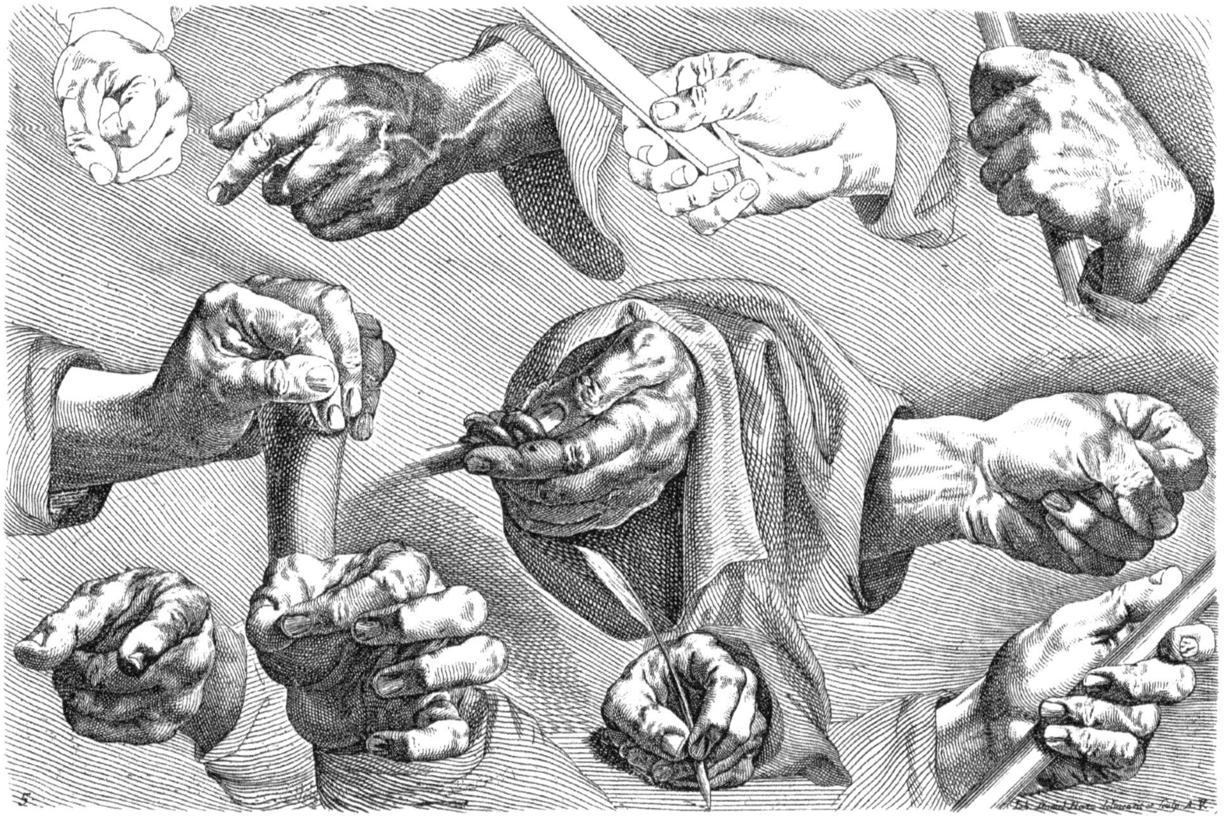

STUDIES OF THE ARM, HAND AND EXTREMITIES

128

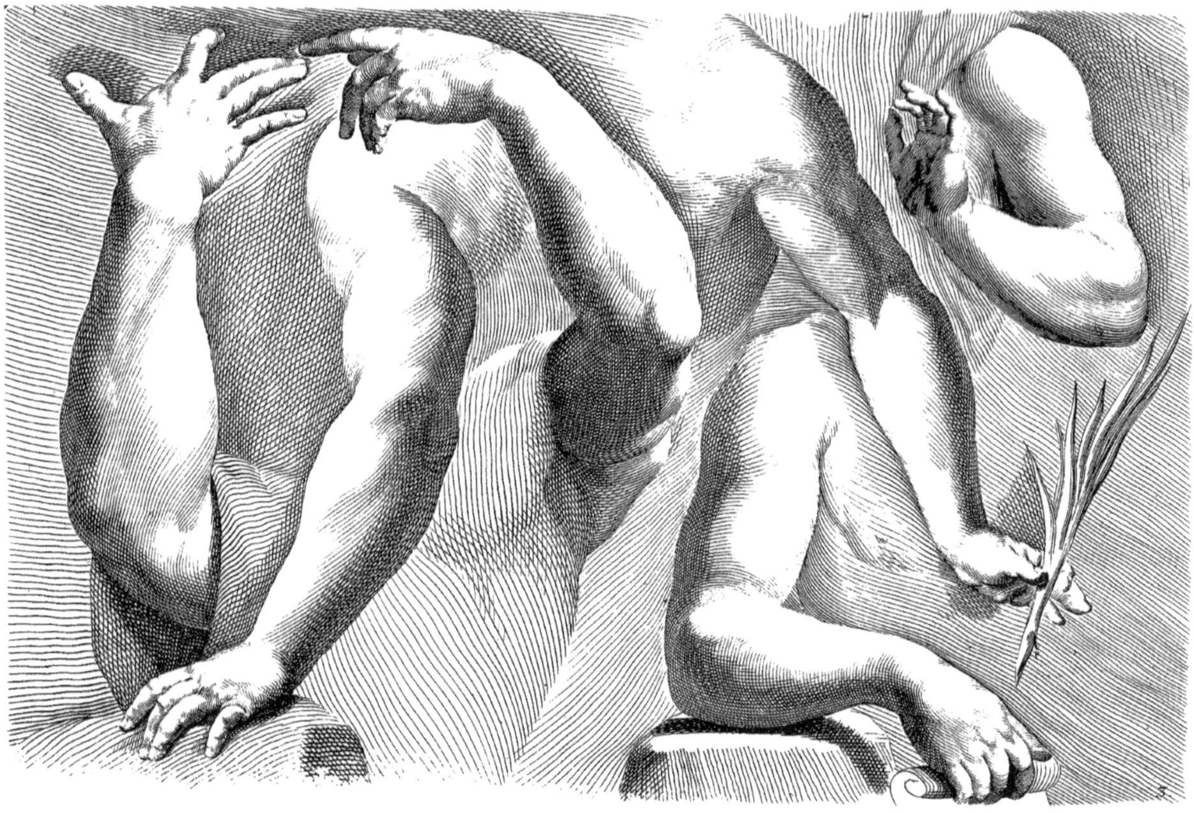

129

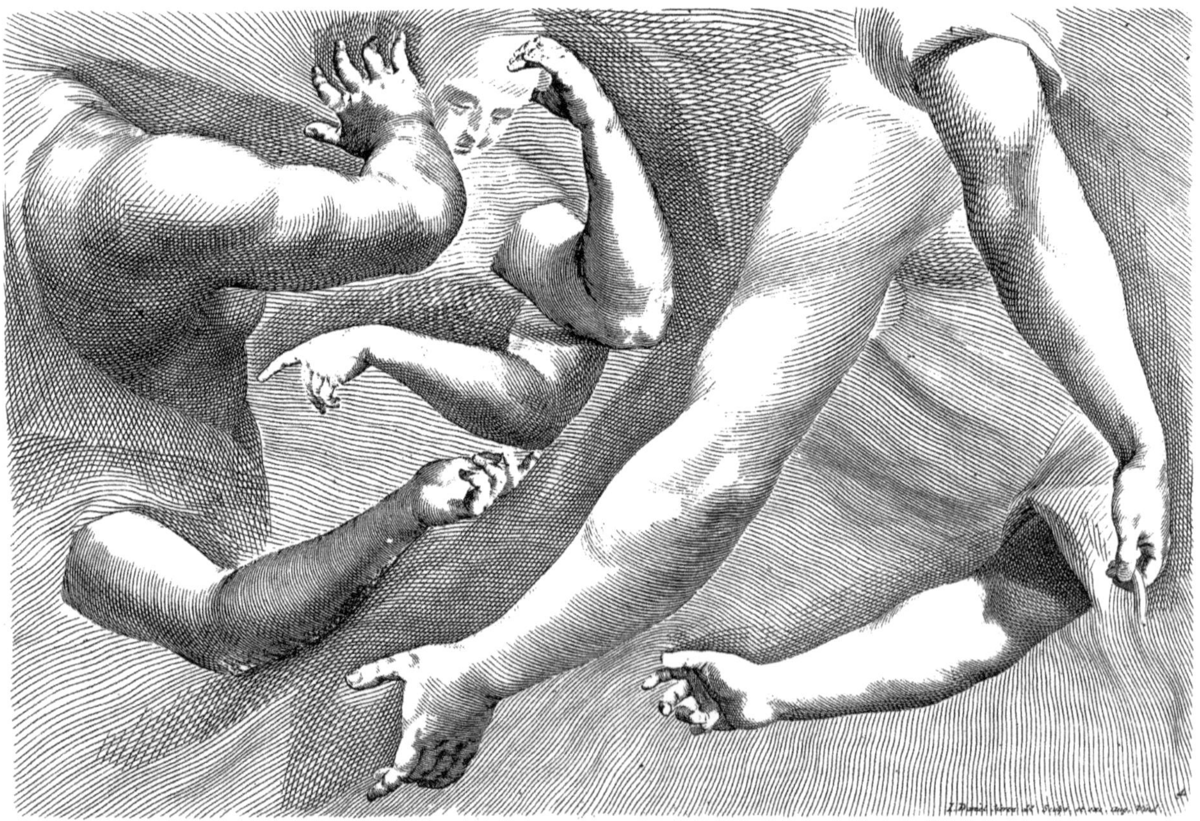

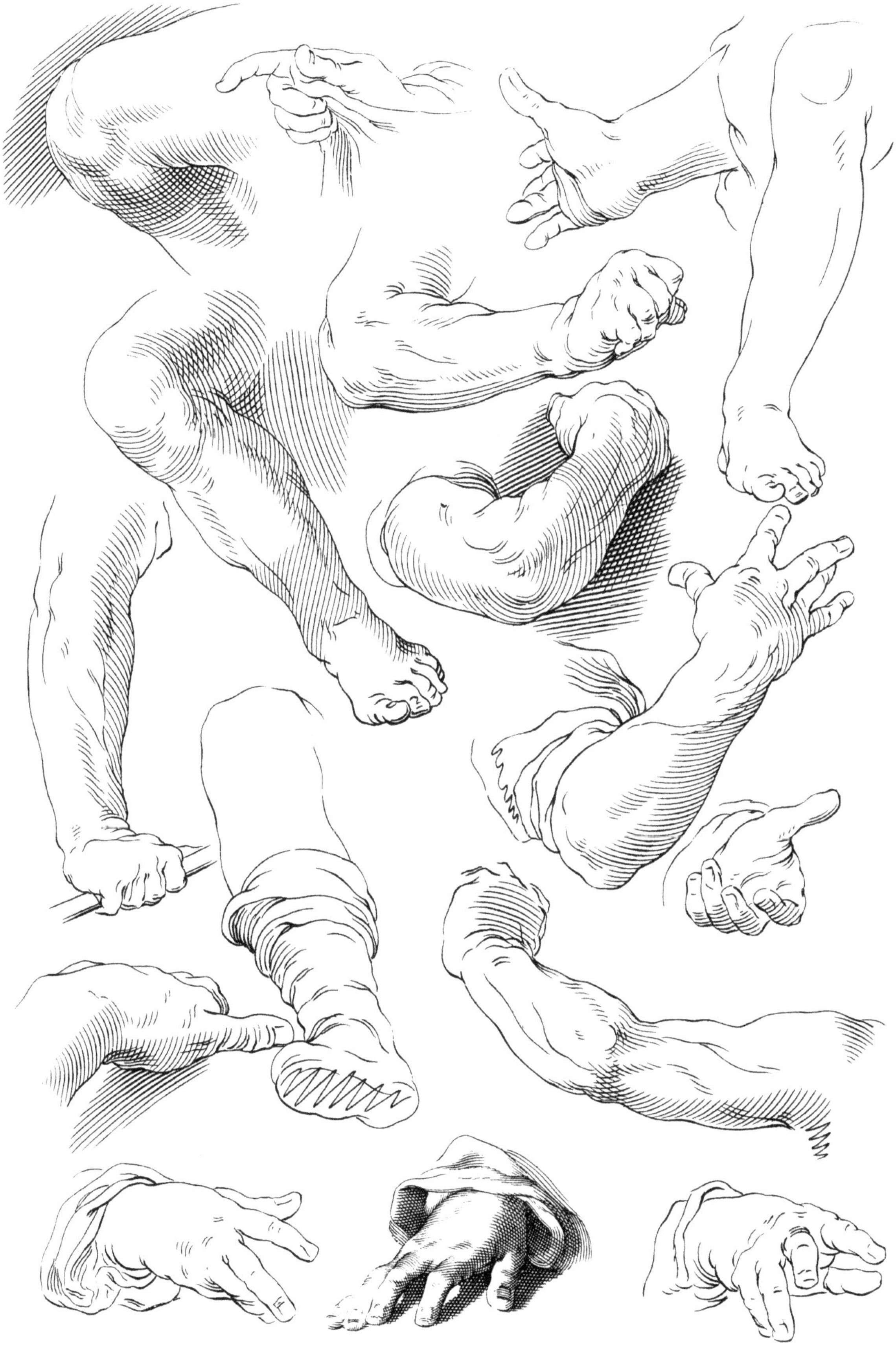

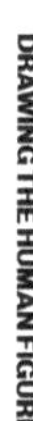

131

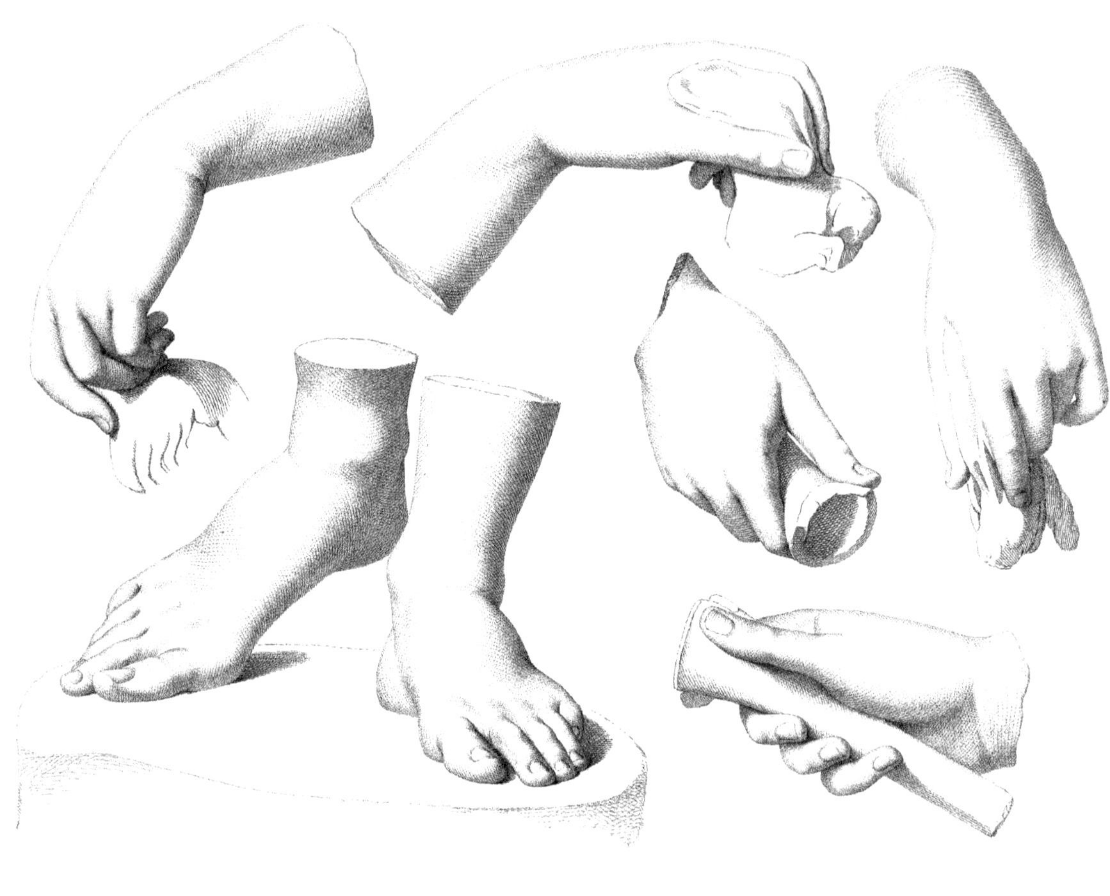

132

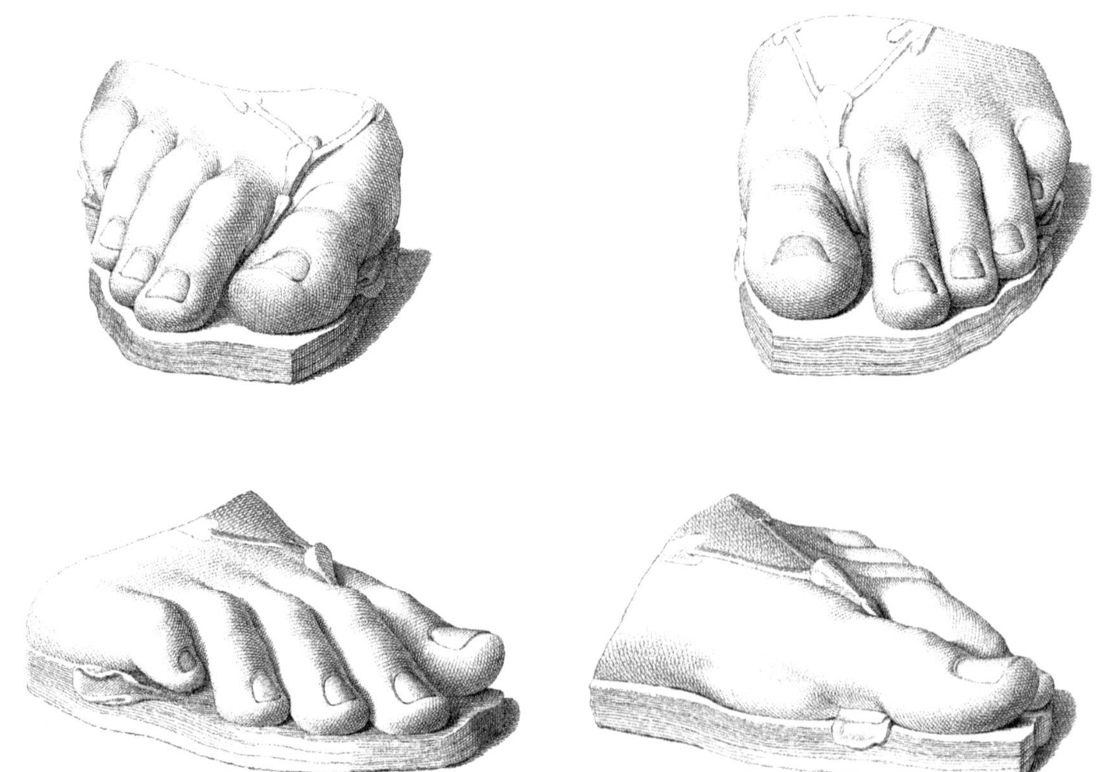

133

134

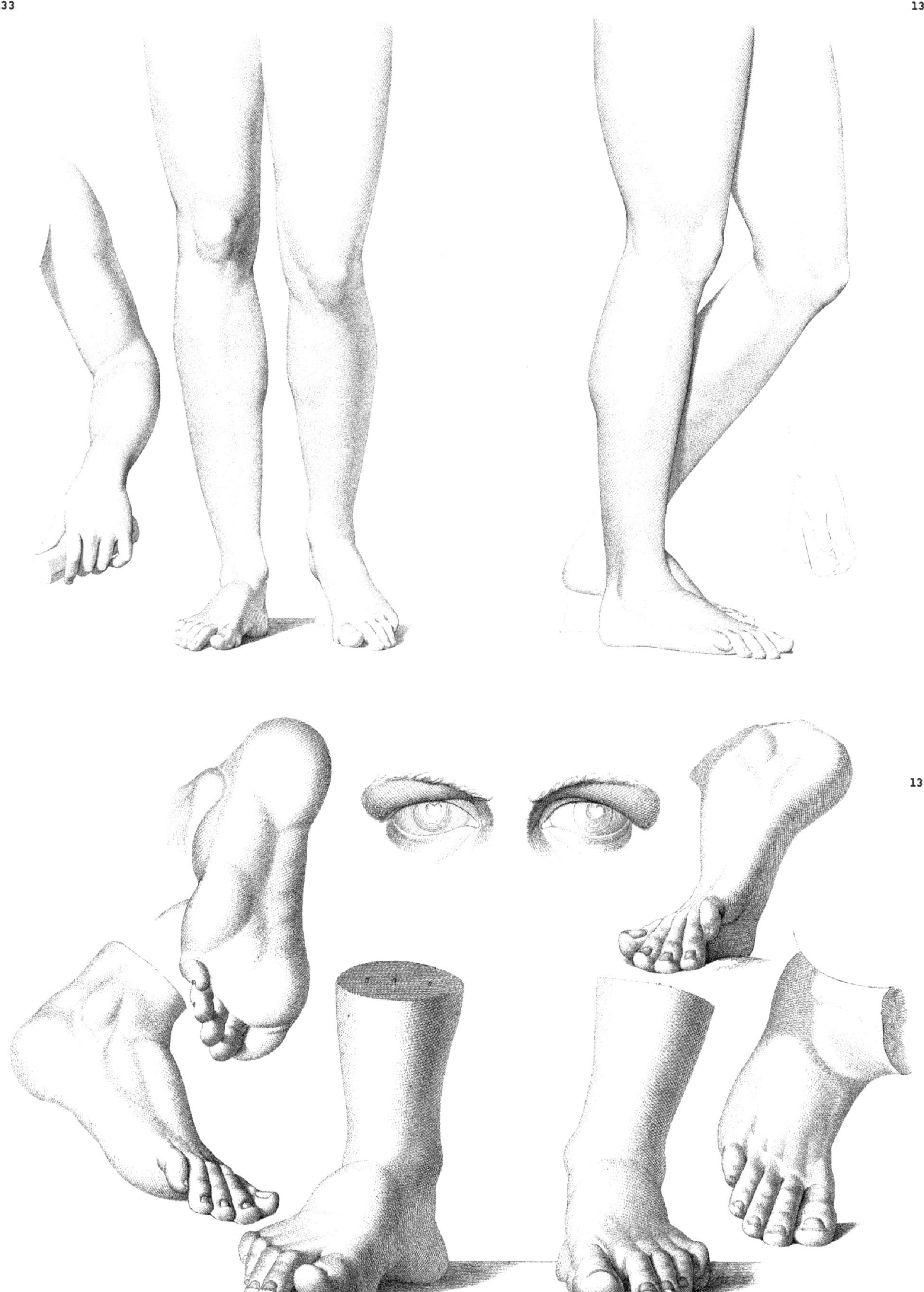

135

136

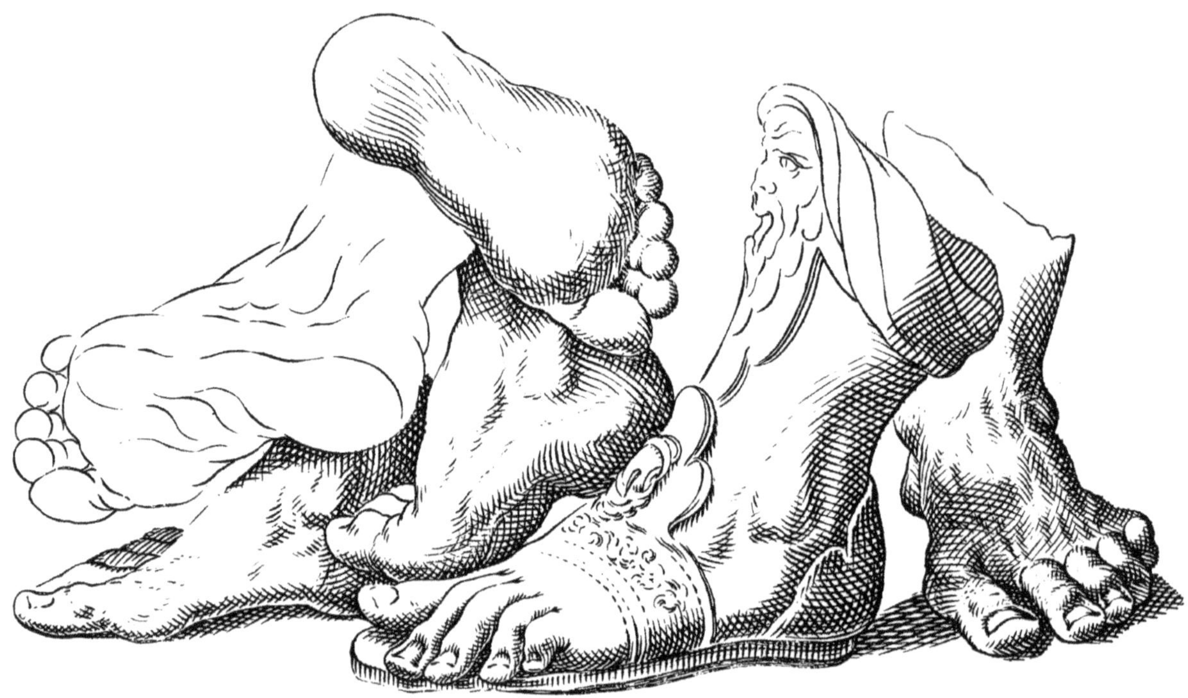

137

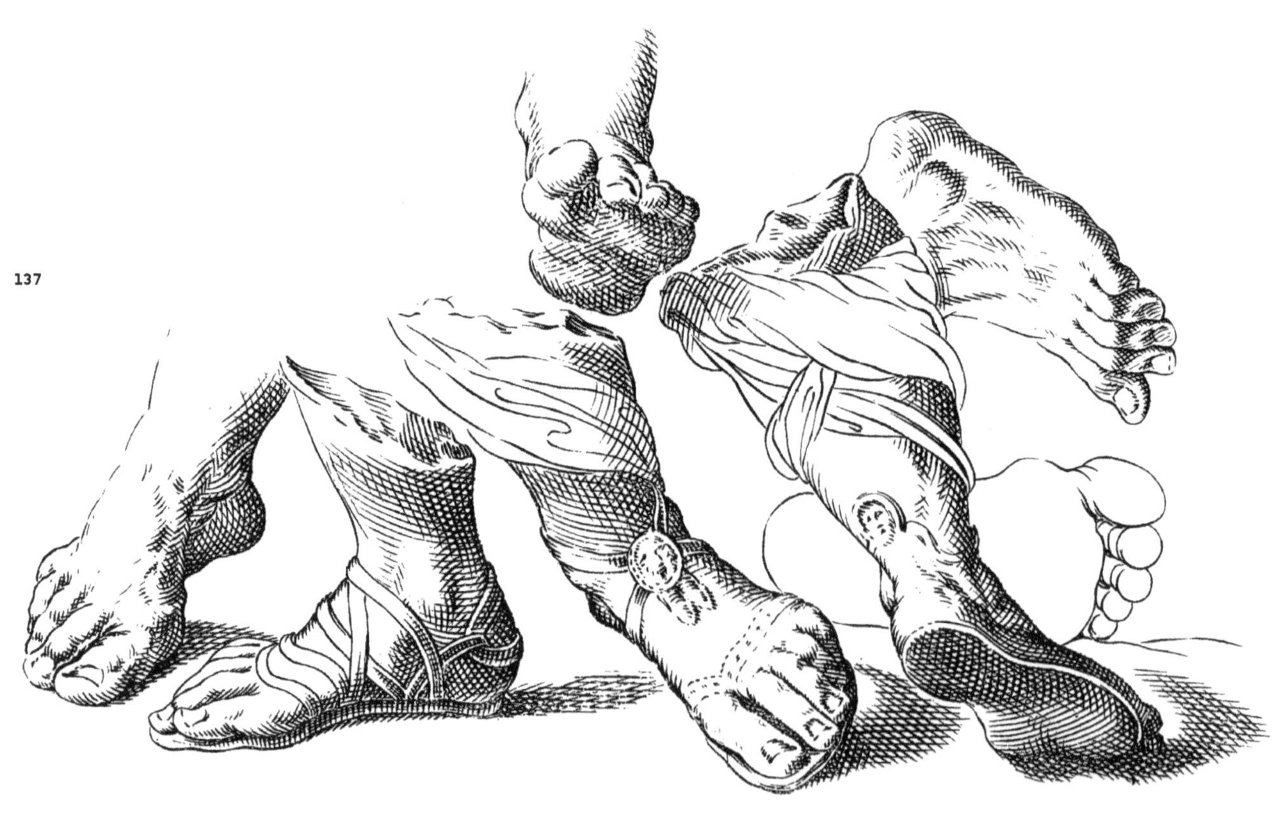

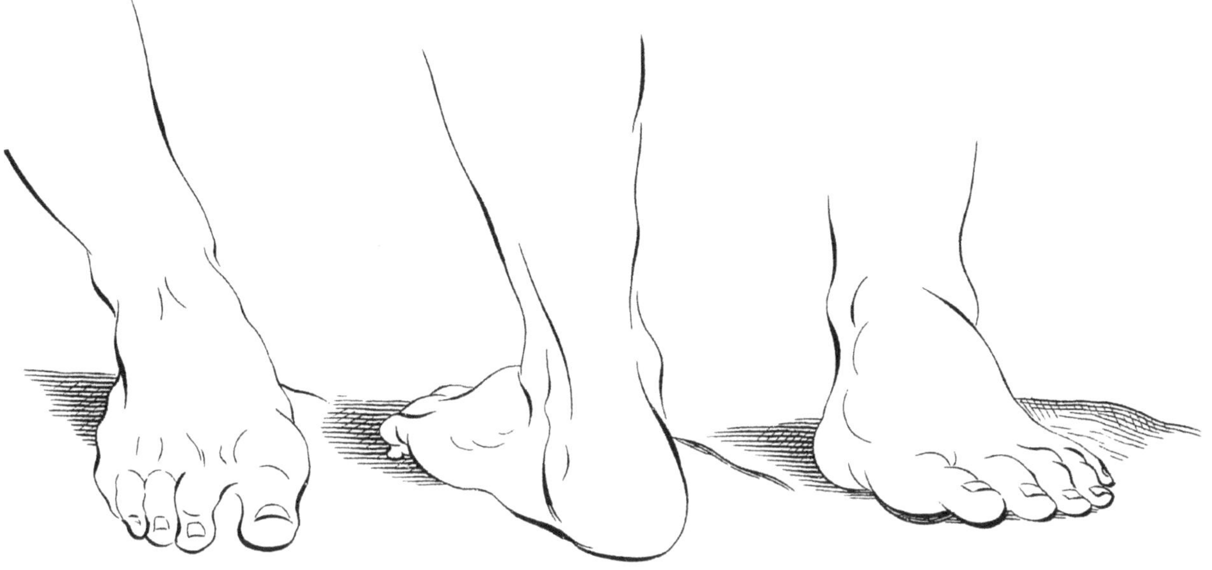

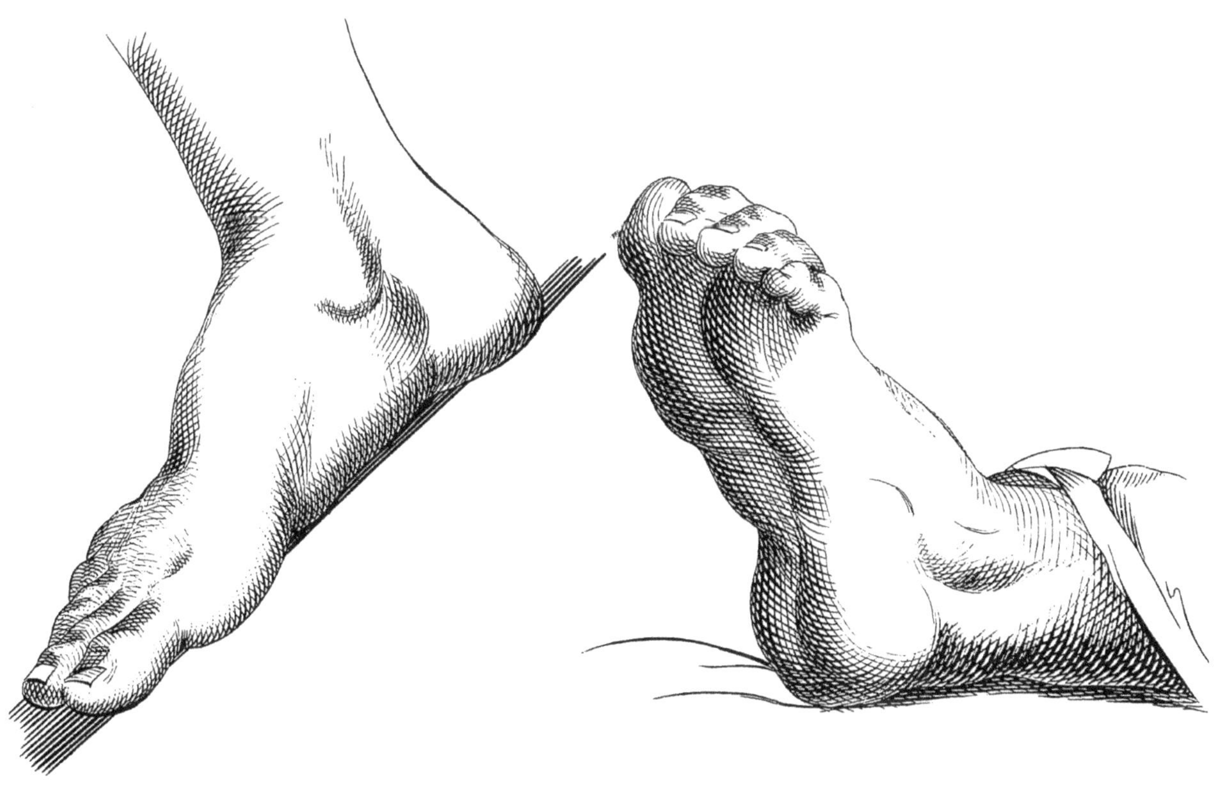

141

142

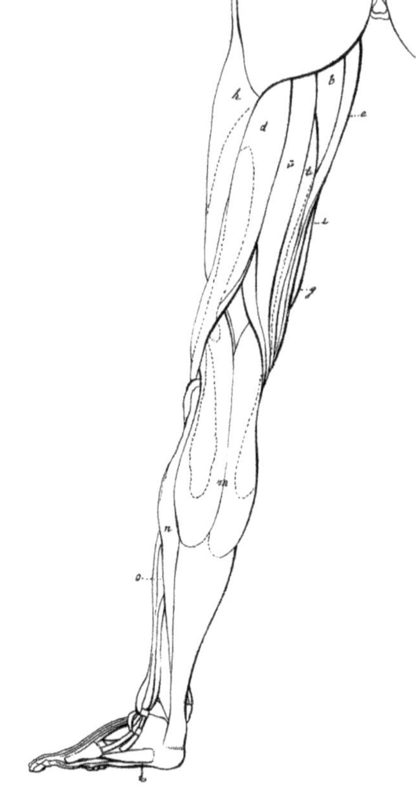

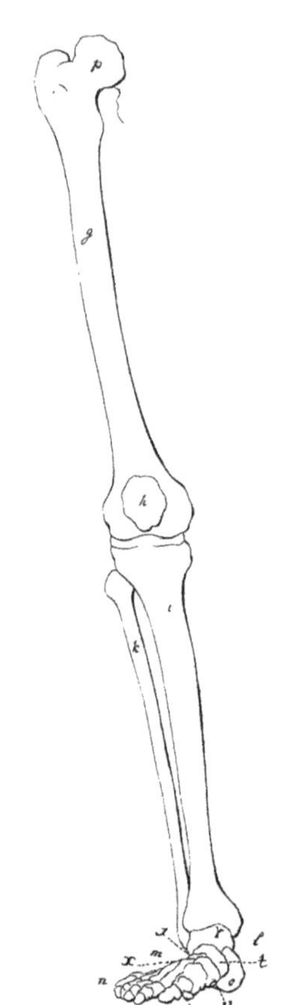

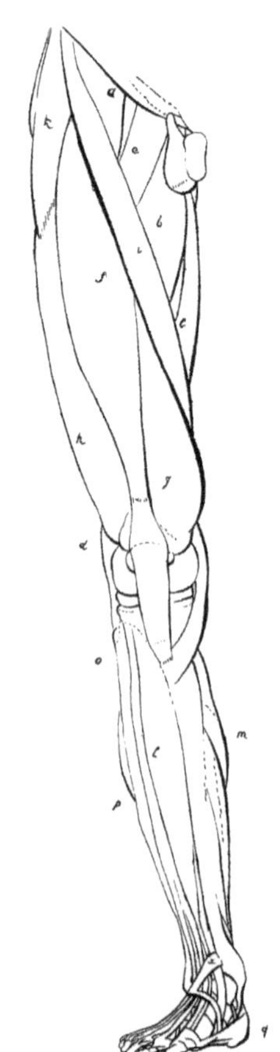

STUDIES OF THE LEGS, FEET AND EXTREMITIES

143

144

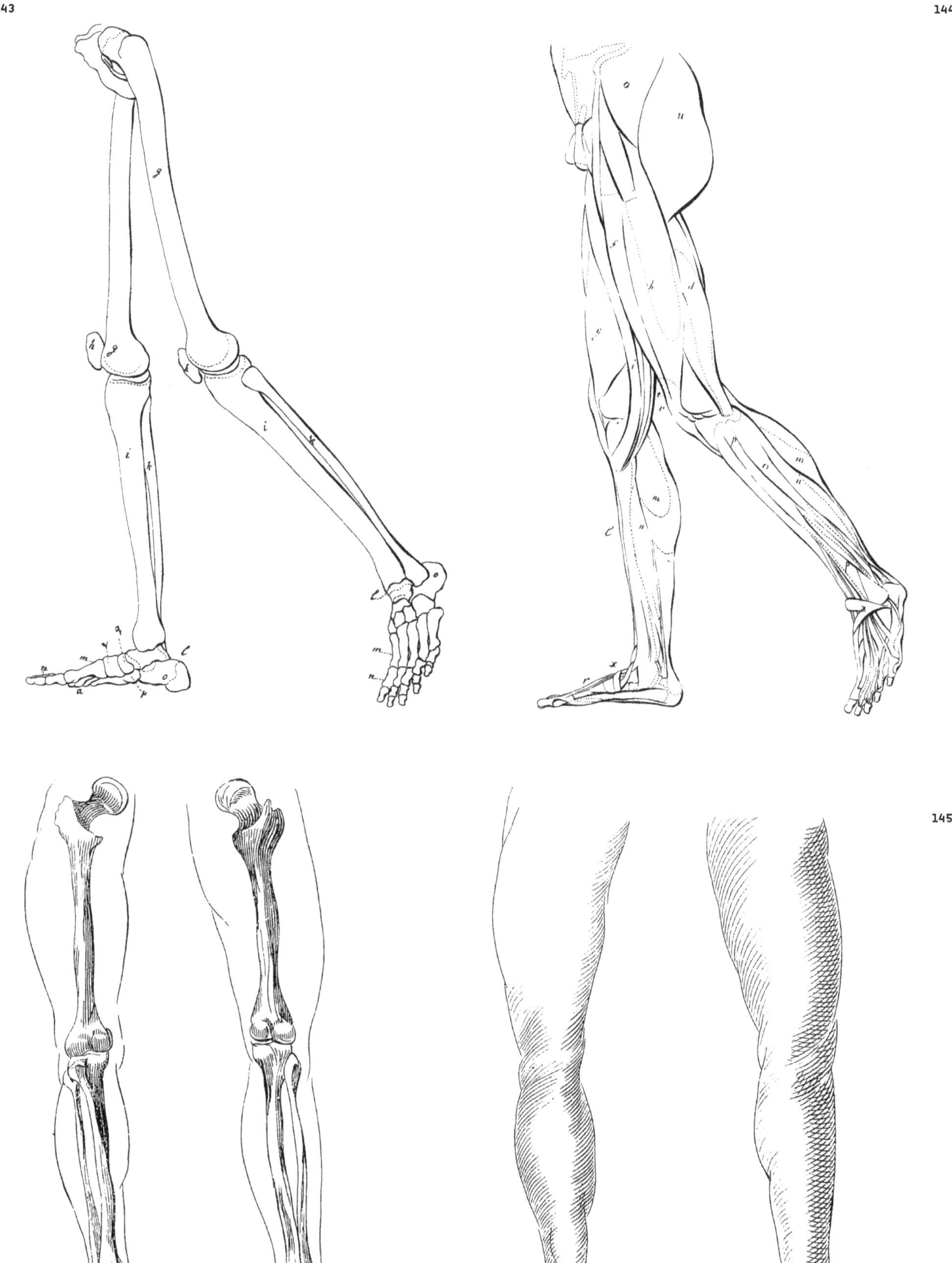

145

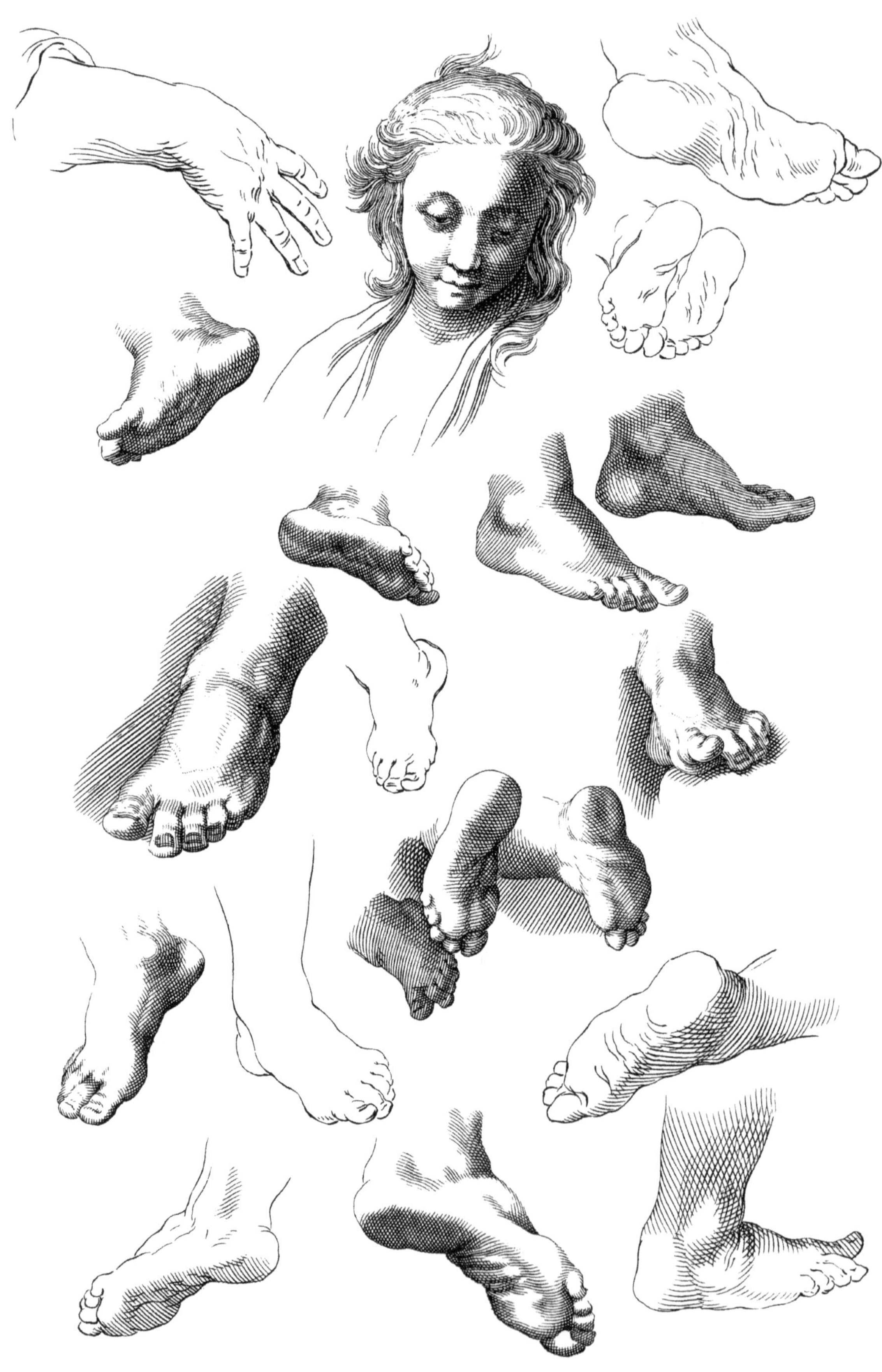

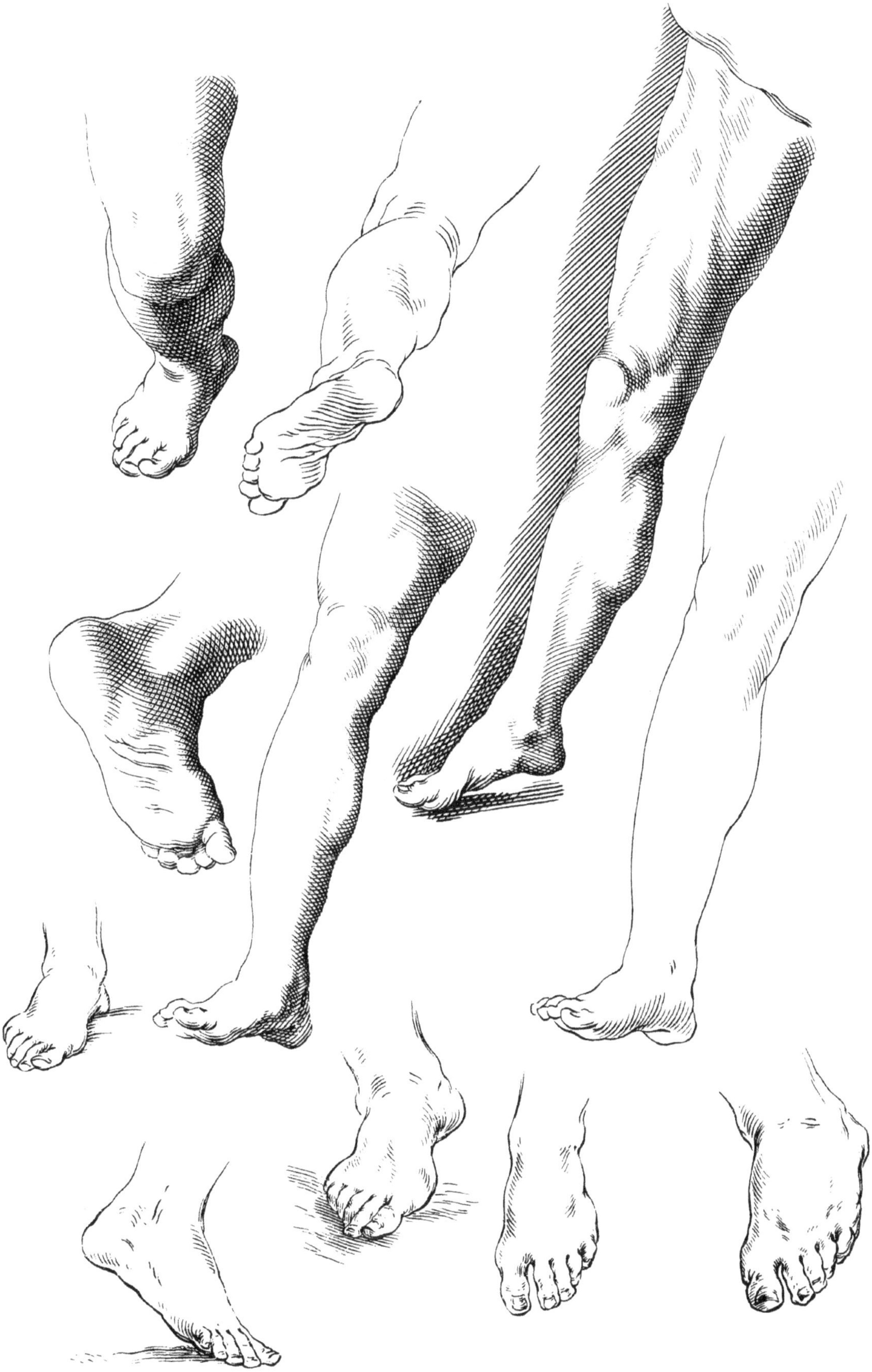

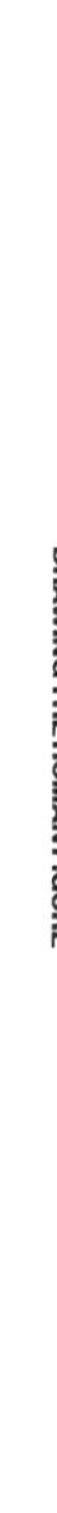
DRAWING THE HUMAN FIGURE

148

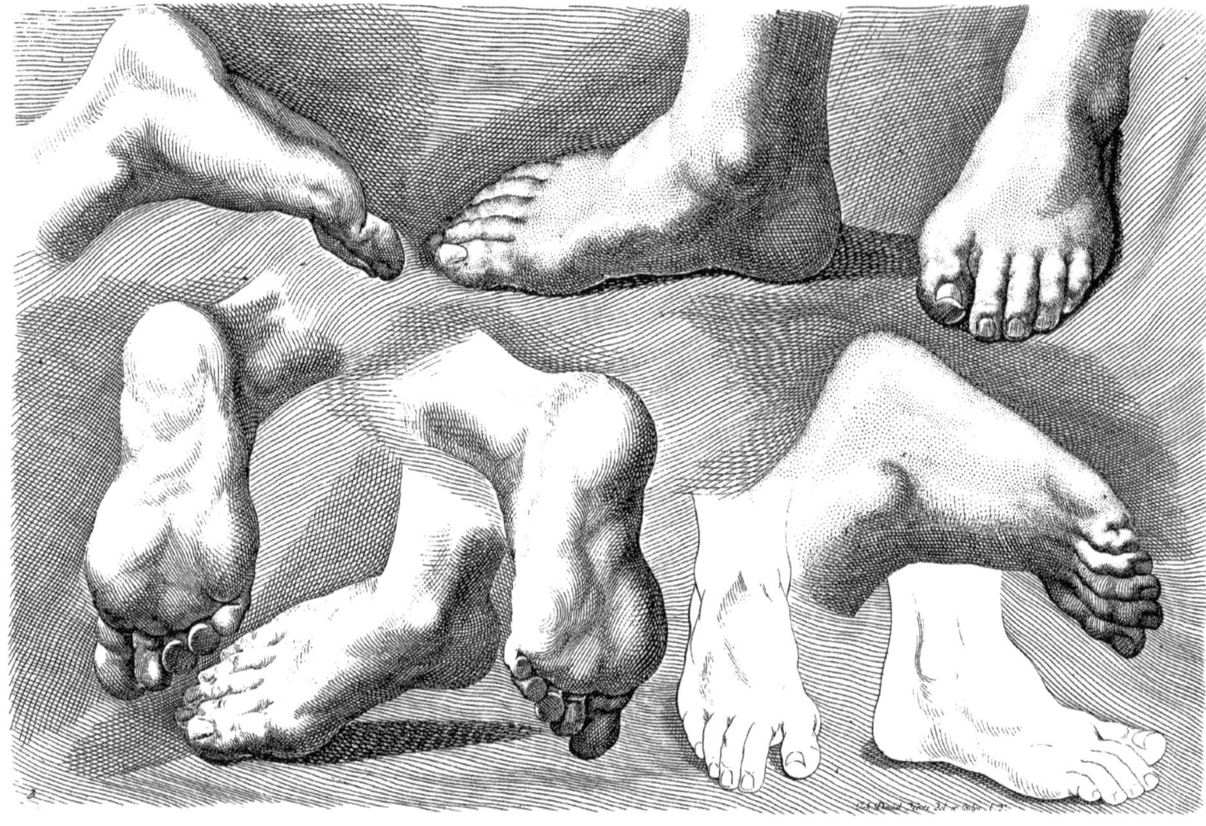

149

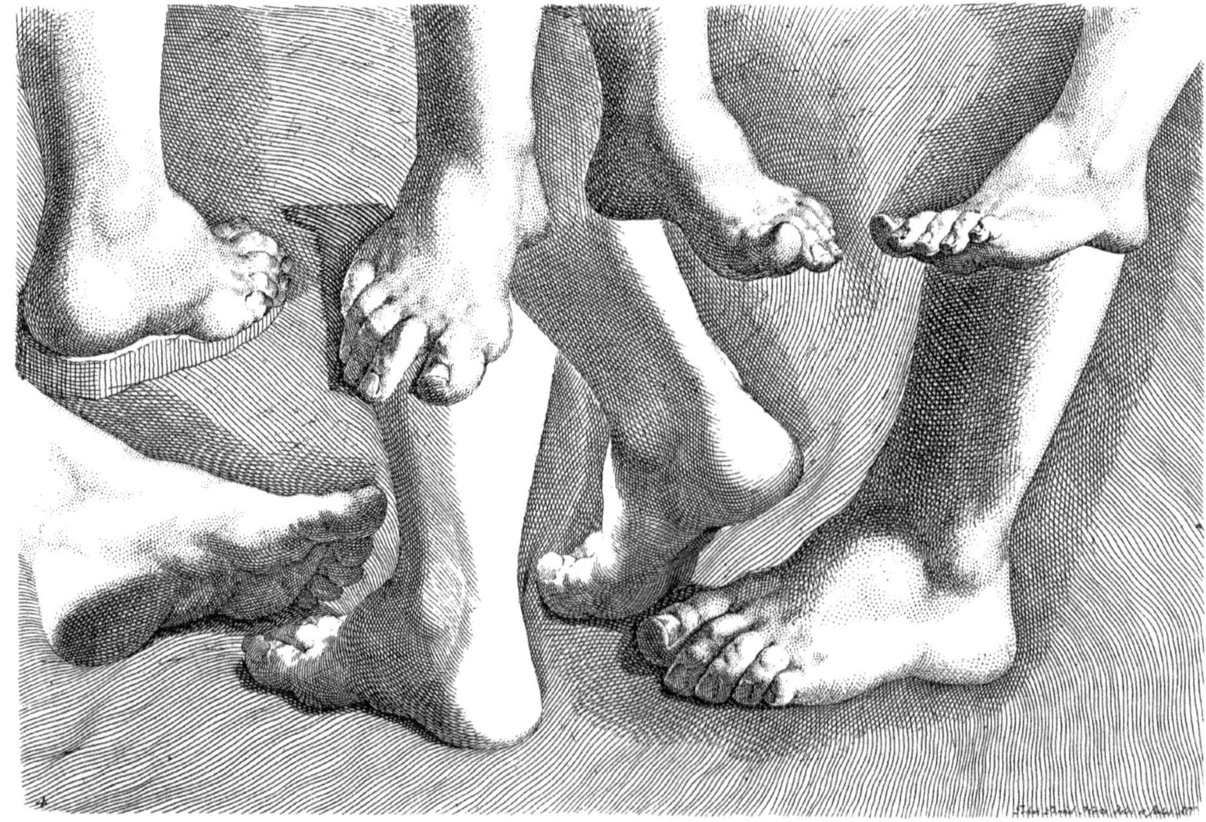

STUDIES OF THE LEGS, FEET AND EXTREMITIES

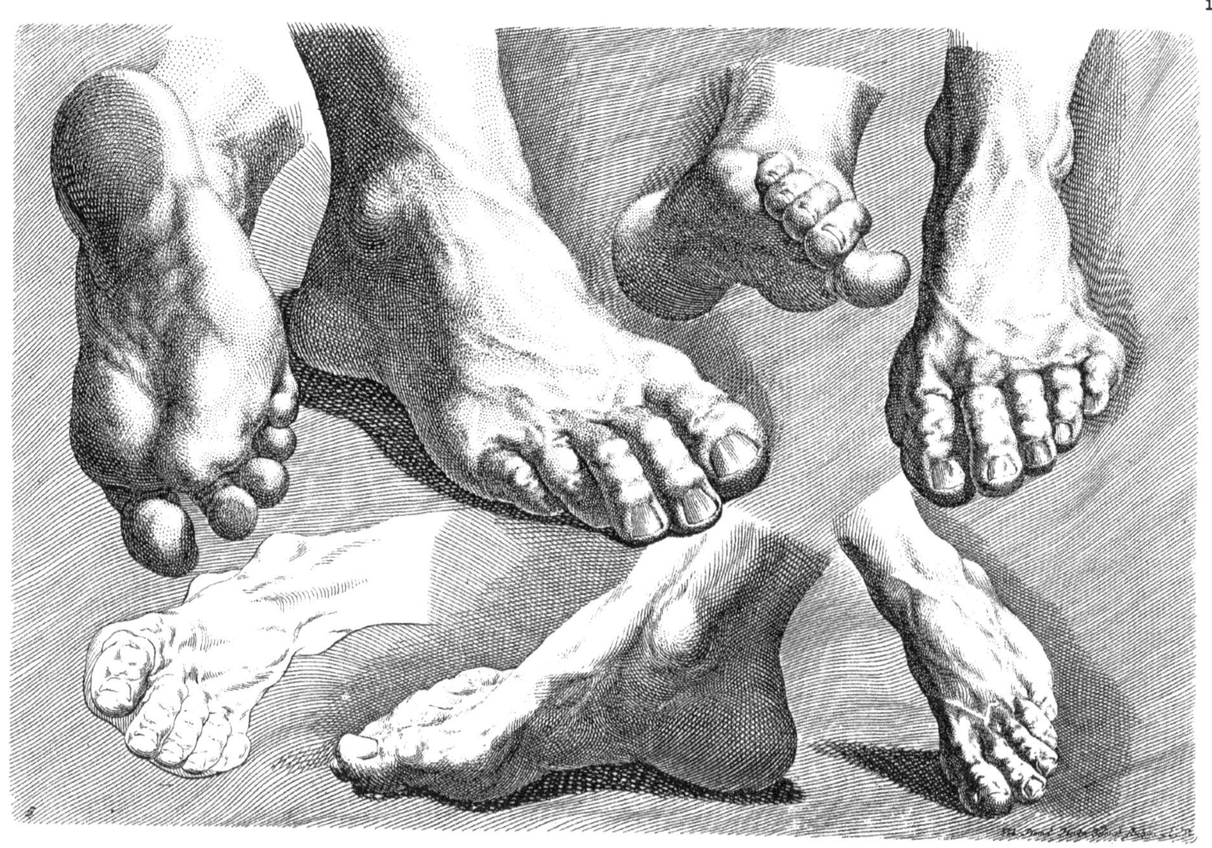

151

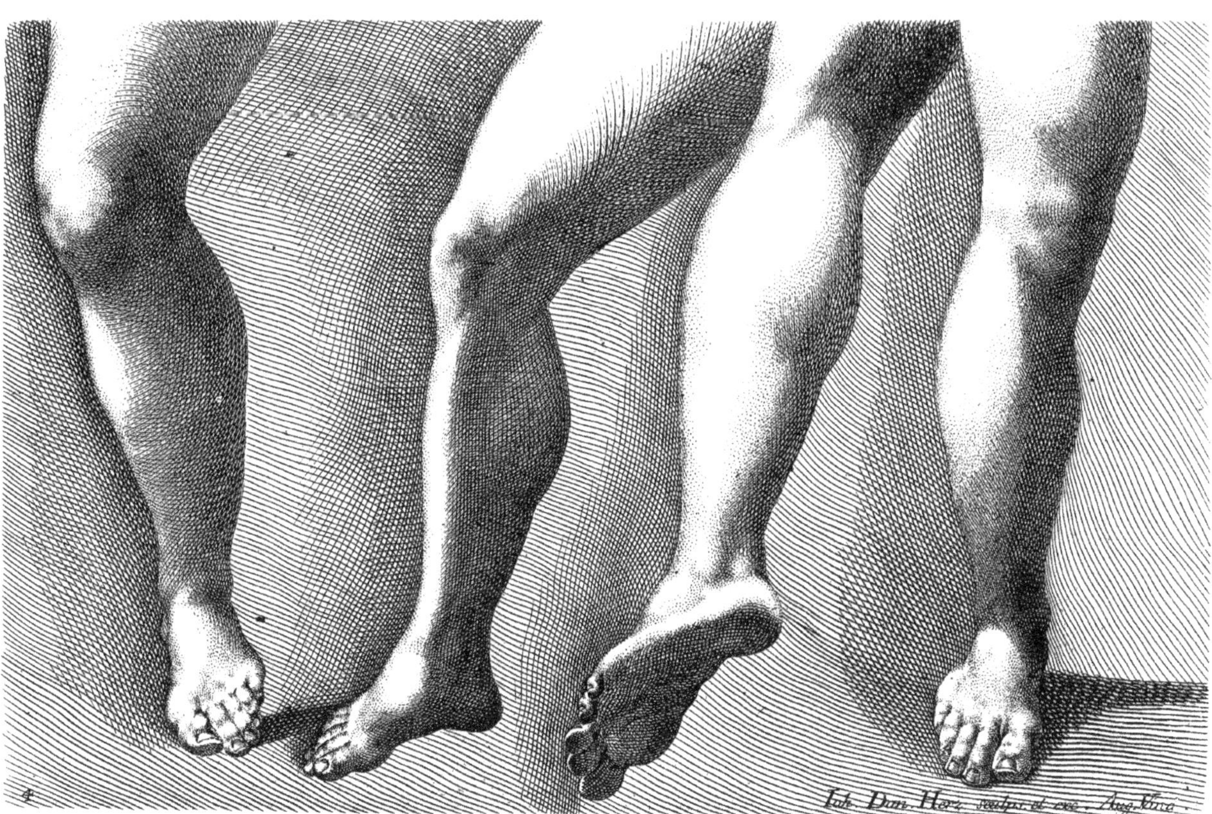

STUDIES OF THE LEGS, FEET AND EXTREMITIES

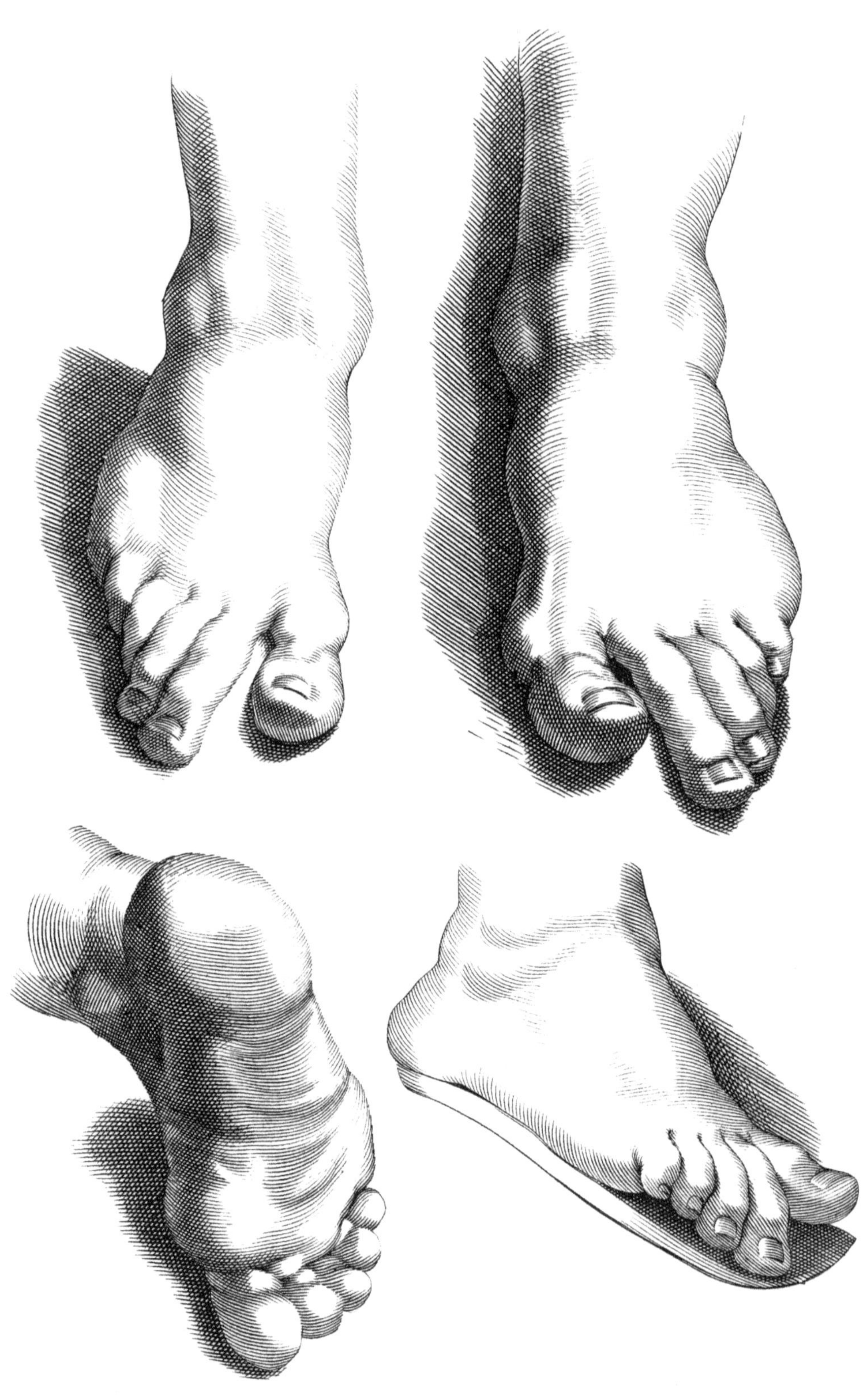

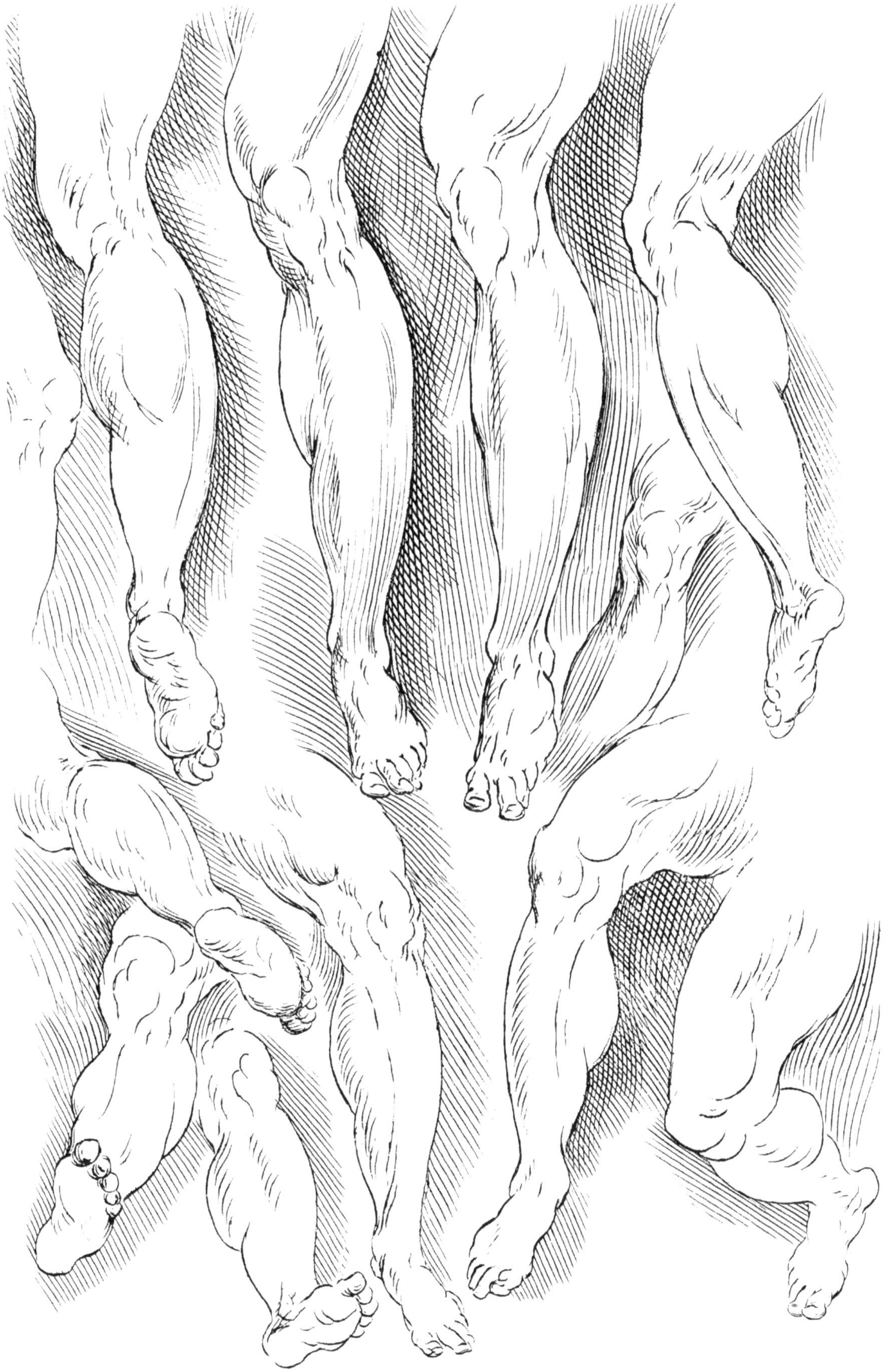

153

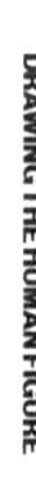

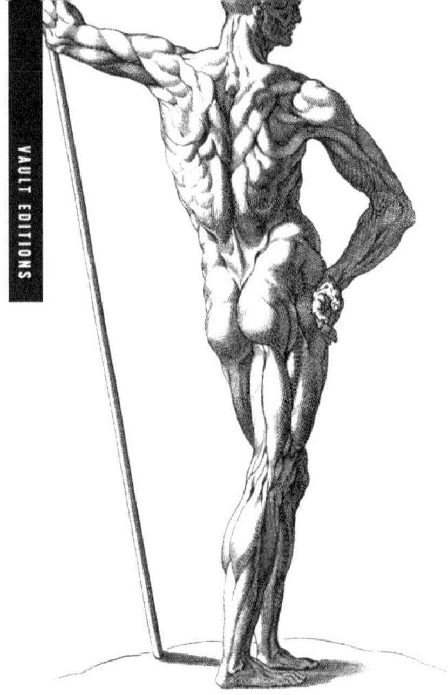

LEARN MORE

At Vault Editions, our mission is to create the world's most diverse and comprehensive collection of image archives available for artists, designers and curious minds. If you have enjoyed this book, you can find more of our titles available at vaulteditions.com.

REVIEW THIS BOOK

As a small, family-owned independent publisher, reviews help spread the word about our work. We would be incredibly grateful if you could leave an honest review of this title wherever you purchased this book.

JOIN OUR COMMUNITY

Are you a creative and curious individual? If so, you will love our community on Instagram. Every day we share bizarre and beautiful artwork ranging from 17th and 18th-century natural history and scientific illustration, to mythical beasts, ornamental designs, anatomical illustration and more. Join our community of 100K+ people today—search @vault_editions on Instagram.

DOWNLOAD YOUR FILES

STEP ONE

Enter the following web address in your web browser on a desktop computer.

www.vaulteditions.com/pages/dth

STEP TWO

Enter the following unique password to access the download page.

dthb23865758sxda

STEP THREE

Follow the prompts to access your high-resolution files.

TECHNICAL ASSISTANCE

For all technical assistance, please email: info@vaulteditions.com

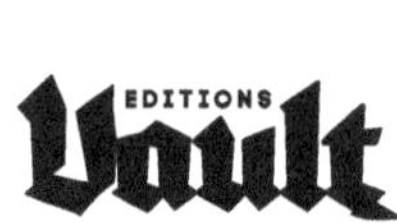

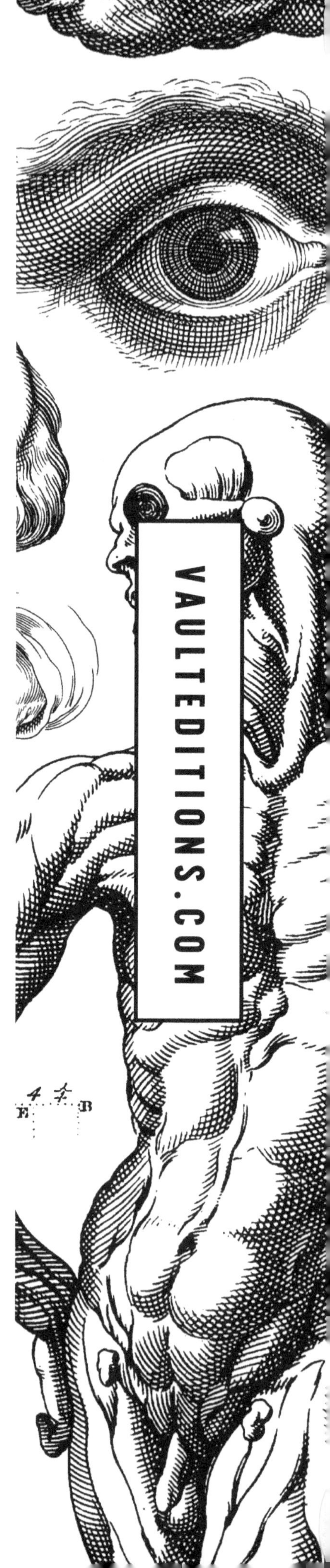